Enterprise Content Management with Microsoft SharePoint

Christopher D. Riley
Shadrach White

ISBN: 978-0-7356-7782-1

Second Printing: July 2014

Printed and bound in the United States of America.

Microsoft Press books are available through booksellers and distributors worldwide. If you need support related to this book, email Microsoft Press Book Support at mspinput@microsoft.com. Please tell us what you think of this book at *http://www.microsoft.com/learning/booksurvey*.

Microsoft and the trademarks listed at *http://www.microsoft.com/about/legal/en/us/IntellectualProperty/ Trademarks/EN-US.aspx* are trademarks of the Microsoft group of companies. All other marks are property of their respective owners.

The example companies, organizations, products, domain names, email addresses, logos, people, places, and events depicted herein are fictitious. No association with any real company, organization, product, domain name, email address, logo, person, place, or event is intended or should be inferred.

This book expresses the author's views and opinions. The information contained in this book is provided without any express, statutory, or implied warranties. Neither the authors, Microsoft Corporation, nor its resellers, or distributors will be held liable for any damages caused or alleged to be caused either directly or indirectly by this book.

Acquisitions and Developmental Editor: Kenyon Brown

Production Editor: Christopher Hearse

Editorial Production: nSight, Inc.

Technical Reviewer: Jeff Shuey

Cover Design: Twist Creative • Seattle and Joel Panchot

Cover Composition: Karen Montgomery

Illustrator: Rebecca Demarest

Contents at a glance

Contents

What do you think of this book? We want to hear from you!

Microsoft is interested in hearing your feedback so we can continually improve our
books and learning resources for you. To participate in a brief online survey, please visit:

microsoft.com/learning/booksurvey

What do you think of this book? We want to hear from you!

Microsoft is interested in hearing your feedback so we can continually improve our
books and learning resources for you. To participate in a brief online survey, please visit:

microsoft.com/learning/booksurvey

Introduction

In this book, you will learn why Enterprise Content Management (ECM) is important and how it can be implemented utilizing the SharePoint platform. When you have completed reading the book, you will have the comfort level to know how to implement ECM inside of SharePoint and to understand why you are doing it. This will also help you bridge the gaps in communication between technology and business needs that exist in most organizations.

As you read the book, you will find that there is more emphasis placed on ECM principles than there is on SharePoint 2013. This is intentional, because as you will soon learn, trying to achieve ECM by simply turning on and configuring SharePoint features is completely the wrong approach. Until you fully understand ECM, you don't stand a chance of making SharePoint's features useful to deploy an ECM solution.

Our research, and more importantly, our practical experience have shown that the difference between successful ECM projects and disasters always points to a people or planning problem. Very often, business users are demanding an ECM solution and expect IT departments to implement it. Without a clear understanding of why they are implementing an ECM solution, IT takes the approach of setting up a SharePoint farm, enabling most, if not all, available features, and leaving the rest to the user. Or, it's taken one step further, and they attempt to configure content management functionality such as versioning and managed metadata, without the guidance from the knowledge workers. This is the definition of "knowing enough to be dangerous."

This results in a SharePoint farm configured, standard features enabled, and users given access. Left to their own devices, users will often blame IT for not seeing what they are looking for, and IT will be stuck without a clue about where to make changes.

Let's hope that at this point the organization gets a clue and does a reset on the project. If not, one of two things can happen: first, the users will not use the system and default to what they did before, and in a year the deployment will be chalked up to failure; or second, the system does get adopted but in a rapid way that mirrors all the mistakes that occur from the use of shared network drives. This is called *SharePoint sprawl* and results in site proliferation and/or the *webification* of already poorly managed shared drives.

The catalyst for these problems is a language gap between IT and business users. When an outside ECM consultant asks you to do an inventory of how knowledge workers operate within your organization, it seems like a mundane and overtly simple question.

However, interestingly enough, when you approach a knowledge worker, requesting a complete description of how they do their job, often the results are a trickle of ideas about the particular tasks a knowledge worker completes in a day, but not really how they are executed. When tasks become routine, their details disappear. This vanishing act results in oversimplification on the part of the knowledge workers of what it takes to manage these tasks. The result is that the IT team has no clearer picture of how content is consumed in the organization than the knowledge workers do, yet everyone's expectations for automation are extremely high.

It is comforting to know that there are very few aspects of ECM that can't be automated, streamlined, and improved with SharePoint 2013. But until an organization knows how the technology fits into their specific modes of operation, it's impossible to go from zero to a successful SharePoint ECM solution.

We are suggesting that planning is the key ingredient to get right early on in ECM projects. But planning usually fails. This is most often because organizations are too nearsighted to do it, because the wrong people are asked to implement ECM, and because the communication between the users and implementers is poor.

Who this book is for

Whether you are a business analyst, IT manager, decision maker, or knowledge worker, by the end of this book you will all be on the same page, speaking the same language, and able to push forward with a proper ECM project. To that end, this book will be part technical and part philosophical. The methodologies of ECM will be followed up with technical examples of how this is accomplished in ECM. This mapping is the exact link that is too often missing in most projects. IT gets the technical SharePoint pieces, and knowledge workers, whether they can state it or not, know the methods of working with the content that SharePoint will be processing and managing.

In addition, we have included a CloudShare demo environment that contains the Information Architecture (IA) discussed extensively in this book.

If you are a business user, you might be tempted to skip the technical bits; please don't. The cursory knowledge of the SharePoint terms and implementation will help you communicate clearly, understand the reasons why SharePoint is being implemented a specific way, and ultimately enable you to get what you want out of the ECM solution.

If you are technical, you might be tempted to skip ahead to the technical pieces and address only those topics that relate to your current project. If so, this is a red flag that your ECM project has already failed and that you are not looking at the solution holistically.

The use cases and labs are meant to help get you started and are in no way designed as a step-by-step guide for building a complete solution. We highly recommend that you read the early chapters first so that you can understand the concepts and best practices for designing and building an ECM solution. Otherwise, you will likely put the technical aspects of SharePoint ahead of the operational business and people aspects of a successful ECM Project.

Ideally, every ECM project stakeholder in your organization will read this book. The project sponsor, power users, IT manager, business analyst, legal counsel, and records management teams will find this as glue to guide the successful execution of the project.

Assumptions about you

The basic assumption of this book is that your organizations needs content management and that you are a stakeholder in getting a content management system deployed. The second primary assumption is that you already own, or will soon own, SharePoint and that your goal is to use SharePoint as the platform for building the required ECM solution.

There are several versions of SharePoint. While most of what is discussed in this book will be relevant for all versions of SharePoint 2010 and SharePoint 2013, both on-premises and in Office 365, the specifics will focus on SharePoint 2013 on-premises standard version or higher. The methodology and process will be relevant whichever version of SharePoint you use. However, if you have SharePoint foundation versions, you will not be able to implement many of the functions required.

Organization of this book

Chapter 1, "ECM defined," begins with a structured definition of ECM. We believe that this will help everyone in the organization use the same nomenclature and concepts. These definitions rely heavily on existing bodies of work that have been established to create a common understanding for ECM professionals to communicate, design, and deploy ECM solutions in a standard and methodical way.

As we move to Chapter 2, "ECM stack: content in," we cover all the aspects of ECM that pertain to the proper capture and storage of content in SharePoint. Next, in Chapter 3, "ECM stack: content control," we cover all the processes associated with properly managing that content throughout its life cycle so that it can provide the most usefulness to the organization. These two chapters will cover all the ECM basics that will require the bulk of your attention and the overall time needed for the planning, implementation, and deployment of your ECM project. These are equally important parts of the ECM stack, but they cover very different subject areas and bodies of knowledge. Therefore, first we discuss how to capture, store, and process content, and then we dive into managing, delivering, and preserving content using SharePoint as the core of your ECM solution.

Now that we have established the same definitions and broken your ECM solution into two distinct stacks, we move on to Chapter 4, "Cases in point." The sections included in this chapter are designed to provide examples that you can point to for best practices as you design your ECM solution. Business processes are never exactly the same for every organization; every Accounts Payable department has unique aspects in how they process work. They might all pay bills, but they do so using a variety of policies, approval methods, financial applications, and Generally Accepted Accounting Principles (GAAP). Note the word "Generally": these aren't laws; they are just guidelines. The same goes for other areas that you are planning to address by deploying SharePoint content management technologies and ECM policies and principles.

As we stated earlier, building a successful ECM solution requires a focus on people. In Chapter 5, "Building an ECM team," we help you identify the right people for your project. To do this, we have provided guidance to help you define specific roles and responsibilities and embrace the need for professional project management. We recommend strongly that you have a PMI certified individual responsible for managing the project from beginning to end. It is also important to identify the technical team members and outline specific subject matter experts who will be responsible for delivering on all the technical requirements outlined in a detailed project plan and architecture design. Finally, we touch on quality control; this will help you understand the importance of unit-testing every deliverable.

Regardless of how well the project is planned, managed, and tested, it will never achieve the desired results without the sections we include in Chapter 6, "User adoption." How many times have you heard someone say, "I have no idea why I do this; IT said that's how it works"? Involving users to provide feedback about usability and helping you to understanding how to listen, not just take notes, will be the one thing you point back to and say that's what made the difference. We will discuss how to incorporate change management practices and create motivation for users. In the end, it might come down to your ability to lead and change user behavior that will enable the ECM solution to manage content easily.

To help you kick your ECM project into high gear, in Chapter 7, "ECM planning guide," we include a complete outline of our recommended IA. You will see that we come back to IA many times during the book; this should illustrate why it is so important. We will cover the importance of governance for the project and the use of the platform as it relates not only to SharePoint but also to content that is used throughout your organization.

The principles covered in Chapter 8, "Records management," and Chapter 9, "eDiscovery," might not be familiar to everyone. However, they are extremely important to understand and, if possible, to include in your ECM solution. Many organizations find out how important these features and the policies needed to implement them effectively are only after a negative litigation, audit, or regulatory event happens.

We round out the book in Chapter 10, "Extending SharePoint 2013 ECM solutions," and Chapter 11, "Tools and final thoughts," by covering some additional areas of interest, including Office 365 and SharePoint user groups. We have also included access to a CloudShare development environment that is a preconfigured SharePoint 2013 environment with the various features and IA discussed in the book, implemented with sample documents.

The purpose of the CloudShare environment is twofold. First, it's to allow the reader to have hands-on access to a SharePoint farm to actually play with the features discussed in the book. The second reason is to foster the best practice of having a sandboxed SharePoint farm when you do any planning, testing, and implementation work. The reader can take the development environment and use it to expand their own ECM design, demonstrate to various stakeholders how certain features will work, or customize it to be more similar to their specific requirements.

CloudShare offers a time-limited trial, with subscriptions starting at a low monthly cost. We recommend that you, at minimum, utilize the trial so that you have access to the virtual environments at your leisure while you read this book.

Acknowledgments

We would like to thank the following people for helping us. Their support and contributions are greatly appreciated.

Shad

The time spent writing this book was substantial and occurred mostly on nights and weekends. It meant sacrificing some pretty sweet powder days at Crystal Mountain with my son Cade or missing out on playing a game of Pokemon cards with my other son Jaxson. Whenever I would retreat to my office, I could hear the family activities occurring without me. Then a knock at the door with a hot cup of coffee, snack, or request to come eat a meal with the family would remind me how supportive my wife and boys were during this effort. I was rarely alone in my office, usually accompanied by either our dogs Luci and Lily at my feet or Chris Riley, who was working via Skype right alongside me. I would like to thank my family for supporting my decision to co-author this book. I had started a new business just a year before the opportunity to write the book came up, so they had already become used to Dad working seven days a week, including late nights and long weekends. My wife Michele is my best friend, and she keeps me honest about most everything I do. My sons are my heart and soul; I cannot thank them enough for letting Daddy focus and work on this book, mostly without interruption.

Chris Riley is downright brilliant, I hope everyone who reads this book has an opportunity to meet him and spend some time getting to know him. He hasn't come by any of his knowledge or core values easily; he has worked tirelessly to achieve success and failure. The results are a person who has amassed a great body of technical knowledge and personal character. He asked me to be his co-author for this book, and I will always be grateful for the opportunity.

I would like to thank my parents Margaret and James White for teaching me that honesty and hard work are the core elements to success. My parents worked hard every day to create a stable and loving home for my sister Serena Kraft and me. My sister is a successful entrepreneur in Alaska, and we both acknowledge that it was core values more than anything that helped us achieve success in life.

Last but certainly not least, I would like to thank the following people who helped me in so many ways both during the process of writing the book and helping to support efforts that allowed me to write it. In addition, I have included individuals who I have worked with during my career that have had a lasting impact and helped shape my opinions about proper design, execution, and teamwork. These people are ECM professionals in their own right, and I am lucky to have worked with them: Kenyon Brown, Christopher Hearse, Jeff Shuey, Cullen Hower, Dennis Brooke, Mathias Eichler, Jeff Doyle, Bob Stellick, Robert Latham, John Dougherty, Al Senzamici, Phong Hoang, Ryan Keller, and Richard Norrell.

– Shadrach White

Chris

I first have to acknowledge the ECM gene for this book. Without the insatiable drive I have to organize vast amounts of information in a way that makes me consume information better and faster, I would never have jumped into ECM because—let's face it—it's a bit boring. Next I have to thank Shad. I've known Shad for many years now; we were introduced as industry peers but quickly became friends. We connect on the fact that the world, despite most Independent Software Vendor (ISV) assertions, is completely behind in technology adoption. He realized, as I have, that companies, although the technology is available, are just not adopting solutions in an effective way. We share the belief that there is no need to further complicate things. Instead, let's make people successful. We also share a drive to help. We know what is possible. Not only because we have implemented it, but because we live it. Shad wants everyone to know this possibility.

One of the reasons I was able to meet Shad was due to a rock-hard industry that is fighting the daily battle of steering organizations correctly. That organization is AIIM. AIIM has been my surrogate industry parent. They have been the source of vast amounts of my applied knowledge in ECM as well as strong relationships that have catapulted my experience and career.

Another big chunk of my drive came from people I've never met but wish I had. These are the figureheads: James Gleick, Richard Feynman, Guy Kawasaki, Ray Kurzweil, and quite substantially, Steve Jobs. While they have not all been directly involved in ECM, they have contributed to my "style," which is critical in my approach to all technical projects.

And finally, I have to thank my wife, Lauren. She sees how I obsessively organize files on my computer and allows me to speak about what to her might seem like gibberish—about the importance of information, avoiding information glut, and the desire to push the world forward into using that great technology that already exists. She is the records manager of my brain and forces me to do what I need to keep my mind from getting cluttered.

– Christopher Riley

Support & feedback

The following sections provide information on errata, book support, feedback, and contact information.

Errata

We've made every effort to ensure the accuracy of this book and its companion content. Any errors that have been reported since this book was published are listed at:

http://aka.ms/S2013ECM/errata

If you find an error that is not already listed, you can report it to us through the same page.

If you need additional support, email Microsoft Press Book Support at *mspinput@microsoft.com*.

Please note that product support for Microsoft software is not offered through the addresses above.

We want to hear from you

At Microsoft Press, your satisfaction is our top priority, and your feedback our most valuable asset. Please tell us what you think of this book at:

http://aka.ms/tellpress

The survey is short, and we read every one of your comments and ideas. Thanks in advance for your input!

Stay in touch

Let's keep the conversation going! We're on Twitter: *http://twitter.com/MicrosoftPress*.

ECM defined

In this chapter, we will lay out the fundamental building blocks of ECM. This will help you understand at a high level what you will need to include as part of a comprehensive strategy for managing content in SharePoint. Almost anyone can create a server farm and then create a site collection and start adding content to a document library. Typically and unfortunately, that's how most SharePoint projects begin to fail. What you will gain from the following sections is a much broader scope of ECM to help you prevent this from happening.

What is Enterprise Content Management?

Enterprise Content Management (ECM) is not a technology, and SharePoint is not an out-of-the-box ECM solution. These two statements contradict what some have thought to be fact and the marketing slicks and PowerPoint presentations so many of us have seen. You might be asking yourself, "What gives, we bought into SharePoint so that we could have an ECM Solution?"

ECM is a set of practices, processes, and methodology that make the technology morph into the most effective way to store, secure, and consume content. SharePoint is a platform, a grab bag of features, and technology that can be molded into a fantastic ECM solution.

ECM is also not moving what has been done in shared drives to a web-based modern platform. Consider how shared drives evolve, how much file duplication and organizational chaos is typically found in shared drives accessed by a community of users. It is extremely hard to find anything resembling structure. Ask yourself the following questions:

- Does your company have a documented File Naming Convention policy?

- Do the Shared Drives you work with follow a common Directory naming structure?

- Can you easily navigate another department or workgroups Directory structure and find a file?

Most will answer no to these questions, and when asked in a group setting these questions usually provoke eye rolling, scoffs, and jeers. The organization and planning of Shared Drives happens in real-time during content creation. This is often impounded by busy workdays, staff changes, and different personal organizational strategies. Ultimately, this approach is not considered a solution for proper content management.

One must acknowledge that unplanned ECM is the process of taking this same structure and lack of planning and modernizing it. Simply doing a one-for-one transposition of the Share Drive into SharePoint results in an even more rapid use of a very bad system.

ECM is the opposite of this; it requires up-front planning and practical application of information architecture. It assumes a standardization of proven methods for capturing, naming, and storing content. In the past, this required a lot of effort and thought on the part of the user. But more and more, technology is taking over for the unfriendly pieces.

Q & A

Q: How many ways can you organize unstructured information?

A: Four—chronologically, alphabetically, numerically, and geographically. These four approaches are compounded by the many ways people use, format, and duplicate them.

In most cases, the information stored in an ECM system is used to support the primary corporate data found in traditional line-of-business (LOB) systems, such as contract management, human resources management (HRMS), customer relationship management (CRM), or enterprise resource planning (ERP) systems. You can commonly find "ECM solutions" with content not attached to LOB applications. Usually, this is a sign of bad ECM, but there can be exceptions. An increasing number of ECM systems are now being used to drive complex LOB activities because people often end up looking for an important document or record to answer a question or to complete a business transaction.

It often takes organizations several failed attempts to realize that without proper ECM no platform can succeed as a content management system. And without a platform with the right set of features, and end-user ease-of-use ECM can't succeed. The core feature sets of an ECM solution are as follows:

- Storage of documents

- Document viewing

- Document editing

- Document security

- Metadata model

- Versioning of documents

- Check-in/check-out of documents

SharePoint today lends itself very nicely as an ECM solution, but that has not always been the case. SharePoint has evolved to provide all the necessary components of an ECM solution, capable of facilitating the complete life cycle of content management. Prior to SharePoint 2010, you could not implement a structured system that would be considered a suitable tool for large scale ECM.

Starting with SharePoint 2007 MOSS, core ECM functionality outlined above was brought into the platform. While SharePoint 2007 could be molded into a reasonable ECM solution for small business, it missed some core functionality in the following areas:

- eDiscovery

- Electronic forms

- Records declarations

- Consistent metadata models

- Business process management

- User and service level audit logs

- Compound documents

With SharePoint 2010, this functionality was introduced, and SharePoint was finally a full-blown ECM solution capable of delivering at almost every level. SharePoint 2010 was still lacking in a few areas, such as more robust business process management, document auditing, information architecture, and capture for document imaging. In these cases, third-party solutions appeared out of the Microsoft Partner community and took the 90 percent to 100 percent. We will highlight some of possibilities for widely used third-party solutions that you will want to evaluate, depending on your specific project requirements.

 Note In this book we will focus on ECM related features. While SharePoint can be used for many information management use cases we will not be including or highlighting areas like Business Intelligence, Web Content Management, or Social Collaboration.

With the release of SharePoint 2013, the following additional features are included:

- Disposition of sites

- Federated eDiscovery

These are two desperately needed ECM tools we will discuss later. SharePoint 2013 also brings some new challenges. The new user interface is better for user adoption but trickier from a governance standpoint. For example, the new "Share" feature, when not properly governed, will cause uncontrolled propagation of site security. Remember SharePoint sprawl, mentioned in the Introduction? The rapid adoption of the Share feature without governance can aggravate sprawl. We will discuss this in greater detail later.

Now that we know that SharePoint 2010 and, more importantly, SharePoint 2013 offer the complete feature set of ECM and then some, we can discuss how organizations can leverage SharePoint as a complete ECM Solution.

A very common misperception about ECM in SharePoint exists with organizations that believe that, by using team sites and collaboration features or by uploading content from shared drives, they are performing ECM. This simply is not the case. These are manifestations of the same bad content habits in a more modern way. This points to one of the primary reasons that ECM projects in SharePoint fail.

Top five reasons ECM in SharePoint fails

- Not understanding that ECM is a methodology, and SharePoint is a platform

- Jumping into adoption with no project planning

- Trying to build an organization-wide ECM solution versus a quick win

- Not balancing technology, business, and user requirements

- Stakeholders speaking different languages of the business, such as technical versus operational

Speaking the same language is a common issue and is the trickiest to identify and mind-bogglingly hard to address. Very often, knowledge workers who request the need for technology for more efficient document processes do not possess the knowledge to ask the right questions of the IT professionals who are responsible for delivering a solution.

To mitigate this, many organizations are utilizing the role of business analyst to bridge the gap between user requirements, IT implementation, and operational benefits to the organization. This role can be justified, but return on investment (ROI) can be hard to measure in terms of hard dollar costs versus savings. The ROI for a position such as business analyst is best determined by looking at the soft costs and opportunity costs of getting it right the first time.

Business Analyst or Information Architect

In most cases, the role of the person who manages the communication between IT and the rest of the business is called a Business Analyst. Traditionally this position focused solely on analyzing the effectiveness of a specific business process and the systems that are used to facilitate that process. There is a difference between analyzing and documenting the outcomes of a business process and providing the upfront planning and guidance for the ECM solution you are designing. If you have seen the Business Analyst role expand to include these types of activities we recommend that you intentionally separate them and assign a new role of Information Architect.

Too often, organizations look only at raw capital expense put into deploying ECM, which is the cost of employee time, professional services, hardware costs, and software licensing. They don't factor in what it will take in terms of change management, user adoption, and the implementation of new policies and amendments. In some cases, the deployment of a SharePoint ECM solution can require changes to job function or description for certain aspects of department operations for individual roles. These are just some of the areas where a business analyst adds tremendous value.

A good Information Architect

- Works with all parties and speaks both IT and Business Operations language

- Helps mitigate misunderstandings between departments

- Navigates a variety of personalities and political turf issues

- Understands the principles of project management

As you can see, the communication gap is not a trivial issue. It requires admission from both the end-users and IT that they are not communicating and perhaps don't know how the organization operates today. And it even sometimes requires an individual just to manage the requirements gathering and communication.

We have defined at a high level what ECM is, why SharePoint is an ECM solution, and the problems organizations face when taking the SharePoint platform and configuring it to deliver a complete ECM solution. Before we go further let's dig into the details of the ECM components.

In this section of the book, we will look at the definitions of each component of the ECM stack, and in later chapters, we will examine the full details about each component's use and implementation in SharePoint.

The ECM stack

We started this chapter telling you that ECM is not a technology, but rather a methodology. This implies that to execute on those methodologies there must be some collection of technology that can do it. The ECM stack is where we stop talking about ECM as a single comprehensive object and start breaking it into its pieces. It's in the pieces that we align the methods to technology.

The ECM Stack includes all the components of an ECM solution. It is sometimes referred to as the document life cycle. The document life cycle is defined as all possible stages that a document can encounter in its life. The primary stages and components are shown in Figure 1-1.

First comes the Capture stage, which puts the content into the system. The next stage, Store, focuses on storing content, which is predominantly achieved automatically with technology. This is the proper committing of the captured content to the system and is both the logical and physical storage of the content and associated metadata. These two stages feed the ECM system with appropriate content. These stages are considered by most knowledge workers to be the least beneficial to their operation, but without them, knowledge workers have nothing to execute on. It's in the Manage, Deliver, and Process stages where the real value of the content becomes obvious.

We have found that in user adoption it's a lot easier to convince users to engage in the management, delivery, and processing of content than in the Capture and Store stages. However, without good capture and storag e of content, effective management, delivery, and processing can't happen. Later we will discuss strategies for user adoption.

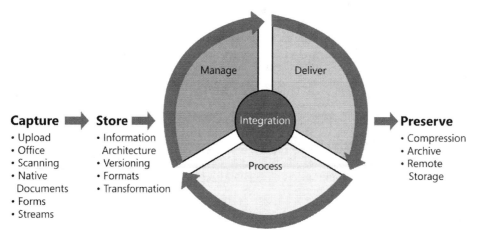

FIGURE 1-1 ECM stages.

The goal is to spend most planning effort on the quality of the Capture, Store, and Manage stages so that very little effort is required for the Delivery, Process, and Preserve stages. Arguably, the lion shares of the planning for ECM are in the Capture, Store, and Manage stages, while the Delivery, Process, and Preserve stages should be nearly effortless, with good content being put into SharePoint.

We have laid out the document life cycle in Figure 1-2. The diagram is laid out to signify two additional aspects. First, on an X-axis, we have outlined features in each of the document life cycle stages and listed them in order of the most commonly used features in SharePoint to the least commonly used. Second, on a Y-axis, we have ordered each document life cycle according to the amount of planning and configuration effort that should be placed on each stage.

It's important to think of these stages, beginning with Capture and ending with Preserve, as having "downstream" effects. What happens, the good and bad, while capturing content directly impacts the quality in the Deliver and Preserve stages. If content is captured and identified inconsistently or if a minimalist approach is taken to applying metadata, the ability to find the content will be greatly diminished.

While the greatest benefits to the majority of users is found by searching and finding content in the Deliver stage, the understanding and adherence to the "downstream" concept will ensure that you take capture seriously. The proper attention to detail in each stage will ensure successful results for knowledge workers when they are searching, processing, or managing content. We will define each of these document life cycle stages in this chapter.

Ultimately, these components align to a feature or combination of features in SharePoint. These technologies/features/aspects combine to make the overall ECM solution. Some deployments can have additional components, and at the later stages of the ECM stack, for example, some organizations can omit preservation and eDiscovery. This inclusion of these later stages is usually driven by specific business needs or regulatory compliance requirements. We find that, for the most part, all organizations will or should deploy some aspect of all these stages.

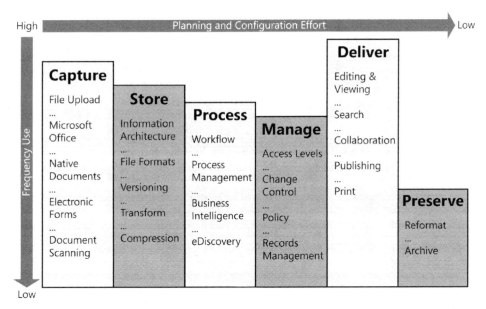

FIGURE 1-2 ECM life cycle.

As we said earlier, each SharePoint component aligns to a feature or combination of features. In later sections of this book, we will explain the alignment and provide examples. Now let's look at each stage in more detail.

Capture

Think of Capture as grabbing information: grabbing it from existing content stored elsewhere, grabbing it from the minds of its curators, or grabbing it from one format and transforming it into another. We capture content constantly without knowing it. Even the process of writing this book is a form of "born-digital" capture.

Capture is the process of preparing, collecting, and indexing content before being stored in an ECM Platform. Capture into SharePoint can happen in the following six distinct ways, ordered by most common to least common:

1. File upload

2. Microsoft documents

3. Document capture

4. Natively created SharePoint documents

5. Electronic forms

6. Data streams

Many tools, forms, formats

During the authoring of this book, we used online document collaboration, email, Microsoft Office, and Skype. These can all be considered forms of Capture.

Without the Capture stage, content does not get into the system. Often this stage is transparent to users because they do it so frequently that they do not realize they are doing it.

This can cause problems in the planning stages of ECM deployment. As depicted in Figure 1-2, Capture is the second-most used stage in ECM, and requires the most planning. We all recognize that this is step one, so failure here results in failure in any downstream stages.

As one of the primary goals for this book, we want to make sure that your ECM team is speaking the same language, so let's look at the specific types of content capture so that we are all on the same page.

From the field

One time I was sitting with a client telling them how great document imaging would be for him. He peered at me from behind a stack of papers on his desk, with filing cabinets at both sides of him, saying, "This technology is cool, but we don't use paper anymore." - Chris

---

File upload

File upload is the most common way users contribute content to SharePoint. Here we are mostly referring to ad hoc user-driven file upload, but the mechanism can also be used in bulk either by a user or by an unattended script.

Users are most accustomed to browsing to a local file location, selecting the file, and uploading it to a designated space in SharePoint. It is one of the slowest capture processes, but it usually results in the greatest quality of content and metadata.

Primarily performed as a singular activity, based on immediate needs to share or manage a document collaboratively with other users, the file upload method is rarely used to bulk load content into SharePoint. Although users might attempt to do so, it is not recommended.

Document uploading can happen by both browsing to a local folder or network directory and selecting a document(s) to upload. In addition, users can simply drag files onto the document library web interface.

Note There is a SharePoint user interface limitation of 100 items for bulk operations in the web interface. You can use scripting tools such as Windows PowerShell to perform bulk-loading operations for larger volumes of content.

Organizations can elect to automate the initial load of content into SharePoint, leveraging either Windows PowerShell scripts or migration tools. In later chapters, we will explain both the risks and the benefits of this approach.

One key element of the manual document upload is the process from the users' perspective. Where are they finding the content? My Documents? A Shared drive? This could highlight some issues that you certainly don't want transferred over. What are they uploading? Certain file formats don't belong in ECM, so do you allow your users to upload anything they have access to? What metadata must they complete for a successful upload? We will address these issues in detail in the next chapter.

Microsoft Office documents

Office documents are a born-digital method of capture. These documents have never known a physical existence. This comes with a lot of advantages. This is when a user creates a document in the Microsoft Office suite (PowerPoint, Word, Excel, and so on), which supports the saving of documents directly into an accessible document library.

The advantages of the born-digital method are improved capture accuracy and, most importantly, ease of use. In this mode of operation, SharePoint libraries are "save as" locations for content. Using Office as a client application to contribute content to SharePoint is also a solution that most end-users embrace, because it's similar to how they have always worked with content.

This encourages knowledge workers to adopt habits leading them away from the storage of content in "My Documents" and "Shared Drives," which is one step closer to better capture. However, this approach works best when knowledge workers are located within the corporate firewall that is connected to the farm 24/7. Lapses in connectivity can cause problems with upload, versioning, and, more painfully, user adoption.

Proper user training can help with this, and SharePoint "Workspaces" is another alternative. Workspaces is a client Office application that allows content saved in a specific location to be auto-matically uploaded to SharePoint. Conversely, it allows the viewing of SharePoint Libraries as a folder on your desktop. This is very similar to "Explorer view" and, for the purposes of this book, is consid-ered the same tool.

While Workspaces and "Explorer view" can be used for project portals and personal file reposito-ries, they should not be used for ECM. From a technical point of view, the functionality in Workspaces actually allows the bypassing of proper ECM functionality such as managed meta data columns. From a strategic point of view, if you offer users Workspaces, they are encouraged to live in a My Documents type structure and not a proper ECM. Give the users Workspaces, and you will never be able to take it away.

While many Office documents are manually created, we recommend coaching users to create documents in Office that are saved directly to SharePoint Libraries or, even better, to create content by using built-in Office Web Applications.

Native SharePoint documents

The second type of born digital document is the native SharePoint document. Native SharePoint documents are those documents created without the use of an external client. They very often are Office documents with the addition of blogs, wikis, and pages. For documents, this is done using a feature in SharePoint called Office Web Applications OWA.

> **Note** Office Web Applications is an add-on in SharePoint 2010 and SharePoint 2013 that allows users to create content in-browser instead of using a client application. It requires Office CALs, and it has some limited functionality compared to client applications. In most cases, it is all a typical knowledge worker needs.

SharePoint now supports the authoring of documents directly in the browser. The majority of the required functionality found in Microsoft Office client applications can be found inside the browser, making content capture of 90 percent of documents very easy to perform directly in SharePoint. Today, this is not the most commonly used form of capture; however, it is the future and the desired method to guide users toward.

As we look to the future of ECM, natively born-digital documents will take over, shortening the time to capture, increasing the accuracy of content capture and its metadata, and being more acceptable to end-users. The challenge of this approach is to make sure that an organization is current in browser and operating system support.

We now move to types of Capture that are more use-case specific and sometimes omitted by organizations.

Electronic form capture

Electronic form submission is one way to get user content into SharePoint. The process enables individuals to complete online forms often referred to as e-forms, and the results of form submission are saved directly to SharePoint. The person completing the form very often will not have access to the form submission content nor necessarily be a named user in SharePoint.

The preferred approach to electronic form submissions in SharePoint is the Microsoft product called InfoPath, because it is a tightly integrated electronic form solution. However, it is also possible to leverage third-party or custom e-form solutions. We will include references to additional resources that can be used for e-form solutions in SharePoint later in this book.

Note Because individuals who submit forms are most often not the consumers of content in this capture scenario, security is a primary concern. Often, it's important that submissions are not accessible to submitters.

One of the most neglected aspects of form capture is form design. Without good electronic form design, the information entered into the form rapidly diminishes in quality. Because electronic forms are one of the best ways to capture structured information and metadata, we encourage organizations to spend considerable time on the usability, presentation, and transformation of their forms.

For purposes of this book, discussion of the specifics of e-forms and InfoPath will be omitted. Rather, forms will be highlighted as a way to get content into SharePoint.

Document scanning

Often, documents are not born digital. They begin as physical entities, but they need to be a part of the ECM system just as critically as born-digital documents. The process of capturing this content is called document imaging or document scanning.

This process occurs in three primary ways: ad hoc, departmental/distributed, or production capture. The process also can include image-only capture or capture with intelligent conversion technology.

The owner of the content at their client workstation performs ad hoc capture with an attached document scanner. Departmental/distributed capture is an extension of this, but shared document imaging stations are usually shared among several knowledge works. Finally, production capture focuses on centralizing all capture operations, controlling the indexing, and performing advanced processing and data collection functions in a predictable manner.

How organizations pick one type of capture over another depends on the document maturity of an organization or their own structure. Later we will go into detail about how the various types of capture can be incorporated into SharePoint. While SharePoint does not have natively built-in scanning functionality, there are several ways to incorporate ad hoc and departmental scanning. Production scanning is often considered as a process outside of SharePoint.

Content streams

Sometimes content is not created by a user but rather by another system. "Integration" is a rather broad term that describes connecting disparate systems. For purposes of ECM, we will define a specific type of integration where only content and metadata are transferred from outside SharePoint into SharePoint and refer to it as *content streams*.

A content stream can come from any electronic source and is defined as the ingestion or publishing of metadata and content via some standard such as Windows PowerShell, REST, XML, and RSS. An example would be the consumption of news feeds inside of a SharePoint page or the publishing of RSS feeds for a list to be consumed by another system.

The functions are broad, covering many different methods for integrating the capture of content in SharePoint. The most important thing to understand is the necessity and governance of such integrations and how it relates to the other forms of capture. For example, surfacing documents that live in another content system impacts the way an organization will plan their ECM environment and train their users.

After content is captured, it has to be properly stored. This moves us to the Store process.

Store

Storage is not just the writing of a document's content to a list or library. It also refers to all aspects of that document, including its security, its history, and its metadata. The following pieces of document storage are listed in the order that they should be implemented and used:

1. Information Architecture

2. Formats

3. Versioning

4. Transformation

Storage is the physical and logical storage of content and associated metadata. The distinction is important. Some might consider storage as equivalent to file shares and databases. The danger in this is that in ECM we add a strong logical component to storage in the form of metadata. It's this metadata that makes downstream ECM processes possible. Without it, you end up neglecting information architecture in favor of a new representation of the old shared drive paradigm or forgetting that the physical file has to be saved somewhere as well. This results both in no planning for scalability and in hitting a wall at some content storage limit.

> ### It's not just Storage
>
> Logical Storage: The metadata model and references that SharePoint uses to find the content—for example, a hyperlink.
>
> Physical Storage: The actual location of the content (technically, the BLOB object)—that is, the combination of server, database, and storage device or server used.

In SharePoint, the physical storage happens in Microsoft SQL databases. These databases are referred to as *content databases*. This is the physical location of the BLOB object that makes up the documents content. Metadata is stored in a separate location and then linked to the content BLOB.

Information Architecture is the logical storage of content. This includes web applications, site collections, sites, list, libraries, and content types. This includes their configuration, number, and relationship to each other.

Arguably, information architecture is one of the most critical components to successful ECM and is where an organization will spend the majority of its time planning.

SharePoint also supports configuration of Remote BLOB (Binary Large Objects) Storage (RBS). We will talk more about this in Chapter 2.

RBS can facilitate a measure of scalability for specific use-cases that involve large individual file sizes and/or high volumes of objects. The configuration of RBS can be targeted to specific SharePoint Web Apps, Site Collections, or individual sites.

An example of this would be large engineering vector files and high-volume document imaging solutions. In most use-cases, RBS is not necessary, and storing the objects in the database has the advantage of providing one source from a backup and disaster recovery perspective.

To continue the theme of making sure that your ECM team is speaking the same language, let's look at the specific aspects of a standard SharePoint information architecture so that we are all on the same page.

Information Architecture

Often, Information Architecture is confused with one of its individual components, such as folders or site collections, rather than looking at it holistically. We find that while many organizations implement Information Architecture organically, very few know what it is. We can visualize all aspects of Information Architecture in Figure 1-3, showing that this is the logical location of content in SharePoint. The figure shows, in a hierarchical order, all aspects that define the logical storage of a document and how its metadata is represented. In later chapters, we will define each of these and their use in detail.

The growing trend is to make the repository portion of Information Architecture as flat as possible and the metadata portion as comprehensive as possible. Later in the book, we will talk about the theoretically ideal Information Architecture and align it with practical implementations of SharePoint. We will come up with guidelines for designing your Information Architecture.

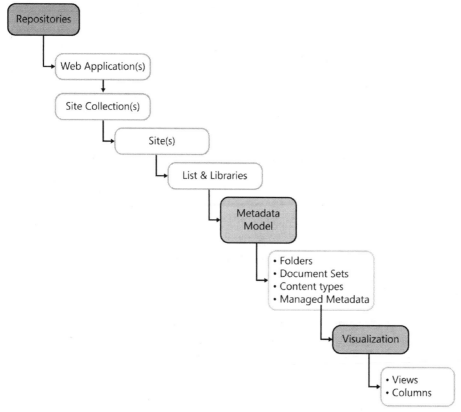

FIGURE 1-3 Information Architecture.

Note What you might not realize is that a folder is just a piece of metadata. To file systems, a folder appears as an extension of the file name. What folders do is offer a single point of view for content, which is too limited because it doesn't provide flexibility in terms of user search. Additionally, in situations that require support for large volumes of content, folders have inherent rendering limitations. By incorporating a flatter information architecture with more metadata, users can slice and dice content according to several variables at the same time, changing that single one-dimensional point of view into a multidimensional, flexible way to browse and search for content.

Q & A

Q: Are folders bad ECM?

A: The trend is to abolish folders as the exclusive method for managing content.

We dare to suggest that Information Architecture is not only the place where you will spend most of your time in planning a good ECM solution, but also a place where you can have fun. For those who strive to be organized, Information Architecture is where it happens.

In contrast, the use of proper metadata in content types instead of folders allows a user to slice and dice content on any number of combinations of information they want. Metadata provides a more flexible means of organizing and reorganizing content on the fly. Surfacing content in visual folder layouts is acceptable, but it must be used in conjunction with metadata and search.

From the field

File formats

One time, I had a client struggling with certain files in SharePoint. I found out that the user was trying to apply ECM logic to .dll and .exe files. I had to stop this practice immediately. - Shad

Every file enters SharePoint as a file format. Most commonly, when we talk about ECM, we are talking about Word documents (.docx), text files (.txt), and compressed portable files (.pdf). A great but often dangerous aspect of SharePoint is that *anything* can be content in Share-Point. As long as there is an electronic way to represent an object, it can live in SharePoint. This includes .dll files, .zip files, and so on. We could even invent a file type (.you) and place it in SharePoint.

Because this is true, the types of files a user can contribute to SharePoint should be controlled. Consider the following:

- Are the files you are storing supported for native SharePoint viewing?

- Do you have the proper management tools (iFilters, Viewers) to support non-native access?

We recommend that ECM planning teams determine approved file formats that are permitted, and the fewer the better. This reduces the overhead of managing the files and opens the doors for more possibilities.

For example, if an organization could ensure that all content contributed to SharePoint consisted of Microsoft Office documents, the organization would then be able to consider the features in SharePoint that allow for the automatic formatting of office documents with barcodes. If the organization can't ensure this, enabling this feature will result in inconsistent content consumption and use.

We will share suggested approaches to file formats and configuration alternatives later in the book. Even in organizations with a variety of specialized content, you can limit the format types to a small subset by using proper conversion and transformation technologies.

Versioning

As documents come in to the right location, in the right format, they often need to be versioned.

Versioning is the process of storing earlier versions of a document with their associated time and date stamps. The earlier versions might be used to revert back to previous version, for comparison across versions and for sharing one version while a more current version is still being edited. This is not to be confused with tracking changes in a Word document; tracking changes is a function that facilitates the creation of versions, but it is not a version control system. In SharePoint, versioning can happen automatically. When a document is saved, it is possible to save a major version or a minor version. The versioning number system is what determines whether it's major or minor. A minor version is everything to the right of the dot or decimal, and the major version is everything on the left side. For example, a document with version 3.5 has a major version of 3 and a minor version of 5.

Because major and minor versioning is usually used only when an organization publishes documents—for example, to an extranet or partner portal—the major version represents the published version while minor versions remain unpublished and continually edited. So while editors are working on version 3.5 and on to 4, the people who have access only to published versions see version 3. When versions are saved, the editor has the ability to add comments to help identify what changed in the version. Some versioning happens upon document upload and is automatic, based on filenames that already exist.

There are two dangers of versioning. The first is blindly enabled versioning, which could result in the overwriting of files without the users knowing. The second and more serious danger of versioning is the impact it has on content databases by adding a separate copy of the document and additional comment metadata. This can cause a site collection to get too large too fast.

One of the huge benefits of the SharePoint Platform is that anything and everything can be content. Besides file size limitations per file, there is no limitation on the type of file you can upload to SharePoint. However, there are best practices for choosing which file formats to support as a policy. The considerations are based on how functional the files are, how they can be viewed or edited, and whether they pose any security risks.

The most common formats used are MS Office documents and PDF files. But it's not uncommon to see media files, CAD files, and other proprietary file formats. Another part of file formats in SharePoint is a mechanism called iFilter. The iFilter is what makes content useful to SharePoint. It exposes the internal content of the document in a way that SharePoint can index and search on it. It also is necessary for third-party products that run within SharePoint to visualize, edit, or otherwise work on the content.

Transformation

As we indicated in the "From the field" sidebar on formatting, transformation, while not always a consideration, often becomes an important consideration when it comes to the types of file formats you allow and the desired formats to have in the ECM system.

Transformation, also referred to as *conversion*, is the process of taking an original file format and converting or transforming it into another. The transformation process often is just a format change, but it can also include other processes, such as optical character recognition, natural language processing, translation, and other types of content manipulation that make the resulting document more useful. SharePoint has some built-in conversion functionality for Office documents and hooks to incorporate other transformation processes.

You now have the documents captured, properly stored in a content database in the right filing location according to your Information Architecture. You have them in the right format with versioning capabilities. Guess what? This is starting to look like a real ECM system. Now let's work on managing the content that has found its way into SharePoint.

Manage

The Manage portion of Enterprise Content Management comprises all aspects around governance of the system. This includes informal and formal policies for users, the requirements for how content is captured, the requirements for how content is stored and secured, what is involved in records management, how and when content is deleted or consumed, and finally, but most ignored, how the system grows.

Governance is defined as bringing together all the elements necessary to facilitate the long-term preservation, accessibility, and disposition of content. This is first accomplished by establishing Organizational Policies and Procedures and often includes authoring and review of a document reviewed and approved by the Legal Department and then formally adopted by the Board of Directors. After this is completed, it can be used as a guideline for implementing a records management plan that includes a formal definition of records, how long they are to be kept, how they are disposed of, who has the authority, and what to do in case of litigation. In conjunction with well-defined Information Architecture, a complete governance plan can help ensure that the user adoption is high and that the extensibility of the ECM solution is straightforward

Governance includes the following elements:

- Records management
- Security and access
- Policies
- Change control

Records management

Records management, like its broader parent, ECM, is a practice and methodology. However, records management requires a far more strict set of principles. Records management includes the following disciplines:

- Records series

- Records declaration

- Retention schedules

A record is a stamp in content, time, location, and metadata for a document. When a document is declared as a record, its content will not change; the metadata, such as last modified data, will not change; and its logical and physical storage location will not change. Very often, there is an additional step that occurs during records declaration, which is a reassignment of security so that individuals who don't have authority cannot access the records.

In the past, SharePoint records management was limited only to record centers. A records center automatically declares all documents as records when they are saved in that site collection designated as a records center. However, now with SharePoint 2013, records declaration can happen in a records center or in any other library automatically, via a workflow, or with manual in-place records management.

Records and non-records alike might be subject to retention schedules. A *retention schedule* is a listing of all document types and their associated life spans. For example, a contract might be deleted five years after the termination date. Retention schedules are required in compliance-driven industries but are not common in smaller business. However, the use of retention schedules is an excellent discipline for any organization and can be a cheat sheet for implementing ECM in SharePoint.

Records management, even when implemented, does not apply to all content. The relevant content is determined by the retention schedule and is usually critical to business operation or contains potential risk/value associated with compliance or litigation. Organizations, even without records managers or records management policies, can choose to learn from the strict organization principles so that the can be better prepared for future compliance restrictions or litigation. The retention schedule also determines which elements of metadata are required or not. This particular practice of deciding what metadata is required or not, while mentioned here in records management, is mandatory for all organizations.

Note Sometimes the enforcement of mandatory metadata is referred to as "management by the red asterisk" because of the symbol placed next to mandatory metadata fields. The plus of this strategy is that you get better metadata when content is added; the minus is that users add less content to avoid it. There is a balance to be achieved.

In your organization, it's not the content you know about that can hurt you; it's the content that you don't know about.

Security and access

Another huge benefit to SharePoint is its ability to manage security at nearly any level. What you learned above about Information Architecture is an absolutely critical element in security considerations. The various site collections, sites, and libraries will all have separate security considerations.

Access levels are among those considerations. Who has access to what? Similar to Information Architecture, the hierarchy of security can spiral out of control. Security and access levels have a direct one-to-one relationship. For example, even though item level security can be achieved in SharePoint, the maintenance and risk of such a policy is high. Also, as with Information Architecture, the trend is to make security envelopes at the top level and flatten and widen the repository where security restrictions are applied. For example, instead of having a site collection for all departments and a site below it per department, organizations are making a site collection per department, with security at the site collection level instead of the site level.

SharePoint has the ability to show to users only content they have access to and also block users out of a repository completely, if necessary. This process is called security trimming and is a tremendous tool that you can use to help protect content and support compliance initiatives.

Security is one way to enforce governance, but it does not solve everything.

> **Note** *Security trimming* is the process of showing only the content that the currently logged in user has access to. For example, if you do a search for documents with the term "security" in it, SharePoint will first find all, for example, 100 documents that have the word "security" in it. But because the user logged in has security access to only 20 of those documents, SharePoint will show only the 20 documents the user has access to. This is true in libraries as well.

Policy

There are certain elements to governance that can be implemented with technology, some can be implemented only with rules, and others could be accomplished with either technology or written rule, so a decision must be made. For example, "management by the red asterisks" is the process of making certain metadata fields required for document upload. But this can encourage users not to use the system when over used, so it might be better for an organization to declare to its knowledge workers which metadata is required and which is not.

A policy is a written rule on how to use the system. What is written in a policy is one thing, but how the policy is implemented is far more important. Most policies will also need to have specific procedures and, in some cases, user training to make sure policies are understood. Policy is usually set at an executive, board, or steering committee level. The department management and knowledge workers familiar with the business process generally develop procedures. A policy that is simply published without documented procedures, training, and, ultimately, enforcement is rarely effective. Therefore, part of a policy system must include the enforcement system. What we mean when we say this is that if you are going to make the policy, you have to take action when it's broken or the policy's value is nullified.

Organizations might want to believe they can do without policy and utilize technology enforcement or rely on the better judgment of their users. This will ultimately lead to great adoption in the wrong way or to no user adoption at all. Not considering the policy system can result in ECM failure.

Change control

When an organization decides to take on a project like SharePoint, the requirements will slowly evolve with time. They actually start to evolve as soon as the project starts. However, if your organization is similar to others and plans for all adaptations along the way, you will be crippled by planning and ultimately finish nothing. There has to be a system that prepares for changes in requirements, technical environment, and business environment so that these changes do not halt the deployment of a system, prevent its adoption, or prevent its extensibility into future solutions for an organization.

Change control is the process of managing this change. In any system, the life of the system can be impacted heavily by change in organization structure, staff, or even just focus. Change control is the tool used to mitigate these negative impacts on the system so that they don't accumulate to reduce the life of the system. In ECM, change control starts at the project kickoff and lasts throughout the life of the system on to the next one. It defines the roles, what happens when a change to the system is requested, and who is responsible for the longevity of the system.

By its very definition, ECM is global in scope, so most business systems and processes have an impact on other departments in one way or another. Truly understanding the impact that poor change management can have is usually felt when a system goes down or a process fails. This happens for a variety of reasons, and we have all been there when things go bad due to a random change made without planning, approval, and documentation.

> ## From the field
>
> *Specific staff such as legal, records managers, clerks, and content managers usually take on the management aspects of ECM. Ideally, when managed and implemented well, taking on these responsibilities has a low impact on its users, with the right amount of control to ensure the success of the system. Users do not like being managed, but they will respect a system that is consistent and always up and running in a proper way. They will also respect the fact that not just the user has to be concerned about their content; the organization has to be concerned with the integrity of the entire catalog of documents contributed by all users. - Shad*

Deliver

The content delivery stage is the process of enhancing content with new information or consuming the content it already has. This includes editing of existing documents, changing of metadata, and sharing of the content with other users. The components of the Deliver stage are as follows:

- Search

- Editing and viewing

- Publishing

Users love the delivery portion of content management. It's where they start to see the value of capture, storage, and management. The biggest value of content comes when it's used effectively in a decision-making processes. To do so efficiently, the user interface and functions need to be created to facilitate the rapid viewing and editing of documents.

These tools should be fast and effective. The knowledge worker should burn as little time as possible getting to the desired content and spend the bulk of time reviewing and/or editing the content. The primary tools for delivery are search, editing, viewing, print, publishing, and collaboration.

Search

Search is the processes of using keywords or Boolean logic to locate content and information. The process of search is to issue a query and to review a set of results to determine an appropriate item. While the actual search query feature is fairly basic, the tools that isolate the correct piece of content or, even further, the correct page in the correct content are very complex. Such features include best bets, search refiners, and relevance.

Search can be both a positive and negative indicator. The more often that users find what they are looking for will imply that the Information Architecture is perfect. Also, the fact that you can search across the enterprise is empowering and reduces the time it takes for you to get to content. Therefore, search and Information Architecture are intimately tied and share joint planning. They are so tied, in fact, that they share components. Facets, also referred to as *refiners*, are components of Information Architecture as well.

The goal of search is to get users to content faster. Search can start out with very basic principles but quickly evolves to topics such as thumbnails, best bets, in-page relevance, and so on. Whatever the cool components of search, the end game is always the same: get the user to the right content with the fewest clicks.

> **Note** The approach we will stress is to put more energy into Information Architecture and encourage the use of other tools rather than search. But when search is needed, keep it simple until a specific requirement arises.

After a user finds the document, either via search or browsing, they have to be able to view and edit it.

Editing and viewing

While users don't often realize where they spend their time or why they do what they do, a simple study will prove that users spend most their day in some sort of viewer. A web browser is a viewer, Outlook is a viewer for email clients, and SharePoint is a viewer for content. An amazing amount of time is spent reading and consuming content as compared to creating it. Most job functions spend the majority of their time consuming rather than creating, while other specific audiences, such as technical writers, business analysts, and publishers, spend a lot of time creating and editing. For this reason, the ability to do this seamlessly is critical.

With the exception for records and archived documents, the majority of content is living. It gets edited and viewed on a regular basis. SharePoint has built in viewers for Office documents. This allows you to work with the documents in the manner in which you are accustomed. For other varied file formats, a different type of editor might be required. It's important in the planning process to understand how content will be consumed, edited, and repurposed.

You need to understand that viewing and editing ties heavily to the formats discussed in the Store stage of ECM. The fewer types of documents, the easier it is for organizations to creating great editing and viewing tools for them. The Office suite has the clear advantage of having essentially bundled viewing and editing capabilities with SharePoint, either with client applications or with Office Web Apps. Documents such as PDF, which is predominantly designed for viewing and not editing, have special considerations when it comes to ease of access. For example, do you allow users to open the PDFs in the browser or client application, or do they have to download to their local machine first?

While the aspects of viewing and editing seem obvious, its considerations are not, which is why it's an essential component to ECM planning.

Publishing

Publishing, which contains aspects of both search and viewing, is the process of pushing content or allowing content to be pulled, by individuals who are not necessarily the curators, for viewing purposes only.

Publishing incorporates versioning in the storage stage, formatting, and ease of access either by targeted search or great Information Architecture. Usually, publishing also includes portals that are branded with basic themes or other more complex branding to make it a great landing page for content consumption. These portals are called intranets or extranets. Content on intranets and extranets is usually read only and comes from another location within the ECM system. This book will discuss in detail creating and managing content for publishing, or rather, the locations from which content is pushed. It will not cover in detail the configuration and branding of such intranet and extranet portals.

Process

Content is not just viewed on an ad hoc basis, or edited, which is essentially another type of capture. Hopefully, it is incorporated into a decision-making process or line-of-business process. The problem is that these types of processes are usually designated for structured information in SharePoint, such as lists. Documents have an additional element of complexity because their content is unstructured, which means incorporating them into any process requires special consideration about their associated metadata.

Process is taking what has been stored in content and incorporating it into another line-of-business activity. These processes are often unmanned and automatic. However, a manually driven process still falls into this aspect of ECM. The elements of process are as follows:

- Workflow
- Business process management
- Business intelligence
- eDiscovery

Workflow

The most common example of process is referred to as *approval workflows*. This is the process of routing a content item or transaction through a series of predefined steps for approval between different layers of management. This is very common in Human Resources, Finance, and Procurement.

For purposes of this book, workflow describes a process that contains one or more states or steps, incorporates user and system tasks, and is routed in a single direction. The purpose of workflows is to take metadata and content and turn them into action. A SharePoint workflow requires an existing business process to be well understood and defined. In most cases, work just gets done, but the flow of how that is accomplished is not documented or fully understood by all knowledge workers. To facilitate that process from beginning to end, there are user driven activities, management decisions, and transactional exceptions that need to be reviewed and completed. Workflows are very high-value items to automate, but most organizations underestimate the amount of due diligence required to prepare for a workflow automation project.

In ECM, the considerations around workflow are not just the content that is moved around via workflow but the steps and considerations of the content flow itself.

Business Process Management (BPM)

Business Process Management looks very similar to workflow, but it differs in that it allows for multidirectional processes, ability to version processes, and change control for processes. It is said that workflow is available out-of-the-box with SharePoint, but BPM usually comes via third-party solutions. The biggest technical difference is not just the workflows that can be created but also the management of those workflows.

In later chapters, workflow and BPM will be discussed together with the assumption that the user is performing out-of-the-box SharePoint functionality.

Business Intelligence and BigData

After content has been captured and processed, gaining insights from the content is a great way to take their value even further. Business intelligence (BI) is a broad category of technology that extracts greater value from content.

The bridge between BI and BigData is very strong. Therefore, we have lumped them together. Both increase the value of the data and assume some sort of structure and good metadata. Arguably, BI is a subset of BigData, although BigData implies manipulation of large datasets, whereas BI could be big or small. We illustrate this in Figure 1-4 by showing content actualization, starting with the most complex and highest cost and moving toward the most commonly used to achieve tangible business value.

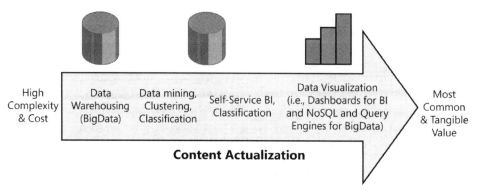

FIGURE 1-4 Content actualization.

BI really falls into the following three types:

- **Dashboards and Key Performance Indicators**   This is most often what people are referring to when they say BI. In SharePoint, this is Performance Point and Conditional Formatting.

- **User-driven BI**   This requires some data expertise and is usually performed using Excel and PowerPivot.

- **Data mining**   Data mining is the intelligent extraction of value, and in SharePoint, it relies on a third-party tool.

Today, most people refer to BI as the ability to visualize large amounts of data in a graphical way, such as a graph. These are referred to as Dashboards or Key Performance Indicators (KPIs). They are fed by structured content, but unstructured content can be incorporated by using technologies such as Natural Language Processing, Text Analytics, Auto-Classification, or incorporating search into the analysis.

User-driven Business intelligence in SharePoint manifests itself as Excel spreadsheets and, more popularly, the PowerPivot add-in for Excel and SharePoint that allows a user to manipulate data in three dimensions or cubes.

Data mining is the most advanced and expensive use of BI. SharePoint can certainly be a source of information for advanced data mining tools but does not natively have data mining tools.

Arguably, BigData is just another definition of, or a broader definition of, a business system that includes and implies larger data sets and the use of a new database approach called NoSQL. Again, SharePoint does not have native BigData support, but it can certainly be used as a source for BigData third-party tools.

eDiscovery

A very specific type of processing of content is called eDiscovery. This particular process is one that organizations hope to avoid. Not only is the process of audits, litigation, and so on painful to the organization, the cost of such processes when not planned for is phenomenal.

> **Note** An organization of 250–500 employees with 2–3 TB of data will pay in excess of $300,000 to cover the cost of just eDiscovery associated with litigation. Organizations well prepared for eDiscovery not only reduce the cost when they are faced with a matter; they improve the overall organization of their ECM system. A *matter* is the subject of legal action, compliance, or content audit. *Discovery* is the process of gathering content associated with the subject.

When planned for, this cost can be dramatically reduced. And the process of planning for eDiscovery, fortunately, is the same as all aspects discussed in search and Information Architecture. Why? Because eDiscovery is essentially search combined with records management.

eDiscovery seems like some abstract term, but it really talks about an advanced form of search. In a later chapter, we will go into more details about what eDiscovery is, how it's used, why it's used, and how it works in SharePoint. eDiscovery is the identification, isolation, and locking of any content that pertains to a matter. The most common instance of a "matter" is litigation. However, a matter could relate to the Freedom of Information Act, content audits, and so on. After eDiscovery is run and content is identified, it must be isolated and separated from content not associated with the matter. The relevant content must be held as a record so that it is not updated or modified, which would make its value null.

It's safe to say that delivery and process are the areas we all enjoy the most when it comes to consuming content. It's also the area where the greatest investments and advances in technology are happening. The goal of ECM is to get users to spend more time in the Process stage and less in the Capture, Store, and Preserve stages of ECM.

Preserve

Content, just like everything else, has a shelf life. Most of the time, content that expires is deleted. This is beneficial to organizations from a compliance and legal perspective and as a part of ECM, but there is some content that is long lived. This type of content, when not consumed regularly, just takes up needless space in an ECM system.

Content preservation is about taking that active content generated as part of ECM and moving it to a location in a format that can be accessed, although infrequently, in the foreseeable future. The important aspect of preservation is storage. In this context, storage refers to both the physical storage of the content and the format that the content will be stored in.

Most organizations prefer to use the high-availability content databases for active and vital content only. For archive content, the preference is to see its metadata but not allow the content to take up space in the content databases. This can be done by using tools such as remote blob storage (RBS).

> **Note** Before active content can become inactive archive content, it must be reformatted.

Reformat

It is very common to reformat content when it's preserved. Ten years ago, the trend was to convert content to microfiche, but today it's PDF/A. The purpose of reformatting is to ensure that it's not editable and to ensure that it can be viewed in the future. The reformat process also includes the purging of unnecessary versions and metadata. In addition to reformatting, many organizations also choose to compress their content.

> **Note** PDF/A is a special PDF format designed for long-time archival of content. It is an open standard that helps ensure the quality of the content and the ability to retrieve the content in any viewer designed to read the format. In addition to the content, it contains standards from metadata.

Reformatting also has the consideration of viewing. How can you be sure that the content you have preserved can be viewed in the future? This is where librarians and content preservationists excel.

Compression

One major consideration for reformatting is the size of files. There is a process of compression that is often considered for reducing the size of files prior to final preservation. The problem is that it's rare to find compression technology that does not alter the content of a document during the compression process. Lossy content, or content that loses quality each time it is converted and/or compressed, is similar to the result of taking a picture of a picture. Over time, information is lost, and the possibilities for editing, consuming, and repurposing content in the future diminish with each iteration.

Compression is just one type of transformation process that is commonly used in ECM. This process reduces the file size of a document without loss of integrity of the content. With graphics, compression can reduce the quality of graphics, but the content of the documents remains. Compression becomes significantly important when discussing ways to save space and archival processes.

Overall, preservation is not all too common, and as the cost of storage reduces and technology for managing content improves, it becomes less and less common. For that reason, preservation will be referred to in this book as a possible end to a document's life in SharePoint, using such tools as RBS and SendTo locations.

Why use ECM?

Now that we have covered all the aspects of ECM, let's talk about the "why" and "who." Specifically, why should your company, department, or team implement ECM? Who will be responsible for implementing ECM, and who will use and benefit from it? The remainder of the book will then cover the "how."

Do not mistake the question of why you should pursue ECM with anything your organization has in terms of current SharePoint implementation. Our goal for "why" you will implement ECM is a question that assumes the perfect hypothetical ECM system, a system where a knowledge worker's effort to capture and categorize content is minimal but the amount of metadata capture is high, and the cost of finding and consuming the content is very low.

These goals are often at odds with each other. For example, expecting a user to enter content into SharePoint in the perfect way means that at time of capture they have to put in additional effort. By not getting the content captured in an ideal manner, the findability of content suffers from long search times and getting, at best, duplicate content and, at worst, the wrong content. In Figure 1-5, we show the contrast in effort between getting content into SharePoint (Capture) and retrieving or finding content (Consumption). Ultimately, you want to automate the process of capturing content to provide enough structured and validated metadata to make the consumption of the content relatively easy.

Note *Findability* is a measure of the effort it takes to locate a document. Content with greater findability enables a user who intends to locate a document to do so with the least amount of effort. Findability can happen at the platform level with tools that improve the quality of all searches, and at the content level with better metadata. You will sometimes hear the term *putability*, which, similar to the term *findability*, is the measure of how easy it is for a user to contribute high-quality, easily findable documents inside of SharePoint.

It was said earlier that it is possible for organizations to plan forever. So it's important to note that all aspects of ECM come with a balance. The emphasis is unique to each organization and its current environment. While it's frustrating, it's a fact of ECM life, and it needs to be accepted.

Therefore, for the sake of this section, we will assume that the ideal ECM solution exists. Your organization's motivating factors for implementing ECM will come from two primary drivers: reactive or proactive.

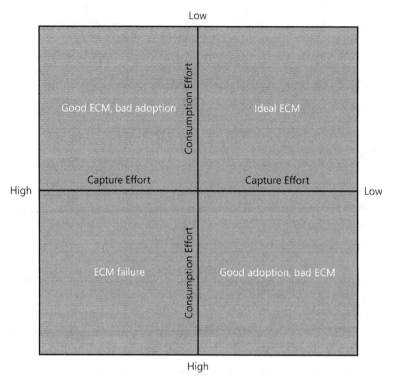

Low

Good ECM, bad adoption | Ideal ECM

Consumption Effort

Capture Effort   Capture Effort

High   Low

Consumption Effort

ECM failure | Good adoption, bad ECM

High

FIGURE 1-5 Capture and consumption.

Proactive driver

It's rare for knowledge workers without the skill set of content management to be interested in ECM without a reactive driver. However, you might have departments or managers that promote a culture that values organization. And from the perspective of being organized, they embrace the methodologies of ECM. Ironically, it's also these departments and this culture that resist change, because they very often have a well-established system for filling content and are not much interested in taking that away.

Another area where organizations are proactive is when ECM has a direct impact on operational costs. This is most often where content touches a line-of-business application. This can be found in health care, insurance, accounting and finance, banking, and so on—that is, organizations where everything has a process and there is content involved. The benefit of these organizations is that they usually already have a retention schedule and content that varies very little in topic, so building an ECM solution is very simple.

And finally, there are the select few, like the book's authors, who love the idea of getting content under control so that greater value can be attained. It is our goal that some readers of this book will finish in this category. Now let's talk about those reactive drivers which are a more common catalyst for ECM.

Reactive driver

Reactive organizations have faced some negative event where the cost of poor ECM was evident. The most common such events are litigation and compliance, where a company was the defendant or claimant in a lawsuit. I'm sure that you can spot something in your organization where you can't help but laugh at the way things are done. At some point, these areas of operation, you hope, are addressed with new approaches.

The second most common is compliance driven. A good example is if your organization operates in an industry that is compliance-heavy, like health care, insurance, or banking. These industries deal with a tremendous amount of regulatory burden. In fact, many of the legislative actions taken to create regulations like SOX (Sarbanes-Oxley), HIPAA (Health Insurance Portability and Accountability Act), and Dodd–Frank (Wall Street Reform and Consumer Protection Act) contain very specific provisions that can be complied with by using components of an ECM solution.

The benefit of the later reactive scenario is that very often, in such cases, the implementation of ECM is very clearly defined, and it's more a matter of conformity. Most often, these organizations, due to their history in the industry, already have a good sense of what needs to be done, and their business challenge is adoption rather than implementation.

For the reactive scenario in litigation, these organizations very often were not aware of what was wrong until it hit them. The process of getting content associated with this litigation is called eDiscovery. Later in this book, we talk in more detail about eDiscovery. The cost associated with eDiscovery is phenomenal. Therefore, to be better prepared and to mitigate these costs in the future, organizations are deploying proper ECM solutions and participating in what is called early discovery.

The reactive scenario is not what the world of ECM hopes companies are using as their primary driver for implementing ECM. The hope is that organizations are thinking about what it takes to best actualize content, get the most value from content, and to make their knowledge workers as effective as they can.

This scenario is very rare and usually combined with one of the above reactive scenarios. There are a handful of organizations who believe that if they better capture, store, and deliver content, their costs of working with content will be reduced, the effectiveness of their staff increased, and finally, that they can move that content into more valuable decision-making processes, such as workflow and BigData.

How can you use information to make better decisions?

Information is just bits of data; it's stored everywhere, and access to the information is abundant. Putting information in context provides the ability to acquire knowledge. Knowing when and where to use the knowledge gained from the information is wisdom. Putting wisdom into action is what differentiates individual performance and enables streamlined decision-making. As shown in Figure 1-6, each step represents a greater degree of meaning derived from content. Departments, workgroups, and knowledge workers who can harness the Information, Knowledge, and Wisdom steps will help an organization to perform at a high level.

FIGURE 1-6 Information steps.

Businesses generally make the mistake of thinking they are managing information by having hardware, software, and communications. In the majority of organizations, information is stuck in silos, duplicated without control and communicated in an inconsistent manner. A well-architected ECM solution can enable the enterprise to overcome the chaos and achieve remarkable results.

It is important to understand the difference between structured and unstructured content.

- **Structured content**   A simple example is the color of red. This can be seen as a keyword value pair and can be used to create lists, tables, and relational context. This type of content is easy to get value from but is harder to create.

- **Unstructured content**   This book is an example of unstructured content. This type of content amounts to 80 percent of all content and is easy to create.

The justification for ECM is to help knowledge workers create structure out of unstructured content. This helps them become more efficient by empowering them with content in the right context at the exact moment they need it. In today's world, the volume of information is exploding at an exponential rate. Knowledge workers at every level of the enterprise are adopting a myriad of devices and technologies. Enterprises understand the value of information; we can all agree that the right information can mean the difference between success and failure. The only way the enterprise can get to the stated benefits of BigData, business intelligence, process efficiency, and business automation is to design, implement, and manage an ECM solution that focuses on helping knowledge workers access information successfully.

What is a *flexible content structure*? This is the ability for anyone to create, name, and store content without policies or requirements for organizing content in a meaningful way. This is what enterprise and knowledge workers have been allowed to do since the rise of the personal computer.

As long as the flexible content structure world exists, you need ECM. Most people think that because they are creating content they are managing it. This is blatantly false, and the end result is nothing short of chaos. Users have no idea where to find content; they spend most of the time searching and sifting through irrelevant and duplicative bits of information that was never stored with any thought of how to find the information later.

Return on investment

The primary drivers that create a positive economic impact on the enterprise are revenue growth and profitability. A secondary driver, like increased productivity, is more difficult to measure but nevertheless creates a substantial return on the investment for a well-structured ECM platform. We know that knowledge workers spend 5 to 15 percent of their time reading information, but up to 50 percent looking for it. The ability for a user to quickly find the information they are looking for is important. Even more important is finding that information in context of the business activities or systems that they already use.

To achieve even larger productivity gains, you have to move beyond just finding information and toward automating the collection, distribution, and processing of the information. ECM platforms provide a distinct advantage for business process improvement by automating common processes and reducing or eliminating redundant activities. Process re-engineering is a fundamental part of implementing a successful ECM platform. This goes beyond the technology and requires a commitment to change management and feedback loops to help determine where inefficiencies exist. Some of the changes will be procedural in nature and might require changes in human behavior, which is always more difficult than configuring the technology.

The duplication of content is pervasive. In a world where storage is cheap and nearly everything has a synchronization option, it's important to think beyond just ease of access. At some point, the original content has to be discarded as it reaches the end of its life cycle. Your ability to ensure that content that needs to be deleted is actually deleted can provide the enterprise with cost avoidance by reducing the risk of having discoverable content in the eventual case of litigation.

Who does ECM target?

ECM targets different people for a variety of reasons and use cases. ECM is a set of disciplines that are used to guide the development of Information Architecture and governance.

A successful ECM platform supports the management of information for operational, transactional, and regulatory purposes. It provides access to the unstructured information assets that complete the record of a transaction, project, person, or activity. The information stored in an ECM platform is supportive in nature to all other systems used in the enterprise, putting structure around this information to control how it is used, who has access to it, and what processes are enabled to leverage it. As a document nears the end of its life cycle, the ECM platform is used to discard information to achieve compliance and reduce risk.

Everyone in the organization benefits from ECM. The key players that are targeted are broken down into those who implement and manage the SharePoint platform and those who access the information stored in SharePoint. Table 1-1 describes how to segment the roles and responsibilities of each of the individuals targeted.

TABLE 1-1 Roles and responsibilities of key individuals

Users	Technical	Management	Governance
Knowledge Workers	IT Operations	Executive	Records
	Developers	Departmental	Legal
	Business Analyst	Project	Procurement

Building expectations

SharePoint offers an amazing set of tools and functions that can be used to deploy a myriad of business solutions. To focus and give you tools that you can use from day one, we are providing an Information Architecture section. In this section, we will discuss the standard building blocks of a SharePoint ECM solution, namely Site Collections, Document Libraries, Content Types, and the Records Center. When you understand what these terms mean and how they work together, you can incorporate the control that every organization wants and needs. Governance can too often be unbalanced, creating either a system that is clunky and difficult to use or one that is too open and ends up being a digital landfill. This is where a well-defined taxonomy that is neither vague, overly granular, nor verbose will help everyone follow the same rules. We will look at types, best practices, and a real use case of taxonomy in action using the Term Store.

SharePoint 2013 is a very powerful on-premise server based solution that is also available as an off-premise Cloud solution. Primarily targeted at small and medium sized organizations, Office 365 takes minutes to sign up for but in the range of a few hours to be fully configured. Administrators will have immediate access to settings for provisioned services. The core Services, Lync and Exchange, are available in minutes, but initial configuration of a multitenant SharePoint site takes around two hours to complete. We will discuss the ins and outs of the configuration options and introduce the concept of the Office Store.

All versions of SharePoint have benefited from a large, talented, and enthusiastic partner community. SharePoint 2013 continues to provide great opportunities for Microsoft Business Partners and Independent Software Vendors to build complementary technologies and vertical solutions that extend the platform. We will outline some vendors and applications that you should evaluate during your project planning and requirements definition. Knowing what technologies are available and how they can help to make your SharePoint ECM solution better will be a real advantage.

The legal and regulatory aspects of ECM from FOIA to SOX can seem like an overwhelming bag of acronyms. To help you navigate what is relevant and what is not, we will introduce the most common laws and practices that you should consider and how to address them in SharePoint. Litigation is a pervasive part of the business landscape, and being able to support eDiscovery requirements in the event of a lawsuit is critical. We will cover the technical aspects of SharePoint that are necessary for performing legal holds, controlling full fidelity of content, and supporting chain of custody.

Next steps

We have covered the difference between SharePoint as a technology platform and ECM as a methodology. In Chapter 2, we will dig deeper into the ECM Stack and uncover in detail the complexities of each stage of the content life cycle. The sections will follow the same structure but include actionable steps you can take to get comfortable planning for ECM in SharePoint. As you're reading through each section, you should be gathering pertinent information about your specific environment and creating a high-level roadmap for implementation.

At this point, you should begin identifying the stakeholders for the ECM solution you will be designing. You need to separate the functions of SharePoint from the information architecture that your organization will use going forward. Identify your existing content repositories both inside and outside of SharePoint, and determine where they meet or fall short of the principles we have outlined in this chapter.

CHAPTER 2

ECM stack: content in

Now that we have established the key components to ECM, we can talk about the individual aspects of contributing content properly to SharePoint.

In this chapter, we will discuss many details about features and settings in SharePoint. In most cases, we will focus on settings and features specific to SharePoint 2013, with site templates of type "Document Center" and content based on the type "Document."

Building a solid foundation

As we stated in the Introduction, everything that happens after the Capture stage has a downstream impact. Creating, storing, and sharing content is easy. However, organizing, managing, and processing content in a manner that is repeatable, findable, and structured takes planning and strategy. Occasionally, we refer to a proper ECM strategy as being like a marriage; it takes work. The rewards for this work are many, but like a marriage, it is a long-term commitment that will only be as successful as what you put into it. If you put little effort into the content that is captured and ultimately stored into your SharePoint ECM solution, you will get little out of it when you start searching for content. This is especially true as the volume of content grows.

> ### From the field
>
> *I was working with a client after they had been using SharePoint for two years, and they simply wanted to throw it out. The users were frustrated, and the IT manager was fed up with the complaints. The problem was that they did not spend enough time planning out the Capture process so that content was structured in a way that was easy to find. - Shad*

The single biggest mistake that you can make when deploying SharePoint as an ECM solution is to underestimate the time required for planning. Every organization and project is unique, so we can't give you an exact formula for determining timeline, resources, and budget. What we can do is give you some guidance for collecting the information you need for developing a plan. After you have a plan based on your organization's needs, you can accurately determine the total budget and resources needed. Following is a list of primary activities that we recommend you complete to get prepared for planning how content will be captured into SharePoint:

- Create a list of electronic and physical file storage locations.

- Prepare a brief written description of the content.

- Interview people in the user groups to determine use cases.

- Begin outlining a standard file naming convention for each file.

Remember that we are only collecting information at this point. The information will be used to begin formulating your Information Architecture. It's important to be realistic about how people use files and systems and why it can be difficult to get control and maintain structure. After all, people like the freedom to name, save, copy, and distribute files in a manner that makes logical sense to them. In an ECM solution, we must tame this natural human instinct by providing methods that support our Information Architecture without becoming cumbersome for the users. This can be accomplished and is generally not a technology problem. It tends to be more of a behavior problem based on bad habits.

In this chapter, we will outline the best practices and methods you can use to get value out of the content that is created, stored, and processed in SharePoint. We can't guarantee that someone won't try to circumvent your perfectly structured ECM stack, but we will outline very compelling examples that you can share with the user community to encourage them to comply with best practices for naming files and uploading documents and related content to SharePoint.

Capture

As we stated in Chapter 1, "ECM defined," capture is the process of getting content into SharePoint content databases with the proper security location and structure, from an existing format such as image or electronic file, or from the minds of its creators, in the form of native SharePoint documents. It is equally important that content is named and tagged in a consistent manner.

File upload

Users can contribute documents to SharePoint by individually selecting them from a file system and storing them into a library. This is referred to as *file upload* and occurs when a person initiates the transfer of content from the local client machine or shared network drive to the SharePoint server(s). To do this, the user must first have read/write access to the library they want to contribute to.

As we outlined earlier, you need to do some planning and also education of people before content capture is initiated. This will ensure that you build a solid foundation prior to files being uploaded randomly by SharePoint users. We recommend that prior to upload you specify for your organization what constitutes a proper file. You should intentionally define a file in the following order:

- Content

- Version

- File naming convention

Often, file naming conventions are more about what to exclude than include. For example, you should never put the initials of individuals, dates, times, or version numbers in a file name. This will seem counterintuitive to you and most people that are using only email and local and network file shares to store and share files. This is because a directory structure does not provide the same metadata and search functions that SharePoint provides. This is what makes Information Architecture so powerful. In general, the file name should pertain only to the topic matter, and perhaps include a business function that the content pertains to. It should not include metadata that is better suited for content types.

> **Note** Defining content type allows for predefined metadata attributes to be applied to a file. Defining and using content types is an essential component of Information Architecture.

When the user knows that a file is appropriate to add to SharePoint, they will browse to the library and use one of the following methods of upload:

- Individual document

- Multiple documents

- From Explorer View

- Dragging from source to destination

When uploading an individual document into SharePoint, a user will specify relevant metadata to be added by using an upload dialog, as shown in Figure 2-1. To upload the document, click the Add Document button at the bottom of a library in SharePoint 2010, or click the New Document button in the top-left section of a library in SharePoint 2013.

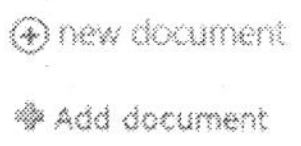

⊕ new document

✤ Add document

FIGURE 2-1 Upload dialog.

Browse the local file system, identify the file to be uploaded, and double-click the file. The next step is for the user to apply appropriate metadata. Fields marked with a red asterisk indicate mandatory fields. These fields will be defined as part of the Information Architecture. By default, the metadata fields for the Document content type are Name, Title, Created Date, Last Modified Date, Created By, and Last Modified By. Remember that Name and Title are the only user editable metadata fields. As we will discuss in Information Architecture, in many cases you will want to add more fields.

Note Depending on the site template you use, the user might experience a different result. For example, using the site template "Team Site" in SharePoint 2013 will result in the ad hoc document upload with the default content type "Document" not prompting the user for any metadata. The examples in this section are based on the document template "Document Center."

Both SharePoint 2010 and SharePoint 2013 support the ability to upload multiple files at once. This feature allows users to contribute batches of documents in SharePoint. The feature can be beneficial when users are guided to upload content that is already strictly organized. But often this feature is used as a quick way to bypass proper addition of content to SharePoint. In 2010 and 2013, this feature can be disabled with some deep modifications to the SharePoint ribbon or via CSS.

Similarly to multiple file uploads, you can upload files from the File Explorer view. The benefits of this are added user adoption and the comfort with file movement that users are accustomed to. The downside is that it also allows the bypassing of metadata and records. For newer deployments of SharePoint, we recommend that you tightly control the use of this method by training users to use only the SharePoint user interface.

In SharePoint 2013, there is the added ability to drag documents into SharePoint from the desktop to the browser. As shown in Figure 2-2, a user can select a file by right-clicking, holding the button, dragging the selected file over the document library in the SharePoint browser interface, and releasing the button. This requires that the user workstation have Microsoft Office installed and a supported browser. For users without these minimum requirements, the drag method for content capture will not function.

The benefit of this feature is greater convenience for the user. The downside is that the user is not given an opportunity to provide the proper metadata, which typically results in no metadata. If features like drag and drop are being used, you will want to adopt policies that promote the proper use of the feature and train the user community to follow the correct steps for uploading content and providing metadata.

FIGURE 2-2 Dragging a file for upload.

Note In SharePoint 2013, if you do not drag the file into the proper location or do not have a supported browser, dropping the file will simply result in the browser opening that file.

Microsoft Office

When organizations can standardize on the Microsoft stack, they get the added benefit of tight integration with SharePoint. Tight integration not only means greater convenience for your users, but it also means great support when there are questions about functionality and configuration options.

For this reason, we strongly recommend that the organization standardize on using Microsoft Office as one of the primary capture sources. You have the option of allowing users to upload existing Office documents to SharePoint. In addition, they can also save them directly from Office into a SharePoint list or library.

SharePoint list and document libraries

SharePoint lists and libraries are often confused, and when to use one versus the other is a common question. In an ECM solution, it's important to remember that you are predominately dealing with libraries. The key difference is that lists are generally populated with structured information. A list item consists of a content type with completed metadata, whereas a library consists of a content type, a file, and associated metadata.

Starting in Office 2007 and subsequent versions, the integration with SharePoint is strong. In Office 2010 with SharePoint 2010, the integration is more than a "Save" location. You also have the ability to modify certain metadata fields, see previous versions, and you have check-in | check-out document management functionality.

When SharePoint is configured to support single sign-on, the integration is seamless. If your organization does not use a single sign-on method or if users are remote, they might be asked during document opening and saving to enter their SharePoint credentials.

Single Sign-On

Single Sign-On is a method for leveraging authentication credentials from Active Directory or LDAP to create seamless access to enterprise applications like SharePoint without prompting users to enter a user ID and password.

The process for creating a new document by using Microsoft Office in SharePoint can be initiated in SharePoint or Office. We recommend that you have users initiate creation in SharePoint. This method is seamless, offers the fewest steps, and avoids confusion about how to save documents. To create an Office document in SharePoint, follow these steps:

1. Navigate to the destination library.

2. Select the Files tab.

3. Select the New Document drop-down.

4. Select New Document. The user will be prompted to accept launching the client application. If no client application is found on the machine, the document will open in-browser.

5. Create and save the document in the designated Microsoft Office Client Application.

 Note By default, libraries created in the Document Center template will have Microsoft Office Word as the new document content type. Your configuration can include any content types you choose.

However, if the user elects to initiate the creation in Office, the user will create the standard blank document. To save the document, the user will click the Browse button and enter the site they want to save to. When they press Enter, they will be able to browse that site and its libraries directly in Office. They can select the destination library, name the file, and click Save.

In both scenarios, after a document is saved the user will have additional properties available in the Info portion of the document, as shown in Figure 2-3. After a user has saved to a library once, it can be conveniently accessed as a Recent Location for storing documents to SharePoint in the future.

FIGURE 2-3 Document Info page.

It is also possible to save links to documents. A link to a document is a pointer to an alternate save location, normally locally on the user's machine. We strongly recommend that you do not use this feature. It results in confusion about where documents are actually saved. It leads quickly to frustration from the users, missed versions, and duplicate files.

> **Note** Compatibility is a key consideration when working with SharePoint as a "Save" location for Office Documents. We recommend using SharePoint 2013 with Office 2013 or SharePoint 2010 with Office 2010.

Native SharePoint documents

In the last 10 years, there has been a major shift from legacy ECM implemented via client/server applications to ECM implemented via a browser/server infrastructure. In both scenarios, the storage and management of the content was managed by a heavy server-side application, but the interface for the users went from an accompanied thick client that tied users to a specific device to device independence wherever you have a browser. The shift away from legacy ECM applications that require program files loaded on the client workstation is still not complete. The initial feature set transitioned from thick client programs was focused on features like administration, search, and processing of content after being saved to SharePoint. What remained was content authoring that was still tied to thick client programs, like Microsoft Office, installed on individual devices. We are of the opinion that over the next several years, desktop client authoring tools will primarily be used for production level authoring and web interfaces will be used by the vast majority of users who create basic documents. The other consideration is the rise of mobile authoring and content contribution using tablets and smart phones.

Starting in SharePoint 2010, it is now possible to create documents in the browser. For the average user, all required functionality is present in the browser, with the ability to use the new Ribbon toolbar to perform word processing, spreadsheet, and presentation creation. In SharePoint 2010, the ability to do so still relied on the client machine having an install of Microsoft office.

Now, in SharePoint 2013, the reliance on the device having a client Office application is no longer the case, allowing for fully independent creation of content via the web browser. This is a game changer that helps define SharePoint 2013 as a fully cloud-enabled ECM solution.

In either SharePoint 2010 or SharePoint 2013, this requires an additional product called Microsoft Office Web Apps. In SharePoint 2010, this is an add-in to the existing farm, and in SharePoint 2013, this is a separate Microsoft Office Web Apps server, also referred to as Web Applications Companion (WAC). This gives you the ability to interact with a spreadsheet exactly as you would in the thick client Microsoft Excel program, as shown in Figure 2-4.

FIGURE 2-4 Microsoft Excel 2013 Web App.

When this functionality is deployed, it is nearly unnoticeable that the user is not working within a thick client application. In addition, access to this functionality is supported across many mobile devices, including laptops, tablets, and handheld smartphones.

The latest support of Office Web Apps allows for users to simultaneously edit documents. This functionality is useful in a team site scenario when multiple people are contributing to the early drafting of content, where the direction of the content isn't fully outlined. Having multiple contributors, regardless of location, be able to share ideas in real time is extremely powerful.

Note We advise that simultaneous editing be used during the early stages of the content life cycle, such as in initial drafts and brainstorming sessions. As the content becomes more defined, you should begin using the document versioning features of SharePoint.

If at all possible, organizations should take the extra step into native SharePoint document creation. If it is possible for your organization to take this path, we recommend an all-or-nothing approach. That is, if you can deploy Web Apps for your SharePoint 2010 farm or install the Office Web Apps Server 2013 and connect it to your SharePoint 2013 farm, you should also remove the thick client-side applications from your user desktops.

In some scenarios, you might want to give certain power users access to the full Office suite. You need to understand that the combination of the two will make supporting users complex due to the interface similarities of both products. Because there are huge technical differences between thick client programs and browser-based usage, it can make it more difficult for the IT support or help desk staff to triage the issue and troubleshoot.

Electronic forms

As we mentioned in Chapter 1, the use of electronic forms is a great way to capture structured information from submitters. It's important to understand that electronic forms capture is used only for the purpose of capturing data, whereas the capture process using Microsoft Office also facilitates document editing and modification.

Electronic form capture is typically used to receive responses to a specific set of questions submitted by an audience of users. In SharePoint, each submission results in a document saved in a special format located in a library accessible by the publishers of the form and usually not the submitters or respondents of the published form.

In SharePoint, this is most often accomplished by using InfoPath. We will not cover InfoPath in detail in this book and recommend, if you are using electronic forms to capture information, that you get specific training on InfoPath.

Document scanning

The last form of capture we will discuss is image capture. This is the process of taking physical documents, converting them from paper to digital, and storing them in SharePoint.

Document imaging in SharePoint is not a native function or feature of the product. The most common deployment of document imaging for SharePoint is front-loaded using third-party software applications. The two ways to perform document imaging in SharePoint are as follows:

- Use external capture applications that release to SharePoint.

- Use ad hoc capture applications built into SharePoint.

External capture applications allow you to capture and convert documents and then automatically or manually upload them to a SharePoint document library. The primary benefit of these applications is that they can scale to support the capture of large volumes of paper documents. Ideally, an organization should seek such applications that support the conversion of images from image-only files to richer document files such as Word or PDF. This is done by using Optical Character Recognition (OCR), which we will detail below. Your organization should also seek applications that allow the population of metadata to document libraries as content is uploaded to SharePoint. Simply scanning paper and dumping to SharePoint with simple file names is not a best practice and will leave you unable to find, manage, or process the content effectively, if at all.

Note If the software used for document imaging capture does not support the population of metadata values, you should consider replacing it or reverting to a manual upload of the content instead.

There are also a handful of ad hoc capture applications that run natively in SharePoint. These applications allow a user to initiate a scan and store a paper file directly from a document library, just as if the user was creating an Office document from scratch. The same metadata considerations apply for this type of solution. You want to find a solution that offers conversion from image-only file types (TIFF, JPG, BMP) into other more-useful formats, combined with metadata.

Scanner drivers

Do not overlook the fact that a user might have a document scanner at their desk and the software needed to interface with that device will require the installation of a driver to communicate between the browser and the metal.

Hardware drivers are not trivial matters and are packaged or downloadable from each manufacturer's website. Microsoft Windows does support Windows Image Acquisition (WIA), and this works fine for ad hoc low-volume capture.

It is more common that a driver would support either a TWAIN or ISIS based standard and might also include proprietary image cleanup and enhancement software to be installed as well. It is becoming more common that the image cleanup and enhancement is embedded in the hardware devices and is much cleaner and easier to deploy support.

In either type of solution, the considerations of image capture are the same. You must first isolate which of the following type(s) of capture meets your organization's needs:

- Distributed capture
- Production capture

Distributed scanning

Distributed document scanning is close to the user. The scanning is performed by the same user who stores the document into SharePoint libraries. Sometimes document scanners are at individual workstations or shared among users in a departmental fashion. Distributed capture is good for ongoing document imaging at low volume but not particularly good if your organization has large amounts of files.

Multifunction peripherals

Also known as *digital copiers*, today's multifunction peripherals include capabilities for large-volume printing and document scanning. They are often seen as a great method for deploying document imaging features to help businesses go paperless.

There is a big danger in making the assumption that because a device can copy, scan, and print that this will reduce the use of paper or streamline the process for getting physical documents into SharePoint.

We recommend that you walk through the process of using the front panel of the Multifunction Peripheral (MFP) to initiate the capture process before you put your process automation eggs in this basket. It can work, but it's rarely as easy as you might think and often requires third-party application software and customized configurations to produce the results you're looking for.

If you have a large volume of files to be scanned on an ongoing basis, we recommend that you consider planning and implementing a production scanning process.

Production scanning

Production scanning is high-volume capture of paper documents to a repository. This is not common in most organizations and might be an infrequent need. However, some organizations in their quest for ECM technology implement production scanning to convert old paper documents to new digital documents. We recommend before considering such a process with SharePoint that you investigate scanning services to help you offload the technology and process considerations that come with production scanning.

Whether your organizations chooses to use external capture applications or native SharePoint applications, or whether they choose to perform distributed capture, production capture, or both, the considerations on how to capture images into SharePoint are the same.

The most important consideration is image quality. The quality of the scanned image directly impacts a user's ability to view the document and its ability to be converted using OCR technology. First you must decide whether you need color images or black and white images. The benefit of colored images is that they will have better quality when printed or externally shared. The downside is a more than five-time increase in the storage requirements.

Note We recommend using color scanning only when you know that these documents will be later printed or that the color is relevant to the meaning of the document. In some cases, you might need to accurately reflect a watermark or other important attribute of the document that comes across only in color.

Most organizations can scan in black and white images, which provide optimum storage size and the ability to be converted using OCR. OCR engines benefit from color scans only when it comes to identifying graphics in a document. If you are attempting to convert many documents that include a combination of graphics in line with text, you can choose color scanning prior to OCR and black and white post OCR.

Another factor that impacts image quality is the resolution or dots-per-inch (dpi) scan setting. Resolution determines the number of pixels used to represent objects in a document. We recommend that you scan all documents at a resolution of 300 dpi. Lower than 300 dpi gives faster scanning speed but dramatically reduces the ability of the document to be converted via OCR. Even if you are not using OCR technology today, the document might be OCR'ed in the future, so it should be a consideration. Any higher than 300 dpi provides no substantial benefit in OCR accuracy, and there are rare occasions when this is needed.

The next important factor is the file format you choose. Be aware that file format at scanning time does not have to be the same file format that is saved to SharePoint. In fact, in most scenarios, it should not be. The format best suited for document conversion using OCR is not the same desired format for general retrieval viewing and storage into SharePoint. We recommend scanning your images as TIFF Group 4, because this will be the ideal format for OCR engines, but having the output conversion results saved in PDF or Word. You will choose between PDF and Word documents when you determine whether these documents will ever be edited.

PDF or PDF/A

The Portable Document Format is the most pervasive and widely supported viewing format for documents to be presented in a somewhat permanent state or "as printed" representation. There are many varieties of PDF and many viewers that support viewing and annotation of electronic documents. PDF/A was developed as a standard to support the digital preservation of a document in its original form.

Sometimes document scanning is done because the digital/editable version of the physical document no longer exists. In that case, you need to scan the document and get all the text you can to rapidly create an editable version of the document to continue its digital life. In such a scenario, you should scan to Word formats.

However, for the vast majority of document imaging scenarios, the documents are not needed for editing but primarily for the purpose of viewing. In such a case, PDF is the ideal format. OCR text is never 100 percent accurate, and the image of the document will always be the most accurate representation of the original document for users. The OCR results are used to make the text available for copying and indexing into SharePoint to facilitate search.

To accomplish this, PDF supports a format of PDF with text under image. When you view the document, you see the original scanned image, but you can copy the text from the document and the SharePoint index crawler can see the text for indexing.

> **Note** We assume that the PDF iFilter has been installed and configured on your farm. iFilters expose text from documents to SharePoint crawlers. By default, the PDF iFilter is not installed in SharePoint Farms. This is a critical component to any SharePoint ECM solution.

To recap, the recommended best scanning settings should be the following:

- Scan image as: TIFF Group 4

- Scan resolution: 300 dpi

- Convert using OCR to PDF with Text Under Image

Generally, scanned documents are always larger than a born-digital equivalent. Therefore, scanning to SharePoint will create additional storage requirements and configurations on your farm.

Store

The store portion of ECM includes both the logical and physical storage of files and their metadata. While the logical and physical storage of documents are quite separate technically, they are tightly woven together.

Poor planning for physical storage could result in farms not scaling to the needs of an organization and could kill an ECM solution and force a reconfiguration. The logical storage helps plan out this extensibility, but it also is the starting point for users interacting with the system. It's one of several key determining factors of a successful SharePoint ECM solution.

The physical storage of documents happens within SQL databases where objects are stored by default. The logical storage of documents happens with many features in SharePoint and should be collectively referred to as your Information Architecture.

Physical storage

In SharePoint, the physical storage of documents happens in MS SQL. The documents and their associated metadata are stored into content databases. To ensure scalability and performance of the farm, it's recommended to keep content database sizes below 150 GB. To do this, you need to know more about the information you are storing there. In most organizations, the best gauge for how large an ECM platform will grow is to first establish a starting point.

Roughly 40 percent or less of the total size of shared network drives and storage will end up in ECM. After proper evaluation of shared drives, you will find that much of the content is not proper ECM content, contains duplicate files, or has met its retention date. For this reason, it is very important to perform a records inventory of your shared drive content so that you can eliminate redundant and outdated information.

So to begin, take 40 percent of your total shared drive space utilized. This will give you a total estimate. If your organization is lucky enough to have this already at less than 150 GB, you are in good shape, but if it's larger, you need to dig deeper and start calculating that same size, but in sub-units such as departments and/or functional operations within departments.

The results of a records inventory, data cleanup, and segmentation of this information into logical factors will give you a general idea of how many content databases you will need for initial deployment. The tricky part is determining what will be needed as the organization and the information it creates grows. We have a fundamental understanding that there is rapid information growth taking place today. This is supported by the fact that most of the world's information was created in the last five years. If you weren't experiencing the demands this amount of information is putting on your organization, you probably wouldn't be reading this book.

However, for your organization, content can be created only as fast as and with as many knowledge workers that are employed there. Therefore, growth of content should be relatively steady and predictable. There are various means to get to your annual growth, but the easiest way is to take a subset of your shared drive and calculate the total size of it.

Calculate storage growth

No single formula can be used to calculate every situation, and yours could be unique. For example, take a shared drive location belonging to a small but active department and calculate the total size.

Perform a search on that share for all content created within an annual period of time. If today's date is 10/13/12, you will search the range 10/13/11–10/13/12. Next measure the size of all the results. Now you can calculate a percentage of the total size, which gives you the increase in a year. Do this three times in different locations to come up with an average for your organization.

Note The "gotchas" in file storage size are media files. Information Architecture has a methodical way of dealing with this, but be aware of where these files might live in your organization.

If your organization is large and you are fearful of SharePoint's limits on content databases, you need to consider implementing Remote Blob Storage (RBS).

SharePoint supports configuration of Remote BLOB (Binary Large Objects) Storage (RBS) as an option for storing content objects directly in the database. This is actually a function of SQL Server and provides the ability to offload storage from the content database to external non–SQL-based hierarchical storage platforms. It is recommended for content databases 4 GB and larger.

RBS can facilitate a measure of scalability for specific use cases that involve large individual file sizes and/or high volumes of objects. The configuration of RBS can be targeted to specific SharePoint web applications, site collections, or individual sites. An example of this would be large engineering vector files and high-volume document imaging solutions. In most use cases, this is not necessary, and storing the objects in the database has the advantage of providing one source from a backup and disaster recovery perspective.

There are third-party solutions built to take advantage of RBS to reduce the impact of database BLOB I/O performance issues. This can also reduce the overall footprint of the database architecture needed to support SharePoint and enable the use of lower-cost storage devices. Your most accessed and current content can reside as BLOBs in the content database and be migrated to external RBS storage locations based on metadata values, content types, or other configurable parameters. As a side note, External BLOB Storage (EBS) was a hotfix provided for MOSS 2007 that provided entire farm-level externalization of content objects.

Where content databases meet web applications and site collections is where the logical storage of content begins.

Logical storage/Information Architecture

Information Architecture (IA) at first seems to be one of those vague things that people talk about to sound smart. This section will define it in more tangible terms. IA is where your organization will spend most of its time and planning for a SharePoint ECM Solution. If you don't understand, formulate, and execute a sound IA, you are almost certainly destined for failure, or at the very least, you will only duplicate what exists on your shared drive infrastructure.

Like its parent ECM, IA is not a technology or feature. It's a collection of features that, when put together properly, make up the organization of content. IA breaks into the following categories:

- Repositories
- Metadata model
- Presentation layer
- Taxonomy/folksonomy

Repositories are the bridge from the physical storage to the logical storage. Many users don't realize that the folder location of the file has little to do with where it's physically stored. This is an example of how what we see on the screen translates to something very different in the IA.

The metadata model is how the content is tied to its associated metadata. Think of the metadata model as a cell in a spreadsheet, and the metadata is the value placed in the cell; there is an inseparable bond between the two, yet they are distinct in their purpose and their properties. The model also details what metadata a document should have or require during capture and how it should be visible to the user.

The presentation layer is where users can interact with the IA. This layer provides a way to slice and dice content, given good metadata, to better find and interact with it.

Metadata is a separate condition from taxonomy and folksonomy, and they take separate consideration. Together, these are tools that can be used to define ways of organizing content in lieu of folders. Ideally, good-enough taxonomies are created to support any number of combinations to find content. Taxonomy and folksonomy serve the same purpose and are implemented in the same way. However, folksonomy is less strict and more prone to a user's nomenclature, while taxonomy is a strict listing of terms that is very rarely modified.

During the discussion of managed metadata, we will go deeper into how to build these. Table 2-1 shows the various categories and components that need to be considered as part of a complete IA.

TABLE 2-1 SharePoint Information Architecture components

Repositories	Metadata Model	Taxonomy/Folksonomy	Presentation Layer
Web Applications	Content Types	Managed Metadata	Columns
Site collections	Content Type Publishing	Rating	Views
Sites	Folders	Like	Navigation
Libraries	Information Management Policies		
	File Naming		
	Versioning		
	Document IDs		

Even though we have identified the individual components, that alone will not solve the IA challenge. When you bring them all together, they will strongly impact how users will interact with a system, the quality of capture, and the results they find when performing a search. Now let's discuss the goals of IA and then how to approach each individual component.

Ideally, an organization will spend sufficient time planning out the IA for SharePoint; the actual deployment of the farm is just an execution on this plan. Although the IA aligns to SharePoint features, most of the planning work is done outside of SharePoint instead of inside a configuration interface.

From the field

The most successful implementations I've done with ECM in SharePoint have shared the following common principles. We were able to start from scratch. We were able to create a complete design of SharePoint outside of SharePoint and implement once. My advice is: Don't get stuck on using SharePoint features just for the sake of using those features.
- Chris

The first thing you must consider is what will be the determining factor for creating new repositories in SharePoint. It could be related to the type of content, to the size of content, or by organizational structure.

The type of content might determine that it has a special type of security that no other content in the organization uses. Because of this, it might need a more high-level type of organization so that the proper security can be applied. For example, many organizations have "management" portals. While each manager in the portal heads a department with its own separate SharePoint site, all managers have access to information that users in those departments should not have access to. Therefore, managers have access to the portal as well as access to their individual departments, whereas users can have access only to the department to which they belong.

The size of the content might determine some IA because, as we stated earlier, content goes in content databases. The first two portions of SharePoint IA are web applications and site collections, which also determine the number of content databases. For example, a small organization might get away with one web application and a site for each department, whereas an organization with a higher volume of content will need a web application per department. Even assuming security access for both organizations are the same, the size constraints could be the deciding factor.

And finally, what do you organize by? When you consider only purely logical storage of information without any size or security constraints, you are deciding how users access information. We recommend choosing organization in the following two ways:

- By department

- By function

Only in unique verticals and cases will this not work for an organization. In many organizations, they are the same. However, some organizations don't have departments that align directly with function. Generally, if departments are more tied to management than to function, you will want to organize by function, because users are joined by function. However, most organizations get away with departmental organization. You might be asking, "What if users cross departments?"

They could! And there are several ways to approach this. In organizations where security is a larger concern, you will grant access to those knowledge workers who bridge departments on an individual basis. The other option is to create team sites for cross-functional teams while not altering the security at a departmental or functional level. Finally, there is the recommended approach for the vast majority of organizations, which is tying security not to a department level but to a role. For example, all knowledge workers should have knowledge worker access to all department sites no matter which they belong to. The only real downside of this approach is that users might waste time on content that does not pertain to their function.

Note Security can happen at the item level, but should it? Breaking inheritance on a site collection will increase the cost of managing a SharePoint deployment and is highly discouraged. If you find yourself doing this a lot, there is an issue with the original IA. Keep in mind that this is ultimately a management issue and not a SharePoint ECM Solution issue.

Web applications and site collections

The first thing to consider is the web application, which is where the hand-off from physical to logical storage occurs. Because it's rare to have a web application without a root site collection, we will also consider site collections at this point.

The web application is the first envelope where the user gets involved. It is also the demarcation of new content databases. While web applications can have multiple content databases, they usually have only one. As illustrated in Figure 2-5, the name of the web application and root site should be simple; that is, legal should be "Legal" and human resources should be "Human Resources."

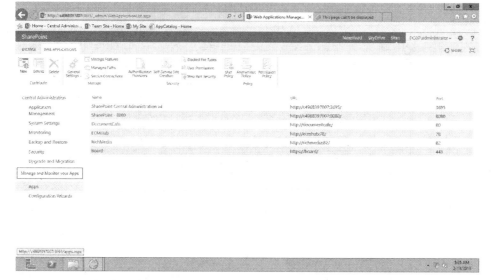

FIGURE 2-5 Legal web application in SharePoint.

If your organization is small and you have a single web application, these will be the names of your sites, and your web application could be a personification of the web application or just your organization name. For example, some companies used \\ECM or \\DocumentCafe. There are some cases where you will have special web application names, such as in the case of content type publishing, which we will discuss later.

Web applications and root site collections go hand and hand. It's rare to have a web application without a site collection. The root site in a site collection is the landing location of the web application URL.

> **Note** When doing anything in SharePoint, you should always have a development, testing, and staging environment separate from your production farm. The development and testing is where the work will happen, and staging is where you test against real use, but with no production implementation. Large projects will have even more testing farms. Never test features or new deployments on a production farm. It seems convenient to do all testing in a separate web application. For simple deployments, this is possible but not advised.

Within each root site collection are sites. Sites, like web applications and site collections, are dependent on how large your SharePoint deployment will be. If you have a single web application for the organization, you will most likely have a site per department and function with the addition of restricted legal and management sites as needed. If you have a web application per department or function, you might not need any subsites, but for very large organizations with nested departments, it might be required.

The rule we would like you to follow in your ECM implementation is to never use sites two layers deep. The most successful user adoption of IA in SharePoint is to be as flat as possible. We find that when you have layers of navigation and repository drilldowns, it's troublesome for users trying to find the content they need and for administrators working to support enterprise governance.

Sites are where you can also differentiate the types of templates you use. A template contains settings and branding for new sites to be built on. In this book, we use almost exclusively the document center site template. However, customized templates can be used in SharePoint to more rapidly deploy a solution. For example, you can build just the ideal ECM site template for a department just once and then easily use that template to create all other departments in much less time. This takes discipline, because it requires that your full deployment happens up front, prior to any content being uploaded.

Libraries

After web applications and root sites are established and all subsites are created, document libraries and lists must be created as well. Unstructured content lives in libraries, and structured content lives in lists. Because most of what ECM addresses is unstructured content, we will focus on document libraries for your ECM solution.

The first mistake organizations make with libraries is allowing them to be created by individual users. Generally, this results in tree navigations that go on forever and library names that are confusing. The benefit of standardizing libraries across ECM sites is that no matter where a user is in the organization's farm, they will understand what goes where.

Note We strongly recommend against allowing users to create libraries themselves. The downside to allowing users to create libraries is that eventually the proficient library-creating user will create libraries like folders. This defeats best ECM practices and only duplicates the problems you have today with a shared drive.

Many organizations will use libraries as the topic matter. Where sites stop at functions, libraries start with topic. However, in the ideal ECM environment, where we are keeping the IA flat, libraries are associated with types of content. The ideal ECM environment will have three libraries per site: Documents, Rich Media, and Email.

From the field

I always introduce the ideal ECM environment to my customers. Often the response I get is, "Yeah, we get it, but we are not there yet." However, I did have one customer fully implement this modern Information Architecture. Their ECM environment today is going strong. They had a larger hurdle to get over with initial adoption, but now the users are working with SharePoint very effectively. - Chris

While this three-library concept, shown in Figure 2-6, seems radical, it allows for the most flexibility and the least amount of clicks to any document. The concept is that libraries are the types of content—that is, unstructured documents in the "Documents" library; for email-enabled farms, email in the "Email" library; and media files in the "Rich Media" library.

Many organizations already have special considerations for email and rich media, so these might be exceptions. For example, it's not uncommon to have a separate web application for the entire organization's rich media files. It is not common to store email in SharePoint, and that takes some serious consideration. Therefore, many organizations might find that the number of libraries they have using the outlined principles in this book are small.

The primary reason that you might choose to expand the listing of libraries would be having too many individual items to contain in a single library. It's recommended not to exceed 5,000 items per library. Often, we find if you are wanting to store this many items in a library in the first place, you did not heed the initial recommendation of not using SharePoint as a shared drive.

A secondary reason is large amounts of specific document types such as invoices or contracts. Although we can address this easily in the library with the metadata model, it might be enough to consider having separate libraries. How you would decide to handle this is based on the processes that surround those documents and the ease of access at the time of retrieval.

FIGURE 2-6 Document libraries.

Metadata

Now our discussion will move from repositories, the local filing location, to metadata. At the library level, content starts to be populated, and as that happens, you need to have metadata properties defined and populated as well. The big difference between the two in the case of SharePoint is that repositories are the paths to content and do not exist as pieces of metadata that belong to a document, whereas the metadata model is associated with the documents themselves.

In this section, we will consider the metadata model as all inclusive. Metadata is data about data. As shown in Figure 2-7, metadata comprises the values that appear in SharePoint columns that allow you to organize, view, and find content without opening files individually.

There are two types of metadata, structured and unstructured, just like types of content. Structured metadata are things like "Last Modified Date" and "Author." These values are usually automatically entered by the system. Unstructured metadata values are created to specifically support the content that will be stored in a particular document library and can be entered at the time of capture during a workflow process or by some other automated means.

Unstructured metadata includes comments, keywords, tags, and so on. The mechanism for entering metadata is via a content type. Content types are the containers of metadata columns. The default content type for a document contains the metadata fields **Name** and **Title**, with the additional fields **Modified** and **Modified By** added by the farm. While it is possible to create new columns on a library level, we recommend that you do not. At minimum, we recommend that you create and modify content types from the root site. Ideally, you will want to use the content type publishing feature in SharePoint.

Columns

A column stores information about each document in the document library. The following columns are currently available in this document library:

Column (click to edit)	Type	Required
Title	Single line of text	
Created	Date and Time	
Modified	Date and Time	
Created By	Person or Group	
Modified By	Person or Group	
Checked Out To	Person or Group	

- Create column
- Add from existing site columns
- Column ordering
- Indexed columns

Views

A view of a document library allows you to see a particular selection of items or to see the items sorted in a particular order. Views currently configured for this document library:

View (click to edit)	Default View	Mobile View	Default Mobile View
All Documents	✓	✓	✓

- Create view

FIGURE 2-7 Metadata properties.

Content type publishing allows you to create content types in a single location and then publish them across the farm. This means that all modifications to the content type will be syndicated. This requires you to set up a Content Type hub with all desired content types, as shown in Figure 2-8, in advance of using them in any site. The benefit of the hub is that you know that all content types and metadata fields will be consistent throughout the farm, which also means that if content moves from one library to another, the experience will be consistent.

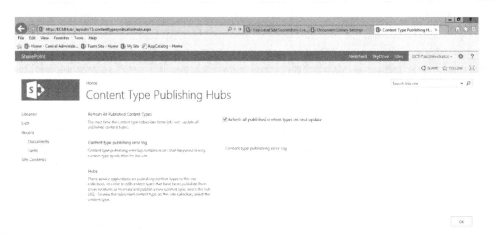

FIGURE 2-8 Content Type hub.

Organizations should use the Document base content type as the starting point for any new content types. New content types will be created based on a heavily used type of document that is specific to a transaction or operation in the organization. This can follow the same examples we used in the discussion of higher volume and repetitive content items such as invoices and contracts.

Content types should not be confused with a method of organization but rather should be seen as the container of the organization criteria. This distinction is a subtle one. For example, an organization might feel that it can create content types for every type of document and use that as a method of organization. The problem is that content types themselves are not metadata, just containers for it. Therefore, the value of that content type goes only as far as the library where it's set up. For organizational purposes, you should create new columns, and those columns will have the metadata you desire.

Before creating a new column, decide on its purpose. During the planning phases of your ECM solution, you might tend to put everything you can possibly think of in a content type for fear of missing something. However, this usually results in too much information that is never used. So before you ever add a new column, decide how the column will be used. You should be able to write out use-case examples of how each new column will be consumed and the purpose for having it.

From the field

Because SharePoint can pretty much be anything, organizations make it everything. Companies tend to want to include whatever they can in their implementations. With my clients, I took the opposite approach and put every desired new feature or configuration on trial. I measured it with the organization, based on how critical it was, how it would be used, and how frequently it would be used. We would end up with a grid of features, and anything that fell below a critical business line, did not have a use case, and was not going to be used frequently was dropped off the list. Surprisingly, this was usually the vast majority of any customization. - Chris

Document ID

To complete our IA, we have two remaining components that are a part of the metadata model. They are rather unique, and it's important to understand the nuances of each. They are document IDs and taxonomy and folksonomy.

The document ID is a relatively simple feature with a very high impact. The document ID service will allow you to implement persistence for documents across the farm, especially in the scenario where your organization has broadened the IA to include a web application per department, knowing that documents have singularity and that the ability to identify a document wherever it's located in SharePoint is critical.

The document ID will automatically generate a unique ID per document uploaded to the farm. The document ID is stored as a searchable piece of metadata associated with the content. The document ID (DocID) is persistent for the life of the content object. Therefore, regardless of where that document is sent, the ID will remain the same. If this weren't the case, Records Management (RecMan) would not work and the chain of custody would be broken. We will cover the importance of legal authenticity and chain of custody in more detail in Chapter 8, "Records Management."

Note In SharePoint 2010, you had the ability to automatically place the document ID and an optional bar code on Office Documents at print time. This is no longer supported in SharePoint 2013.

We recommend that you enable the document ID feature on all your ECM site collections. While you might not always show the ID to the user, the feature supports a best practice for your overall content governance strategy. To enable document IDs, you will turn on the document ID site collection feature for all site collections in the farm that you're planning to use for your ECM solution. When the feature is enabled, a new setting option will appear on the site collection level called "Document ID Settings." As shown in Figure 2-9, you can specify the prefix for the document ideas to be created. Using custom code, you can also customize these IDs even further to support your enterprise governance requirements.

FIGURE 2-9 Document ID Settings page.

Note If you decide to enable document IDs on a farm with existing content, it might take some time for existing content to be populated with new IDs.

Taxonomy and folksonomy

When we talk about the terms *taxonomy* and *folksonomy,* we're usually greeted with some blank stares and quizzical expressions. They are uncommon pieces of the natural English language but are used very commonly in the discipline of Records Management and content organization. To make it more familiar, think of a folder structure that you might see when you use File Explorer to navigate and find documents in your local My Documents folder. This is likely the closest thing to a taxonomy structure that anyone should be able to relate to. The file system that the folders and the documents are stored in is just a piece of metadata, and nested folders are a hierarchical organizational structure.

Taxonomy implies a collection of terms and their hierarchy. This creates a relationship that allows you to save content and find it later in a repeatable and logical manner. Taxonomies also branch into areas of synonyms (ontologies) and relationship of terms. But the general purpose of taxonomy is to organize your content based on specific department or operational terminology.

Folksonomy is implemented as a taxonomy that gives departments or operational units more flexibility. Folksonomies tend to be more personal, while taxonomy is stricter and applied to an entire organization. In SharePoint, both are implemented as managed metadata columns as shown in Figure 2-10. When you have mastered how to create and manage your taxonomy, the process is simple. The hard part is the concepts behind these tools.

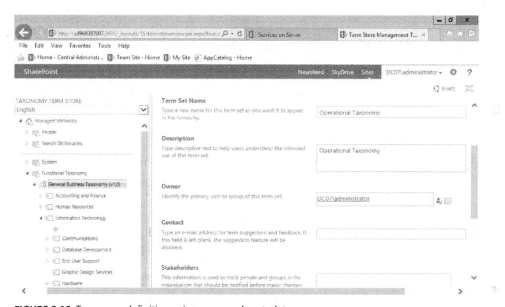

FIGURE 2-10 Taxonomy definition using managed metadata.

As we stated already, taxonomy is stricter and folksonomy is more flexible. The biggest mistake organizations make is to build a taxonomy for the entire organization. Not only is this extremely time-consuming, it is very difficult to get consensus between departments, whether or not they are cross-functionally dependent. In your taxonomy, we strongly urge you to abide by the following guidelines:

- No "Other," "Miscellaneous," or any generalized terms

- No terms from parent to child deeper than four levels

- No transient terms or terms that could change over time

There are essentially three types of taxonomies. These are functional, regional, and time based. A functional taxonomy for the organization is possible only when it's simply a listing of the organization's structure. Each organization is unique, and yours might not fit exactly into a taxonomy as we describe it, but we have found that for the vast majority of organizations, taxonomy per department is required.

Many organizations choose to employ types of taxonomy. A document will be assigned to only one term per taxonomy. For example, if I upload an employment agreement to the HR department's ECM site and I'm located in the New York office, I would apply "New York" from the regional taxonomy, "HR" from the organization-level taxonomy, and "Legal >> Agreements >> Signed Contract" from the HR-level functional taxonomy.

Taxonomies are stricter. Because of this, you will want to create them up front, and for the most part, they will remain unmodified. Instead of introducing new terms to the taxonomy, you will add synonyms to existing terms to help user adoption.

We have worked with many companies that struggle with the strict nature of taxonomies, and you might find that your organization encounters a similar experience as you start to define them. Therefore, you might elect to incorporate a strict taxonomy with a more flexible folksonomy, or skip taxonomy altogether.

Folksonomy is implemented via managed metadata just like its stricter cousin, taxonomy. The big difference is that the terms are usually user contributed and not assigned up front but as the users interact with the content stored in the ECM solution. The benefit is that the terms more closely align with the terms and idioms that the users commonly call content. You could even think of it as corporate slang or operational lingo. It's important not to get too carried away with folksonomy because you could end up with term sprawl as terms are rapidly adopted and applied to content to support every spelling variation of every term possible.

The ease of administration of taxonomies and folksonomies in SharePoint doesn't do justice to how powerful and dangerous they can be. Simply creating a set of terms and publishing to your users without validating language and use can be extremely problematic and difficult to unravel. Your organization needs to spend considerable time planning the use of taxonomies and folksonomies.

The metadata elements "Like" and "Rating" fall roughly into the category of folksonomy, which is the lose tagging of content by users. They also show up as metadata but have their own functions inside of SharePoint.

Would you ever "Rate" your boss's document with 1-star? Rating documents is the ability for users in a library to note how useful a particular document is with a granular 1–5 rating.

> **Note** We have found that the "Rating" feature is useful only for organizations with hundreds of users. The obvious reason is the feature is powerful only when many people are rating documents. Otherwise, it does not surface as a meaningful way to get at content. The funny thing, you will find, is that people think it's a cool feature during demos but the practical use of it will be dependent on a high degree of user interaction.

Similar to rating content is the ability to like content, which is a binary way of flagging content. The biggest difference is that "Like" creates a collection of favorite documents for individual users that are presented in their profile pages as a part of MySites. For this particular feature to be useful, the organization has to plan to use and be effective with MySites.

In this book, we are not going deeply into MySites. However, we do want to assert a position on them so that you can properly prepare if you do decide to implement them. MySites should be carefully planned out, and the benefits and drawbacks should be weighed prior to turning on the Profile Services and MySite features. We have defined the IA that should be followed for an ECM solution. MySites should also be defined and planned in a similar fashion, and it should be considered a project in and of itself.

As you can see, IA, although usually the most ignored element in ECM planning, is an absolutely critical component that will largely define the successful user adoption, content findability, and governance objectives in ECM. Later, we will see examples of SharePoint deployments where the full deployment is executed using the best practices and principles we have covered in this section.

Process

Processing content requires an understanding of what we call the *as-is* state. Before we can begin to build technical and functional requirements for automating a business process, or the *to-be* state in SharePoint, we need to complete some discovery with the people who are currently performing the job functions and tasks associated with the process. This also gives us an early opportunity to start building a relationship with the users who will ultimately be the judge of the ECM solutions that we roll out in SharePoint.

We recommend as a best practice to complete the following three steps:

1. Interview and observation

2. Process white-boarding

3. Documentation and review

It's important to select the right people from your ECM team to perform these steps. Depending on the scope of the process that is being automated, it could require multiple people and skill sets to complete the discovery effectively.

In general, the person performing process discovery should either already have or be capable of creating rapport with the users. In some cases, we have found that using an outside resource that has experience in process design and business consulting can be very beneficial. They often take a fresh look and don't carry any internal or historical organizational baggage with them. If they are good at building rapport, as we stated earlier, the users might share things with them that they wouldn't otherwise be comfortable telling someone from IT. The person(s) assigned to perform the process discovery needs to be proficient with the following activities, techniques, and tools:

- Business Process Modeling and Notation (BPMN)

- Using Visio for process flow-charting

- Leading group discussions in white-boarding sessions

- Creating written documentation that is easily understood by various stakeholders

 Note The team of people selected to lead your SharePoint ECM solution project are critical to its success. In subsequent chapters of this book, we will discuss how to build out your ECM team and give you some examples of how to generate successful user involvement in process design.

When mapping processes to SharePoint, the most important thing to remember is to take advantage of the fact that old processes can be revisited and improved on. Creating a modern version of a bad process further propagates and delays the evolution of the organization. This is often referred to as "paving the cow path." That is, always look for opportunities to improve the process before you implement a bad as-is state in SharePoint.

We expect that when you are at the point of choosing how to implement your processes that you have already decided that the process meets the requirements of the organization, is as optimal as possible, and the process is relevant to day-to-day operation. It might seem obvious that a process needs to be relevant, but you might be surprised at the number of processes that exist that add no value whatsoever. This is often referred to as the seven worst words in business, or "We have always done it this way."

From the field

I am reminded of a process that was used by a local government entity to manage the processing of applicant licenses. They received nightly FTP uploads from another department, containing IBM 32100 print stream files. The files contained applicant information. The process was to print these files every morning and manually enter the data into an applicant tracking system. The original plan was to continue keying the data and then capture the documents for archival storage, which would require keying in indexing information for the image archive. We had no control over the sender, but we did have control over the end point. This is a bad process. Instead, we changed the end point, electronically parsed the incoming print stream files, loaded the data to a newly designed workflow process, and archived the reports automatically. This completely eliminated printing, data entry, and document scanning. - Shad

Now you can start thinking about how that process will map to SharePoint features. To help you prepare, we have outlined the most common out-of-the-box (OOTB) types of processes that are available for you to implement in SharePoint.

Content routing

When new documents are uploaded to SharePoint, they can be automatically routed, automatically initiate a workflow, or be modified based on specific criteria. This is a basic way to enrich content and reduce burden on users at time of document upload. In SharePoint, this is achieved with a feature called the content organizer. There are many use cases for this feature, and we recommend this as a good place to start automating notifications for users that new documents have been uploaded. In Figure 2-11, we show a simple configuration that will notify Chris that a new document has been added to the Press Release document library and needs his review.

FIGURE 2-11 Notification trigger is set using the Content Organizer.

Disposition workflow

This type of workflow manages document expiration and retention by allowing participants to decide what action to take on expired content. The expiration is determined by information management policies that trigger an event. This usually results in a task created for someone, and a workflow process is initiated to track the completion of the assigned task.

As shown in Figure 2-12, when a document has expired (in this case, a Press Release [PR]), a task is assigned to Chris to review the PR document and approve its expiration. This will remove it from the extranet website that it is published to.

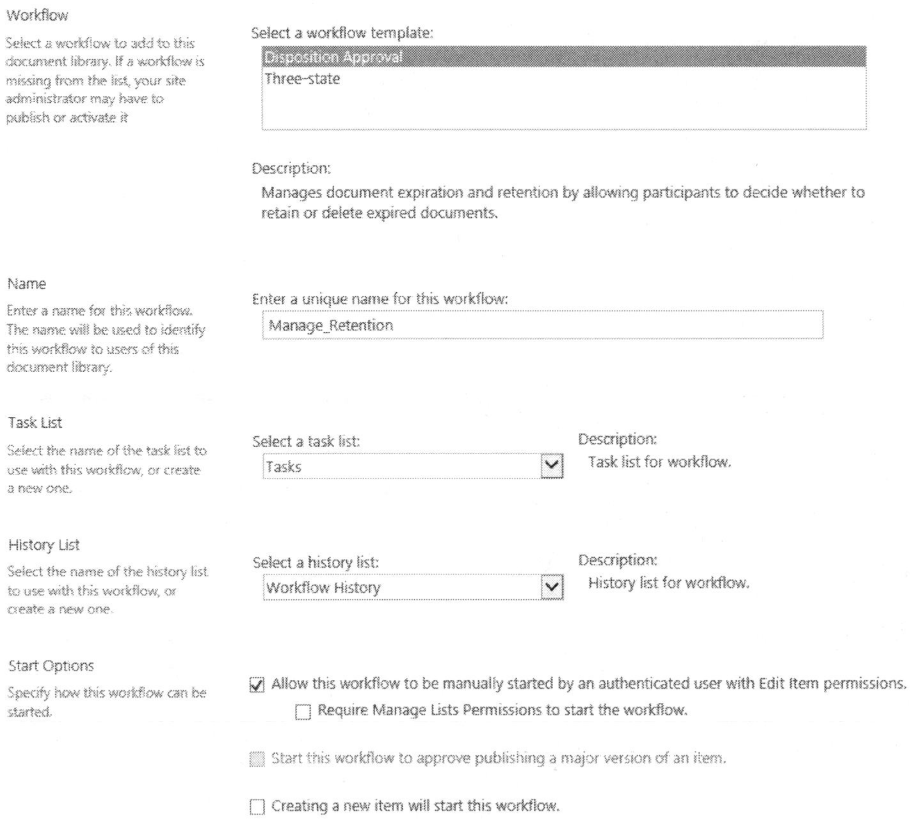

Workflow

Select a workflow to add to this document library. If a workflow is missing from the list, your site administrator may have to publish or activate it

Select a workflow template:

Disposition Approval
Three-state

Description:

Manages document expiration and retention by allowing participants to decide whether to retain or delete expired documents.

Name

Enter a name for this workflow. The name will be used to identify this workflow to users of this document library.

Enter a unique name for this workflow:

Manage_Retention

Task List

Select the name of the task list to use with this workflow, or create a new one.

Select a task list:

Tasks

Description:

Task list for workflow.

History List

Select the name of the history list to use with this workflow, or create a new one.

Select a history list:

Workflow History

Description:

History list for workflow.

Start Options

Specify how this workflow can be started.

☑ Allow this workflow to be manually started by an authenticated user with Edit Item permissions.
☐ Require Manage Lists Permissions to start the workflow.

☐ Start this workflow to approve publishing a major version of an item.

☐ Creating a new item will start this workflow.

FIGURE 2-12 Press Release document expiration triggers a review task.

Three-state workflow

This workflow is typical of a waterfall workflow, but with limited states. (The term *waterfall* infers that you can move forward in actions, with limited ability to send documents backward.) The individual states are the steps the document will take based on human decisions or systematic actions. The uses for this workflow are primarily document approval. In the following example, shown in Figure 2-13, a document needs to be approved by three individuals prior to being published to an extranet site.

Workflow states:

Select a 'Choice' field, and then select a value for the initial, middle, and final states. For an Issues list, the states for an item are specified by the Status field, where:
Initial State = Active
Middle State = Resolved
Final State = Closed
As the item moves through the various stages of the workflow, the item is updated automatically.

Select a 'Choice' field:
[_____ ▾]

Initial state
[_____ ▾]

Middle state
[_____ ▾]

Final state
[_____ ▾]

The list or content type requires at least one single value choice field with three or more choices.

Specify what you want to happen when a workflow is initiated:

For example, when a workflow is initiated on an issue in an Issues list, Microsoft SharePoint Foundation creates a task for the assigned user. When the user completes the task, the workflow changes from its initial state (Active) to its middle state (Resolved). You can also choose to send an e-mail message to notify the assigned user of the task.

Task Details:
Task Title:

Custom message: [Workflow initiated:]

☑ Include list field: [Name ▾]

The value for the field selected is concatenated to the custom message.

Task Description:
Custom message: [A workflow has been initiate]

☑ Include list field: [Title ▾]
☑ Insert link to List item

Task Due Date:
☑ Include list field: [Created ▾]

Task Assigned To:
◉ Include list field: [Created By ▾]

○ Custom: [_____] &⃝ ▣

FIGURE 2-13 Press Release document is routed to three individuals for approval.

Conditional formatting

Conditional formatting is used highlight specific content, based on rules and triggers applied to metadata. Many users are already used to conditional formatting, because it is commonly used in Microsoft Excel, and can be similarly used in SharePoint in libraries and lists. It's most common in lists of data but also very useful in a library of documents to "flag" or highlight content.

Note Conditional formatting from SharePoint 2010 to SharePoint 2013 changed dramatically with revisions to SharePoint Designer. In SharePoint 2010, conditional formatting was a feature available in SharePoint Designer as a part of "Design View." In SharePoint 2013 SharePoint Designer, "Design View" was removed. Because of this, the only method for conditional formatting in SharePoint 2013 is to modify XSLT templates or to implement third-party solutions.

Workflow

This more general form of workflow is a very powerful tool to create many types of more advanced workflows. This type of workflow is created outside of SharePoint, using SharePoint Designer and Visio for flowcharting to create a visual representation of the process. After design, they are published to a SharePoint site for use on content. The more advanced workflow allows the use of variables, multiple column data, parallel actions, Boolean logic, and basic conditions. After the workflow has been published, it's available to be scheduled or used on content in an ad hoc manner. A good illustration of creating a workflow in SharePoint Designer is shown in Figure 2-14.

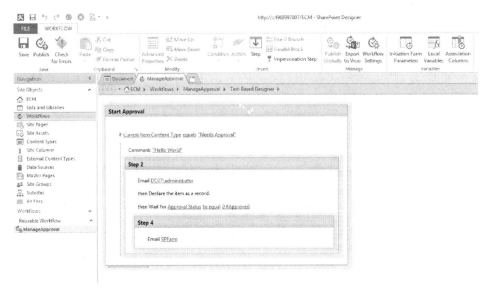

FIGURE 2-14 Visio flowcharting.

Note Using Visio to assist in workflow design requires Visio 2010 Premium or later.

Content routing, disposition workflow, and three-state workflow can all be achieved in the browser with any authorized user. Conditional formatting and general workflow are created by using SharePoint Designer. It's an external client application that connects to the sites on the farm for more advanced modification. This tool is not for typical users and can be used to modify many more complex features of SharePoint besides core ECM functionality.

We recommend limiting the use of workflows in ECM to the features and example given, if at all possible. You should also try limiting the number of features and third-party tools to as few as possible. We have found that the key to successful process implementation is simplicity. The general workflow is based on the Windows Workflow Foundation. The administrator will most likely create this workflow in SharePoint Designer with the addition of a Visio flowchart if needed. Obviously, this can be taken further with code, but we caution you to keep it as simple and straightforward as possible. Otherwise, you will follow in a long line of projects that never seem to end.

Note We recommend that you use the 80/20 rule. Most processes and transactions go smoothly and follow a defined path to completion. If you can solve and automate 80 percent of your non-exception-based workflow processing needs in a simple manner, you will be successful. If you spend all your time focusing on the 20 percent of transactions that are exception based, you will create an overcomplicated and difficult-to-maintain workflow process.

Organizations can conceivably build any workflow scenario they can dream up by using the methods and features we have covered. Use caution when designing and implementing your workflow, and remember that you will have to provide maintenance in the form of updates and modifications. Some best practices to follow when designing workflow include the following:

- Document and make available a listing of all public workflows, their purpose, use-case examples, assumptions of using it, and any special considerations. This can often be made available as a SharePoint list.

- Determine a simple naming convention for workflows that allows for non-creators to understand what a workflow does.

- Never label steps by using individual's real names. When they leave, you will likely have to update the process.

- Do not overcomplicate workflows; keep them as simple as you can. For example, do not automatically jump to SharePoint designer when OOTB 3-state workflow will do fine. Do not automatically jump to Visio when SharePoint Designer will do fine.

- Unless mandated for security reasons, always make workflows reusable.

- Avoid using custom actions. Not only do you need to support the workflow, you will need to actually document how custom actions work. There's also a high risk that custom actions have not been fully tested and could result in failure during workflow processing. For this reason, we recommend avoiding them in ECM.

It's not uncommon for individuals who create a workflow and have intimate knowledge of how it works to leave an organization, leaving the company stuck with one option, which is to discontinue the use of a workflow. This could be very disruptive to the usage of the ECM platform. It's uncommon in ECM to need advanced workflows beyond approval workflows based on states. Such custom workflows are best suited for custom line-of-business applications built on SharePoint. We therefore recommend that if the workflow cannot be easily created using OOTB methods or SharePoint Designer, the organization should consider a third-party tool for managing and building the workflows.

The subtle difference between Business Process Management (BPM) and workflow is the maintenance of workflows. The "Management" part of BPM separates it from standard workflow creation. In a standard workflow creation, a workflow is published without regard to previous workflow versions, without regard for who created it, and without regard for when it needs to be updated, and so on.

Note If your organization has many workflows, it's best to consider a solution that allows the WYSIWYG administration of all workflows. In addition, BPM tools offer versioning of workflows and many more state options that integrate with variables even outside of SharePoint. Unless you are going to be building a completely custom business application or if you have many workflows, we recommend seeking a third-party BPM solution.

We further extend process into the area of Business Intelligence (BI). Although it's not terribly common on documents, BI in SharePoint is very powerful. Like conditional formatting, BI is a way to visualize content to surface key data and performance metrics that can be used to improve business decisions and outcomes. BI is most common on list data and not content, but some organizations find ways to leverage BI also on documents. More specifically, we are referring to the visualization form of BI, not self-service BI or data mining.

The differences between BI in SharePoint 2010 and SharePoint 2013 are fairly substantial. The subset of features to accomplish this is called PerformancePoint. Typically, an organization will have a separate site collection for data reporting. To be successful with PerformancePoint features and documents, the metadata has to be a top consideration. To achieve relevant and meaningful visualization of the business data, you must have a well-structured, consistent, and accurate metadata model for document content types.

Next steps

We have moved content into SharePoint, stored it, organized it, and set it into motion. Now it's time to start managing the activity around content and how users interact with content. It's also time to start making sure that users can efficiently and effectively access content for editing and consumption. In the next chapter, we will cover the Manage portion of the content life cycle.

CHAPTER 3

ECM stack: content control

After content is in the system, it's time to put it to work. You might think this is the easy part. Functionally, it is much easier than the creation and capture portions of the ECM life cycle, but strategically, it's very difficult. We have found many organizations that are several years past an initial SharePoint deployment looking back and realizing that the adoption of this technology has not really improved a business process. In many cases, it has either become a web version of a shared drive silo or a collection of mismatched sites that aren't easily navigated by users.

As we mentioned in Chapter 1, "ECM defined," an ideal EMC solution is a balance between the effort to capture content and the effort to consume or find content. The preceding chapter was all about getting content into SharePoint; this chapter is all about consumption and accessing the content you need in an intuitive and structured manner. After content is stored in SharePoint, you have to pay particular attention to how content is managed, who manages that content, and how the content will be delivered and consumed. Last but not least, you need to determine how the content completes its life cycle, through disposition or long-term preservation.

Management of content

When we talk about the management of content, we are not just referring to who is in charge of SharePoint. Yes, we will discuss how to make sure your content is being treated properly. But we are also talking about how to manage its value, the people who use it, and setting proper expectations.

Two extremes prevail when organizations start implementing SharePoint. It either is seldom used, or it's used prolifically without governance. Being aware of both of these opposing outcomes will guide your ECM team's planning and help determine where to focus their primary efforts. You can start by answering the following four questions:

1. Is your organization one that embraces new technology or resists?

2. Does your organization process work at a macro or micro level?

3. Are shared drives the primary source of information management today?

4. What other systems or processes are used to manage content today?

Being honest about whether or not your organization can embrace new technology is an important question. In general, younger organizations are more adept and open to change, adopting new technologies, and improving processes. This is also true about people, so being realistic about who, where, and how you will implement and be successful with change is vitally important. Be aware of signals that people are resistant to change. These signals can come in the form of availability for meetings, a consistent focus on exception processing during design meetings, and the use of phrases like *"If it isn't broke, don't fix it"* or *"This is how we have always done it."*

It's important to work within the confines of how your organization adopts and addresses change. Specifically, in question 2, we ask whether your organization processes work at a micro or macro level. What we mean is this: How are decisions made, and who can effect change in work processes most effectively? In some organizations, groups and departments are given a fair amount of autonomy to get work done in the most efficient manner, using the tools and techniques that suit them best. In other more structured organizations, everything is mandated from the top down and there is a great deal of command and control.

Depending on your situation, you need to know how and where to start scoping the management aspects of content in your SharePoint ECM solution. This will also help you determine what individuals need to be on the ECM team, which we will cover in Chapter 5, "Building an ECM team."

Change opposition or support

We implied earlier that ECM is as much, if not more, of a people problem as it is a technology problem. Although we use common nomenclature for business processes, like "expense approval," and for departments, like "accounting," no two organizations are alike. Because of this, it's important to use principles and methods to guide your ECM solution design and not necessarily defined steps or configuration outlines.

We have found that there are companies who love new technology and, as an aspect of the culture, cannot wait to get their hands on it. These types of organizations or groups will be very excited to start using SharePoint and will be your early adopters. You can leverage their enthusiasm, but you will need to contain it, because this is usually the beginning of how viral use of SharePoint starts. Without Information Architecture (IA) or governance, these users will adopt bad habits and the ECM solution will turn out poorly. When this group establishes a bad habit, it's hard to stop it.

You might find that the organization in its entirety or in specific groups is very used to process and control. These control-conscious groups are welcoming and normally not opposed to systematic ways to organize information. If you look at their shared drives, they tend to be very organized already, which we hinted could help with IA planning we cover in Chapter 4, "Cases in point." While this group will be great for adopting SharePoint for ECM in the correct way, they will be hard to get moving, and they tend to not like change.

The other interesting element in this group is the nature of their content; it is typically more transactional and repetitive, as opposed to unstructured information. Most organizations have one or more of these types of groups. Some common examples are in finance, engineering, operations, legal, and human resources. Also, many industries are very used to structured processes and governance such as healthcare, insurance, and financial sectors.

Both types of groups, if already using shared drives as the vast majority of the content world does, believe that they have a system for organizing content and that it's just fine. Whether a knowledge worker admits it or not, their slice of the shared drive pie is a dumping ground for content. Sometimes it's organized, and at other times it was created while on a conference call. The net result is a system that they know because they built it, but one that does not serve the overall organization well. To understand how people might want to use your SharePoint ECM solution, it's important to understand how content is being stored in these shared drives today.

How users currently manage their content is a good indication of how they will want to manage it in SharePoint. Habits are very hard to change, and if a person has been doing a particular job function for many years, they are used to adopting workarounds to get the job done. At the first sign of any struggle, a user may revert to old habits, such as looking for a workaround or complaining that the new system just doesn't work. This is compounded by daily stress and workload that make the burden of using a fancy ECM solution even higher.

The four questions we asked at the beginning of this chapter were not outlined to establish any specific components of your implementation. Rather, they are meant to generate introspection so that you will begin to understand where your problem areas will be. You should use this knowledge to identify what groups will provide opposition or support for your ECM team's planning of a successful implementation and extension of SharePoint. The next step is to use this information to address the specific areas of the Management portion of the content life cycle. The following outlines the primary areas to consider for who manages the content. Please keep in mind that the management of content is not the same thing as who manages the security or access levels to the content.

- Security

- Document types/retention schedule

- Document audits

- Managing bad habits

- Policy creation and implementation

Who manages content?

As a best practice, we recommend that the individual(s) in charge of managing content in SharePoint should not be the same people who maintain SharePoint, typically the IT department. In fact, depending on how large your deployment is, you can and should have many people who are responsible for managing content. The more people who are active managers of content, who understand the principles and benefits of your IA, the better chance you have of maintaining control of your information.

SharePoint as the ECM platform is the responsibility of the IT department, from the server and storage infrastructure to the farm installation and configuration. Their involvement or, rather, responsibility should stop at the site collection level. This is typically a blurry line, where IT responsibility ends, and your IA and general ECM governance begins. Below the site collection, an individual(s) who has a vested interest in the success of ECM in your organization should manage your ECM solution.

In many organizations, this person is the Records Manager, Content Manager, or Information Architect. Some small organizations don't have the luxury of such a position for budgetary reasons. Even some larger organizations haven't identified the need for this specific position. There are a variety of reasons why this might be the case—for example, there is little regulatory oversight or the organization has never been party to litigation. In such cases, you have to consider appointing a team that is responsible for the content or, if the organization is large enough, individuals in each functional unit, often referred to as *Super Users*.

This is challenging in many organizations because both IT and the Content Manager or Super Users have, or should have, a stake in the ECM solutions performance. For example, it should be a defined part of their regular responsibilities or tied to a Managed Business Objective (MBO). In some cases, this can create challenges between IT and the Content Managers because they often do not have the technical know-how to take over at the site collection level.

> **Note** Managed Business Objective (MBO) is a tool used by many organizations to establish goals above and beyond personnel job description. Monetary incentives usually accompany achieved MBOs to help acknowledge the extra effort required to meet the objectives. For example, a portion of the quarterly employee bonus can be based on MBO. Including MBOs for the effective use of the ECM platform is one technique that organizations are using to encourage proper adoption without the use of technology.

The first problem is usually addressed by creating synergy between Content Mangers and the IT staff. Both should be on the *ECM Committee,* which we will talk about in Chapter 5, "Building an ECM team," and both should be bound by the common goal to make the ECM solution work, both technically and operationally. In most organizations, this works out well, but it also always helps to draw a clear line in the sand stating that IT is responsible for everything up to site collections and the overall performance and uptime of the farm and that Content Managers are responsible for everything below site collections.

> **Note** Specific roles and responsibilities should be part of a well-defined governance plan and formalized documentation. Having a person(s) assigned to the role of Records/Content Manager or Information Architect is the best scenario and can help further define the organization's commitment to ECM.

The second problem is much harder to address, and organizations can really address this issue only when they identify and recruit the required staff well, before SharePoint is selected as a platform. Many organizations luck out and can identify users in each function who aren't in IT but are technically savvy and eager to be a part of this exciting new technology initiative. As for officially titled Records Managers and Content Managers, it is good to make sure that they have sufficient

SharePoint experience and training. A rule of thumb is that it takes about one year with hands-on experience with SharePoint to really begin as an administrator.

Security

If you have ever attended a SharePoint event, you know that one of the most common topics or common subjects within a given topic or track is security. This is both good and bad. The good news is that there are many individuals out there who know a lot about SharePoint security. The bad news is that the number of sessions at any conference on a particular topic is a gauge of how complex that topic can be.

Our approach is different. When it comes to ECM security, the best principle is that less is more, so keep it simple. This is one of the many areas of building an ECM solution in SharePoint that could result in planning paralysis.

From the field

Over-architecting security or any portion of SharePoint can result in a solution that is difficult to manage and use. During a recent project I worked on, it was clear that the security team was more interested in creating a complex security hierarchy that only they could understand and manage, this caused the project to stall. It finally came down to usability of the site collection, and the business unit was able to convince the CIO to override the security team. In the end, the security model established was good enough and the ability to get content in and then manage and use it was excellent. - Shad

We know and can recommend that simple is better because indirectly, while you are designing a fantastic IA (covered in Chapter 2, "ECM stack: content in"), you are determining security. That's right: security users and groups are very similar to IA. And fortunately, IA in SharePoint indirectly helps determine your security structure. So with a well-designed IA, part of the security work is already done for you. Now let's cover the two basic types of security in SharePoint: repository level and document.

Repository

Repository level security is the shared responsibility of the Content Manager(s) and IT. The repository level security should map to functional or departmental security groups in your organization's active directory. Active directory most often is where users and access levels are assigned. Typically, users are added to groups based on their department or function. Most organizations have this well established, which also means it cannot be changed. Although every organization is different and therefore every active directory forest, tree, and domain structure is different, the goal is to have these high-level functional groups align with the SharePoint repositories.

As we explained in Chapter 2, repositories are both the logical and physical location of content. The top-level repository is the web application, also known as the site collection. The next level is the site, and the final level is the library. The number of web applications is roughly determined by the size of the organization and the amount of content. While it's certainly possible to have multiple content databases, in this book we will assume that there is one content database per web application.

This means that the site collection is the first point, or envelope, that you can apply security to. For ECM, three general principles to follow for security are as follows:

1. Never assign user level security.

2. Never assign security lower than the site.

3. Never break inheritance lower than the site.

In general, one of the biggest challenges of security is the administration of it. Alarm bells go off in every organization when the security topic comes up; multiple people want to take ownership, and frankly, it becomes overthought.

When you think about it in simple terms, it's rare to find an organization where everyone in a department or group can't see all documents. Of course, there are exceptions; for example, Executive Management. However, the proposed approaches for IA that we outline in Chapter 4, "Cases in point," will show how this is addressed by having a specific site collection or site for the organization's leadership groups.

Therefore, the primary consideration is the groups, what the groups are applied to, and cross-functional sharing.

The ideal scenario

Based on our experience, we propose that each group gets assigned their portion of the IA. For example, the Human Resources security group gets assigned to the HR site collection or, for small organizations, to just a single site. The Engineering security group gets assigned to the Engineering site collection for large organizations or to a single site for small organizations. The manager of both of these functions should belong to a separate security group called Managers, and that group should be assigned to the Managers site collection for large organizations or to a single site for small organizations.

Our goal is that you begin to see a pattern emerging that will become very clear in Chapter 4 as you work through the practical examples. You should also be able to guide each group as they build out their portions of the IA by using the examples and templates we provide in this book.

This will also allow you to adhere to principle number 1, which is to never assign user-level security. With this method, you should never have to apply ad hoc security to individual users in the organization. The primary reason that we do not want you to do this is because managing it is very problematic, if not impossible. Without a third-party management tool, it's impossible to know where these ad hoc users have been assigned. It is also very difficult to make sure, when security is no longer needed or when the user is no longer with the company, that the user can be or is removed.

Team site

Cross-functional projects/repositories needing many users to be involved should be created in a separate site collection for teams. In this site collection, the root-level security is the entire organization, and the team leader will solely determine the individual team site security in an ad hoc manner.

This seems like an exception to the rule, and it is. But the concept is still within the principles of ECM. The result of the project—that is, the individual team site—is the document that belongs to ECM. Therefore, the team site itself is a sort of record. The team site collection is an ECM system for all projects, and because projects have short lives, the project and all activity within that project live and die there.

The biggest challenge with this approach is to make sure that team sites are deleted when the project is over and, if the result of the project was a document, that the final document ends up in the approach function in the organization. For this, in SharePoint 2013, we recommend using the new site disposition functionality, and in SharePoint 2010, we recommend looking at third-party tools or relying on the team leaders, via policy, to clean up after themselves.

This approach addresses the need for cross-functional work, keeps the principles of ECM in their designated functions, and makes IA and ECM management flexible. Figure 3-1 shows an example of a project team site used as a cross-functional repository for the Projects team site.

FIGURE 3-1 Projects team site.

The final two principles we established for repository security were never to break inheritance below the site level and never to assign groups lower than site level. Both are established because of the fact that security is very hard to manage, and as soon as management is lost, it's a rapid downward spiral in security and sprawl issues. This is especially true with the new share functionalities present in SharePoint 2013. Therefore, to keep security very clear and administration clean, we recommend that security be applied only at the lowest repository envelope, which would be the site collection for large or document-heavy organizations and a single site for smaller organizations. After this has been enabled on these repositories, it should not be broken out any lower.

It is even possible to get item-level security, and while it sounds fun, it's not. We have yet to find a fully justified use case for when item level security is right.

Site administration and recycling

In addition to repository security, the following SharePoint-specific security considerations will be important to understand and plan for when implementing your ECM solution:

- Site collection
- Site administrators
- Recycle bin

Who has access to administration functions on the site and, more importantly, the site collection is an important consideration, primarily because of the risk it could impose on the stability of SharePoint. A site collection and site administrator have the ability to modify security, enable and disable features, navigate to terms sets, modify content types, and so on. Without malicious intent, it's very easy to change something small, such as a content type, and harm the user's ability to use the system.

The process we recommend is to have no more than three site collection and site administrators. If at all possible, assign only site collection roles, and no ad hoc site administrators. Your ECM solution, when established, should not change often, so the need for a site administrator should be minimal. The group of three should include two Super Users or Content Managers and an individual from IT—most likely the farm administrator. The purpose of three is redundancy and accountability. In the governance section of Chapter 7, "ECM planning guide," we will talk about tracking these users and changes.

> **Note** These three individuals don't need to be 100 percent sure of all the functionality available in site settings, but they should be aware of the risk of changing things suddenly and have an appropriate level of cautiousness when making any changes.

From the field

Every time I open up SharePoint Site Settings, it takes about five seconds before I know where I am, and I will be delayed trying to remember where that pesky link I want to use is located. There I am, stuck on the site settings page looking for "Term Store Management." From an administration level, SharePoint can be daunting to navigate even for the most experienced. - Chris

The recycle bin in SharePoint has special considerations at the site and site collection level. The recycle bin is where documents go when they have been deleted. By default, recycle bins are set up in two stages. This means that there are two recycle bins: the site recycle bin and the site collection recycle bin. The settings for this are found on the web applications settings page in central administration, as shown in Figure 3-2. It's possible to turn off the second stage recycle bin, and it's also possible to set a purge date for when the recycle bin is cleared: by default, 30 days.

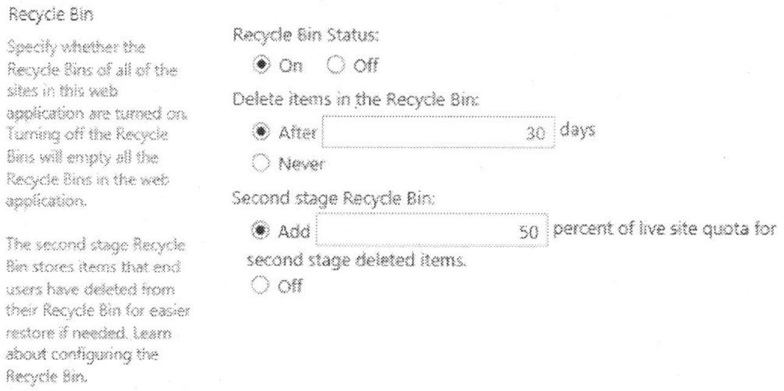

Recycle Bin

Specify whether the Recycle Bins of all of the sites in this web application are turned on. Turning off the Recycle Bins will empty all the Recycle Bins in the web application.

The second stage Recycle Bin stores items that end users have deleted from their Recycle Bin for easier restore if needed. Learn about configuring the Recycle Bin.

Recycle Bin Status:
◉ On ○ Off

Delete items in the Recycle Bin:
◉ After [30] days
○ Never

Second stage Recycle Bin:
◉ Add [50] percent of live site quota for second stage deleted items.
○ Off

FIGURE 3-2 Recycle Bin settings.

This method is useful because it's not uncommon for users to delete a document in the site and, on day 31, realize that they should not have. The consideration that needs to be made is who can restore, empty, and administer the recycle bin? Typically, the same three site collection administrators we outlined are the same who have access to administer the recycle bin. There are also two separate types of bins at each level: the end-user recycle bin and the administrators recycle bin.

> **Note** There are unique scenarios for some companies where even the site collection administrators should not see the content of deleted items. In this scenario, if acceptable, we recommend enforcing with policy, due to the small number of site collection administrators. Otherwise, a custom solution is required to modify the security of the recycle bin.

It is also good to plan the limit size of recycle bins and to have a policy for when, if ever, they are emptied separate from the defined purge period. Ideally, organizations will establish a time period and adhere strictly to this rule because, as we will see in Chapter 8, "Records management," following your own policies is critical for remaining compliant.

Document

We have established security to the repository, so now it's time to consider what a user can and cannot do with the documents that are stored in the repositories.

On a site and library level, you can manage different types of security groups. These groups, separate from those in Active Directory, determine what can be done on a document level. For example, you can decide which users can edit documents and which users can only read documents. These settings should not be viewed as tools for producing content; rather, this is the security that happens on the repository. They should be viewed as a way to protect the content of documents from unfortunate editing by the wrong people.

From the field

I'm never surprised when I audit a SharePoint environment and I see a user belonging to multiple security groups, custom security levels on every site, individual users assigned to a site, and more document-level security options than I could ever imagine. With SharePoint, keeping it simple is the only way to succeed. Fortunately, in ECM, it's structured enough that there is really no reason to break this rule or the principles we outlined. - Chris

You will find many approaches and views on this. Unfortunately, most organizations mimic security levels in their active directory. This is OK, but it usually results in too many groups to manage. Then there is the approach to consider just the types of activities that can happen to a document. For example, a user could perform any one of the following activities:

- **Design a document** Provide the ability to view, create, delete, approve, edit, and customize.

- **Edit a document** Make modifications to existing documents and delete them.

- **Contribute to a document** View, create, update, and delete existing and new documents.

- **Read a document** View and download existing documents.

- **View only** This is similar to read, but you cannot download.

- **Moderate a document** View, add, update, and delete items.

There are a few special actions that are reserved for custom solutions and web services that we are not covering in this book. All of these options distill to the ability to create, delete, modify, read, download, approve, and customize.

Because we have isolated document-level security as a way to protect the content of documents, we have included a decision tree in Figure 3-3 to illustrate a process of defining document-level security.

Even between experts, this approach can be quite controversial. The reason for such a radical approach is to maintain the ease of administration that SharePoint needs to have so as to ensure that the platform is adopted and extended. We believe that most organizations will have the requirement for the minimum level content security groups, which are Full Control and Read-Only.

 Note The most important thing in your ECM solution is to make the approach the same for all sites, and make sure that you also consider how hard it will be to administer.

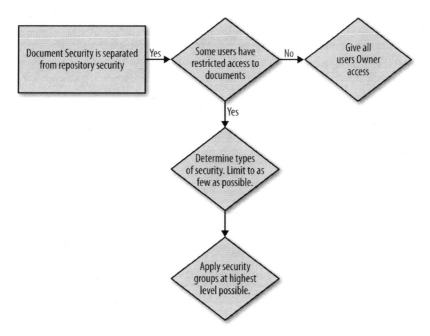

FIGURE 3-3 Document security decision tree.

Document management

Also at the content protection level are the check in/out functions and the versioning functions. Checking out a document is a very important yet simple tool in ECM that ensures that as a document is being edited by a user, the editing process is not impacted by another user who views the document.

From the field

When we were writing this book, we strictly adhered to the check in/out principle. There was not a time where we were working on chapters and the documents were not checked out. In the event Chris or I wanted to view progress, we would not impact each other's updates. - Shad

If you use default settings in SharePoint, it is up to the user to check out documents and to make sure to check them back in, at which point they should also add comments. Because it's at the user's discretion, you will find that when they own the content, they will tend to use this feature, because all users are sensitive to the additional work that could be created if someone else saves a version while they are editing. However, it's not guaranteed, so we recommend that you enforce that whenever a document is being edited, it is automatically checked out. As shown in Figure 3-4, you can do this on a library level in library settings and by selecting versioning settings. You can select Yes for the option Require Documents To Be Checked Out Before They Can Be Edited?

Settings › Versioning Settings

FIGURE 3-4 Versioning settings.

A side effect of this important feature is users forgetting to check documents back in. This should first be addressed with training, and eventually there will be enough social disruption around popular documents that users will make it a habit. Administrators do have the ability to force checked-in documents. We have even seen some unique customizations that run on a daily basis to find checked-out items and remind users to check them back in via email. This is another people and technology problem that is better to address with people first.

> **Note** Custom solutions add a variable to SharePoint that could impact extensibility, migration, and stability of the system. From time to time, we talk about custom solutions. By default, we recommend always using out-of-the-box features to ensure the life of your platform and that the ability to migrate to future versions is as easy as possible. When we talk about these recommendations, we are only hinting at some interesting possibilities; they should be considered carefully.

While in the versioning settings, we have something else to look at here. The next important consideration in protecting content, and a very common ECM feature is versioning. There are two types of versions, as we noted in earlier chapters. The first type is *major versions*, and the second is *minor versions*. A major version is everything to the left of the ".", and a minor version is everything after. For example, if a document has version 3-2, it has major version of three and a minor version of 2. Both sides of the decimal can be essentially infinite. Therefore, version 3-125, the 125th minor version of major version 3 of this document, is possible but not advised.

The first consideration is whether you should use versioning. In our experience, it's hard to find an ECM scenario where versioning is not a necessary feature. This helps make sure that the activity associated with the edits to a document is well contained and that you can revert to old versions if you need to. We did a study that shows that about 1 in every 20 documents has a need to be reverted back to a previous version. Only if documents are read-only, if you have technical limitations on your content database, or if you are advised by legal counsel (because every version is admissible content and available for eDiscovery) should you consider not using the feature.

When an organization has decided to use versioning, it must consider whether or not to implement minor versions. It's rare for an organization to have a need for minor versions unless they have implemented publishing. Publishing is the process of taking major versions of content and publishing them to other users in the same site or to intranet/extranet sites. This allows major version of documents to be published while the creator of the document can continually modify working versions. In most cases, organizations need only major versions. Unless you have strong documented reasons for doing otherwise, we recommend sticking with major versions only.

The final item to consider for content security is draft item security. It is possible to limit which users or groups can see draft versions of documents. In ECM, we feel that any setting other than "Any User who can read items" is dangerous. Does your organization use drafts and, if so, why? We find that most organizations, unless utilizing publishing features in SharePoint, don't need to use the draft feature in most cases. If you are utilizing drafts, because this is such a subtle feature, it's very difficult to document whether or not there is a special security consideration. As a result, if multiple editors are collaborating on a document, with some having draft privileges and others without, the problem of lost content will not be easily identified. It might be necessary at times for people without proper edit security to know about the existence of draft content. For these reasons, we recommend that, when using drafts, you should allow everyone to see the draft versions that exist.

We have outlined all the considerations for managing document repository security, ensuring integrity of the content, and special considerations as it relates to working with content in ECM. Now that your users have captured the content, your ECM solution is managing it because of the IA the ECM team put in place, and the users are putting the content to use. In the next section, we will explore the best practices associated with productive use of content.

Delivery of content

We have covered a lot of ground so far, but none as important to the people in your organization as the delivery of useful content. Content is useful when it is delivered to you and others in a familiar and consistent manner. The beauty of consistency is getting what you expect, whether it's your favorite restaurant, a solid relationship, or relevant content. When you don't get the experience you expect, especially if it is foreign to your common practices, whether it be in daily life or in business, you're going to shy away from that experience.

In this section, we will build on the Capture and Manage aspects of ECM by emphasizing a strong method for delivering content to your users. You want this to be a fast and effective experience for them, getting them the content they are looking for in a consistent manner. This is very important for user adoption, which is the ultimate factor in achieving success for your SharePoint ECM solution. Searching, finding, and consuming content is where organizations get beyond all the parts of ECM meant solely for the input and management of content and into actually using it for daily activities. It is where the mass of unstructured content will begin to meet all the back office line-of-business systems and processes used in daily operations. We recommend that you adhere to the following three elements:

1. **Consistency**   Leverage your IA.

2. **Focus**   For example, focus on the rule and not the exception.

3. **Users**   Involve them early and often.

Consistency

The benefits of being consistent in your SharePoint deployment have been made clear throughout the book regarding consistency in how sites and IA are set up per department and consistency of content types and libraries. The same is true when you think about the ways you will put content in the hands of users for editing and consuming. The benefits to remaining consistent will be measured in the ease of maintenance, decreased help desk support, happy users, and the ability to expand the ECM solution in repeatable ways that can truly benefit the organization. This will happen by planning for and incorporating consistent file formats based on need, consistent views and viewing, search functions, and web app updates.

From the field

During the final go-live week of a recent project, the document preview feature for SharePoint was identified as useful by a key stakeholder but it had not been included in the initial design for document library searching. This required Office Web Apps and some additional configuration. The hands-on user training had not included this new feature, but it was included in the final rollout. The help desk was immediately answering questions related to the install of the plugin required for preview; some users liked it and others didn't. Ultimately, the feature was turned off to reduce remedial training efforts. - Shad

Consistency of updates means that when you change the system you change it in repeatable and expected ways. End users fear change; this is a truth that will not go away. You should avoid changing the system frequently or in ways that alter the familiarity or steps required to interact with your SharePoint ECM solution. When you make changes, they should be regular periodic small updates, and any large changes should involve a prior notification. A fair amount of selling the change should be done with the users long before the change is made. Most updates to a farm that are visible to the user relate to consumption of content, which is why change is considered as a topic here.

To interact with content, users have to access it first. Access to content happens in two ways: by browsing or by search. Unfortunately, we find that the current trend is "throw it in the bucket and search for it." In a traditional line-of-business operation, this is not extremely effective. It is ineffective because search is the most subjective way of accessing content. In search, the burden is on the user to know the proper terms and format of a search query to get the document they seek. We would like to pose this question for you: If a user knows this much about the document, should they need to search? It's rare to find documents with enough content, or content in the right place, for search to be a highly effective method of accessing content. A single search is usually a 50/50 event, but after multiple searches, the user gets the feel of results and can dial in the results they are looking for much faster.

Therefore, we encourage organizations to consider search as the alternative when browsing does not work, rather than as the initial approach. In content browsing, a user drills down into the document they know they need, and because you have designed a good IA, they will get there very quickly. Indirectly, the more users need to search, the greater indication of poor IA planning.

Browsing and navigation

Browsing for content starts at the web application level. Users have to first identify where the document repository content lives and then the logical location of that content. Fortunately, we have explained why good IA is going to help you make sure that users spend most of their time in a single web application, making the need for extended navigation irrelevant.

The three main ways to navigate content are as follows:

1. Top link bar

2. Quick launch

3. Tree view

The first two are very common, and the last more common than it should be, because it implies problems with IA.

The top link bar, as shown in Figure 3-5, is the navigation at the top of the site. This navigation is generally reserved for physical repositories or subsites. It can be customized to link to any location via URL, but we recommend isolating to other web applications on the farm and subsites within the current site collection. You might also consider linking here to common resources that every employee in the organization can benefit from. As stated earlier, the key here is consistency. This is true for all navigation. Be consistent in how you name and order headings in navigation. Also be consistent about what the headings are. Navigation methods that are regularly changing will result in users finding another way to browse for content.

FIGURE 3-5 Top link bar.

The quick launch pane is on the left side of the browser. It is typically used to show all lists and libraries. Our recommendation is that quick launch be used *only* for listing libraries and lists in ECM sites, with the exception of cross-functional site links such as extranet/intranet quick access—that is, locations that you know a user will frequent. You can do this by creating a new navigation link, as shown in Figure 3-6. Navigation links can link to locations in the farm or locations outside the farm that are accessible and referenced by a URL.

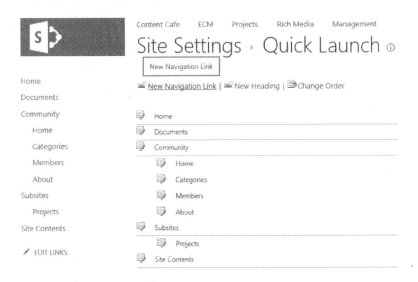

FIGURE 3-6 Quick launch links.

All the links in the quick launch are grouped by headings. Usually, headings are limited to Home, Libraries, Lists, Tasks, and Calendar items. In ECM, we generally do not see the Task or Calendar item in sites; these are reserved for the team sites discussed previously in the context of the Manage section, so these headings are often removed in favor of just Libraries and Lists. Because headings are also linkable, it's possible to have the headings themselves be the logical storage—for example, the "docs" library instead of "docs" being under "libraries." The benefit of this is streamlined navigation, but it becomes troublesome if you mix varied types such as lists and libraries. The primary recommendation, as stated earlier, is be consistent and keep your navigation simple. As a best-practices approach to simplicity, we recommend that your SharePoint ECM solution include only headings that link to libraries such as "Documents," "Rich Media," and "Email."

Tree view is an additional feature that can be enabled on SharePoint 2013 and is a way to visualize the relationship between logical and physical storage to its parent logical and physical storage. Essentially, when you turn tree view on, you get a new web part, as shown in Figure 3-7.

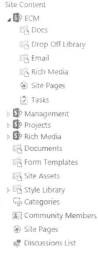

FIGURE 3-7 Tree view.

Another huge aspect of content view is library views, another tool that is either used not enough or in excess.

Many organizations are not aware of the extent that views in SharePoint can be modified. You can change columns by removing and adding which are visible. You can group content based on metadata, and you can create views that essentially filter content. Organizations that tend to use this in excess will have upwards of 10 views for any one library. This is an indication of bad IA. Organizations that are using the out-of-the-box views are using the tool too little and not leveraging the power of sorting by columns and filtering. These organizations will tend to be the same ones that use folders to organize their content.

There is no magic bullet on views, but there are a few guidelines. Every column shown should provide value to the user in the following ways:

1. If a column is useful only for some automation process or special type of user, it should be hidden or a part of a special view just for those types of users.

2. Columns should never exceed the right side of the page on a typical browser. Columns that are not visible in a single window are not usable.

3. Grouping is very powerful, but use this feature with caution and provide adequate user training as to the purpose of grouping. Grouping is used to aid a user who is browsing for content, while lists are used for more robust processes.

4. Limit the types of users who can create views, and make views consistent in all similar libraries across the entire SharePoint farm.

Site contents

Next on the navigation list is the viewing of site contents. In SharePoint 2010, this is called "View All content," and in SharePoint 2013, it's called "Site Contents." Asking one to "Click View Contents" is a common phrase, but we feel a crutch. It should not be required for the typical ECM user to navigate to lists/libraries or contents that are not otherwise accessible via the quick launch. Typically, if this is being used, it's a training problem, usually the result of someone far more experienced with SharePoint teaching how they use SharePoint, instead of how an end user should be finding and viewing content. Unfortunately, it is very common for a SharePoint site to have so many places to navigate from that an entire separate window to show all the contents is required. Both situations are not sustainable for widespread user adoption or simple browsing. We recommend keeping this tool a little secret, to be used by your super users only.

When IA fails or bad content somehow gets added to the system, the only option for accessing that content is search. Full-text search enables an index to be created from content stored in the body of a document. The goal is to get the user to the content with as few clicks as possible. With good consistency of content across the farm stored in a well-designed IA, a user is more familiar with content, and users can find that content based on keywords, where it's located in the farm, and other metadata searching.

Search

We have all experienced light and overloaded search results or getting too few results or too many. To eliminate the problem of having too few results, you want to make sure that indexing across the farm is adequate and that all the content in the farm has the appropriate iFilter activated so that it can be indexed. We can eliminate the problem of having too many results by filtering results using Boolean logic search terms, if/and/else/equal to, or search refiners.

Note Now search in SharePoint has evolved to include Boolean logic. For example, I can make a query for documents where the title starts with SharePoint but has the word ECM in the body. It would look something like this: ("title:SharePoint*" AND "ECM").

Because Boolean searching is not a common tool, something more is needed. Users are often in too much of a hurry or not advanced enough to use Boolean logic. One way you can help them get to their results faster is by using search refiners.

Search refiners are generated automatically based on a document's structured metadata. When you do a search for documents that start with "SharePoint" and contain the word "ECM" and you get too many results, you can refine your results by knowing simple things about the document, such as the author or when it was created.

Refiners can be taken even further, by including keywords and tags. Specific terms from the body of the document can also be generated on the left portion of a search panel, as well as their hierarchy. There is some customization required to get this feature to work, but it is one that is well worth the effort.

Note Remember that structured metadata is metadata that is generated by the system, such as author and modified date.

Farm administrators can do even more to assist the user in finding content. They can do things like *visual best bets*. This is where a particular document is highlighted at the top of a search based on a keyword. The relationship between the keyword and the best bet has to be established manually. This helps users know what is the most important document for that search term.

The trick with the best bets option is keeping it current and relevant. This usually requires an administrator specializing exclusively in search and who has the relevant operational domain knowledge or knows how to obtain that knowledge within the organization.

Another common feature is linking content to individuals by including people search in the search results. By default, this appears on the right side of the search results and is effective only if you have active MySite pages for your users.

Viewing

After a user has browsed to or searched for a document, they need to have access to view and edit the content.

In SharePoint, there are two options for viewing content: either via the client application or via the browser. Surprisingly, the answer as to which to use is highly dependent on the licenses your organization owns and the makeup of your users' desktops. For example, if your users have Microsoft Office installed on their PCs, viewing via client application might be very convenient. If you have users accessing content on mobile devices, you need to spend time on a great browser viewing experience.

It also depends on your SharePoint licenses. To get the most robust experience with in-browser viewing and editing, the organization should invest in licenses to the Microsoft Web App server. This is a separate SKU and server on the farm that manages the real-time editing of documents in a browser. This tool allows both mobile users and PC users to have 80 percent of what is available in any client application for office documents.

To help ease your decisions, we recommend being consistent. Supporting various types of clients can be difficult. For example, if your organization is dominated by local network PCs with Microsoft Office installed, it's recommended to make the "open in client" application the default use case. Additionally, this will help if you have other file formats that are not a part of the Microsoft Suite.

If you can purchase licenses to add Microsoft Web Apps Server, we recommend that you standardize on editing and viewing in the browser, to the extent where you remove Microsoft Office from the users' desktops or laptop PCs. For unique circumstances for some users, you might allow the client integration with the local version of Office.

 Note Separate the readers from the creators. In many organizations, those who create the content and those who read the content are not the same. It is possible to consider different modes of operation for each. For example, readers should be able to work with all in-browser viewing of content, while creators might need Office client applications.

Finally, there are third-party viewing tools available that cross a spectrum of file formats. When your users are doing a lot of read-only access to documents, these tools might be useful.

Preservation

Preservation of content is an aspect of delivery, because typically preservation is a process of document conversion and movement to another location.

Preservation focuses on content that has historical importance to your organization. The types of content can be diverse and vary depending on the type of organization, enterprise governance, and any regulatory considerations you might have to contend with. The breadth and depth of preservation is very noticeable in the government arena, where many documents have historical importance and, in some cases, need to be kept forever.

For example, the documents associated with city planning could have a life cycle that requires them to be kept forever, to retain the historical significance of when, where, and how land use decisions were made. It's key to understand where SharePoint ECM begins and should end in terms of active content and archiving.

In the case of historical documents, the importance of managing a content life cycle does not generally have an impact for a SharePoint ECM solution, because many of the historical documents should be stored either on permanent media or on microform.

Note We recommend that you focus your SharePoint ECM solution on active content. This is content that is being created, reviewed, and shared and that has value to the organization at large for completing a job function or transaction. We do not recommend that you use SharePoint as an archive or long-term preservation solution.

Even if preserved content is still a part of SharePoint, it's recommended it be moved to a completely different SharePoint farm or, at minimum, to a site collection. The reason for this is that SharePoint is built for high activity and interaction from users, whereas preservation is about content that is interacted with very rarely or only for research purposes.

If you are keeping this content in the active SharePoint environment, there is a large opportunity cost that is taking valuable resources away from other high-value content. It is taking up space from your primary storage that should be dedicated to active content. Also, it could be impacting the performance of the farm, but most importantly, it's accessible by users who might or might not know the difference between preserved content and active content.

We recommend the following steps when determining how content moves from the active portion of its life cycle to the preservation stage:

1. Determine where the preserved content will live. It is assumed that as a part of the process of preservation the content will move. If you are saying to yourself that preserved content will simply be placed in a separate library in the same location as active content, this alone is not considered preservation.

2. Determine the long-term preservable format that the content requires.

3. Determine the automated or manual process that will move and convert the content.

4. Determine a custodian for preserved content. This will be an individual or external organization.

5. Determine the format of metadata for preserved content, and include in that metadata the last location where the content was saved in SharePoint. This is important to establish the chain of custody.

If you choose SharePoint as the final location for preserved content, consider methods of remote blob storage (RBS) for the preserved content. RBS is a database configuration that allows certain content to live outside of the SharePoint database while maintaining its accessibility through SharePoint. This allows you to keep the content in the SharePoint user interface without the load on the database. Using RBS is not recommended for active content but only for site collections where you have moved or are referencing preserved content.

It is a great practice for organizations to start either preserving or offloading inactive content, or disposing of it according to a predetermined retention schedule. This ensures the efficiency of the system and prevents users from being overloaded with content that is no longer relevant. This should be done in accordance with the following activities performed by an experienced Records Manager:

1. Create a records inventory to determine the breadth and depth of all your organizations records, both physical and electronic.

2. Create a retention schedule that clearly outlines the definitions of content, based on several parameters that are relevant to your organization. At a minimum, this usually includes document type, records series, retention period, active date, and inactive date.

   Legal Holds can also be established for items identified during litigation discovery processes. These are known as *Interrogatories* and *Requests for Production* (*ROGs*). In this case, content objects can be placed on hold with a timer. If they are touched or further requests are made before expiration of the timer, it can be reset accordingly.

3. Create a records retention policy that clearly outlines the procedures and governance of records for your organization. This usually includes the review and blessing of your legal department and executive branch.

After these activities have been performed, you can use the information in the retention schedule to configure SharePoint to support the preservation of content at the appropriate stage of its life cycle.

You have now completed the reading necessary to understand all the series of stages that content traverses during its life cycle. We began with defining Enterprise Content Management in our introduction. We then walked you through each of the major steps required for a SharePoint ECM solution. To recap, we have covered the following areas:

- **Getting content in, or Capture**   Upload, MS Office, scanning, native documents, forms, and streams

- **Configuring site(s) collections and document libraries, or Store**   IA, versioning, formats, and transformation

- **Moving content from person to person, or Process**   Business process management, workflow, business intelligence, and eDiscovery

- **Finding and collaborating on content, or Manage & Deliver**   Navigation, editing, viewing, searching, and preserving

Next steps

We will now outline two different strategies for using your newly acquired ECM knowledge. First we will look at a small or departmental deployment of SharePoint ECM, and then we will make the necessary adjustments for a much larger scale project. We will be providing step-by-step instructions and giving you some nice outlines that you can use for documenting your IA.

CHAPTER 4

Cases in point

We have covered the fundamental stages that all content in SharePoint should pass through to leverage a fully functioning ECM solution with a solid and well-planned Information Architecture (IA). You should now understand the methodologies and approaches to getting content into SharePoint, storing it in a meaningful way, and managing and tracking the content to its final preservation stage. Now it's time to put everything you have learned together by outlining some example deployments that can be used in real-world scenarios.

To do this, we will consider three broad categories of deployments: small scale, large scale, and line-of-business (LOB) applications. The key difference between a small-scale and large-scale deployment is in the capacity of the farm to support a given volume of content. While it is not always the case, the type of deployment a company chooses is roughly determined by its size—more specifically, the amount of content it plans on storing in SharePoint.

Deployment assumptions

A content database should not exceed 150 GB of content. Previously, we outlined a method to estimate the size of your farm. If you know that you will easily exceed 150 GB of content, you should consider a large-scale deployment and leave plenty of space for growth. Remember that the amount of effort to set up and maintain a large-scale deployment will require significantly more time and resources, so carefully validate that it's the right thing for your organization. We also want to make sure that your SharePoint ECM solution will meet the current and future needs of active content.

How small scale and large scale differ technically is that a small-scale deployment will contain all physical and logical storage in a single web application and site collection, whereas large scale, at minimum, will have a web application or site collection per function or department and perhaps even require additional granularity, depending on content volume.

There are many methods for expanding the storage capabilities within a single site collection as well, but the assumption here is that we are not using third-party tools. We are relying on no-code, only out-of-the box configuration possibilities, and designing with the concept of keeping it simple, thinking about migration and upgrade paths for our SharePoint ECM solution later on.

The other assumption that extends into the LOB applications is that we are working with an on-premise SharePoint 2013 Enterprise Edition small farm configuration. The small farm should have two web front ends and an application server. When the configurations get to the logical storage level only, the server-level configurations will be left to the IT team for general support and maintenance.

The LOB deployments are considered separate of ECM because they address not general content management but business processes that are content driven. They solve specific problems, such as human resources recruiting, contract management, or accounts payable.

All these deployments will be created for a hypothetical company called "Coho Winery." The company is a conglomerate and owns multiple wineries throughout the United States. Sales are generated in both the B2B and B2C marketplace. They produce their own brands and produce private label wine for some of the largest big box outlets. Their corporate offices have the following standard organizational and functional departments:

- Legal

- IT

- Executive Management

- HR

- Accounting

- Sales & Marketing

- Operations

Important Your organization's environment and requirements might differ from the one presented in the book. As you follow along in the chapter, be sure to note those differences and then adjust your project planning documents and ECM solution design accordingly.

In the small-scale example, the size of the organization in terms of content is roughly 30 GB, with 150 employees. In the large-scale deployment, it's roughly 3 TB and 1,000 employees. The company is setting up a brand new SharePoint deployment and, after it's been configured, moving content from shared drives to the new SharePoint ECM solution. They have never had SharePoint before, and the vast majority of the knowledge workers, those who have access to the ECM solution, are located in the corporate offices, while most regional store employees do not need access.

Besides the LOB applications, the portion of the farm being addressed is purely ECM. You can assume that there are custom applications living elsewhere in the organization.

We will now step through the initial web apps setup process. Both deployments start the same, with the creation of the Port 80 web application called "ECM Café." The Café is the landing page for the entire ECM system. As illustrated in Figure 4-1, we start in Central Administration and click Manage Web Applications under the heading Application Management.

FIGURE 4-1 Central Administration.

We then create a new web application, as shown in Figure 4-2, by clicking the New button in the upper-left corner of the Web Applications tab.

FIGURE 4-2 Create a new web application.

You will be given a dialog box, as shown in Figure 4-3, with all settings to create the new web application. Many of these settings will be determined by your IT department, and such recommendations should override anything stated here. However, the naming of the web applications should be in full control of the ECM team because this is a component of IA.

The settings we are going to change for our deployment are as follows: Name: "ECM Café," Port: 80, Public URL: *http://cafe*, Application Pool Name: "ECM café," Database Name: "ECM_CAFE." Your organization might have already established a database naming convention. If not, this is a red flag. The convention we are using here for all ECM web applications is "ECM" underscore "_" web application "café." This should match the name of the web application outlined in your IA. After you have set all these parameters, you can click OK, and the web application is built.

There are two other web applications we will use that are the same for either large scale or small scale and for the LOB applications. These web applications are *http://ECMHub* and *http://Projects*, respectively. Again, the naming will fall in line with the naming you have established as a part of your IA, as shown in Figure 4-4. The ECM hub will be accessible to only the ECM team responsible for setting up and maintaining the ECM portion of SharePoint. This is where some testing and the content type syndication will come from. The project's web application is the location of all the self-service team sites. These are considered cross-functional activities, where the results will be put in ECM but the project itself is a living document within this web application.

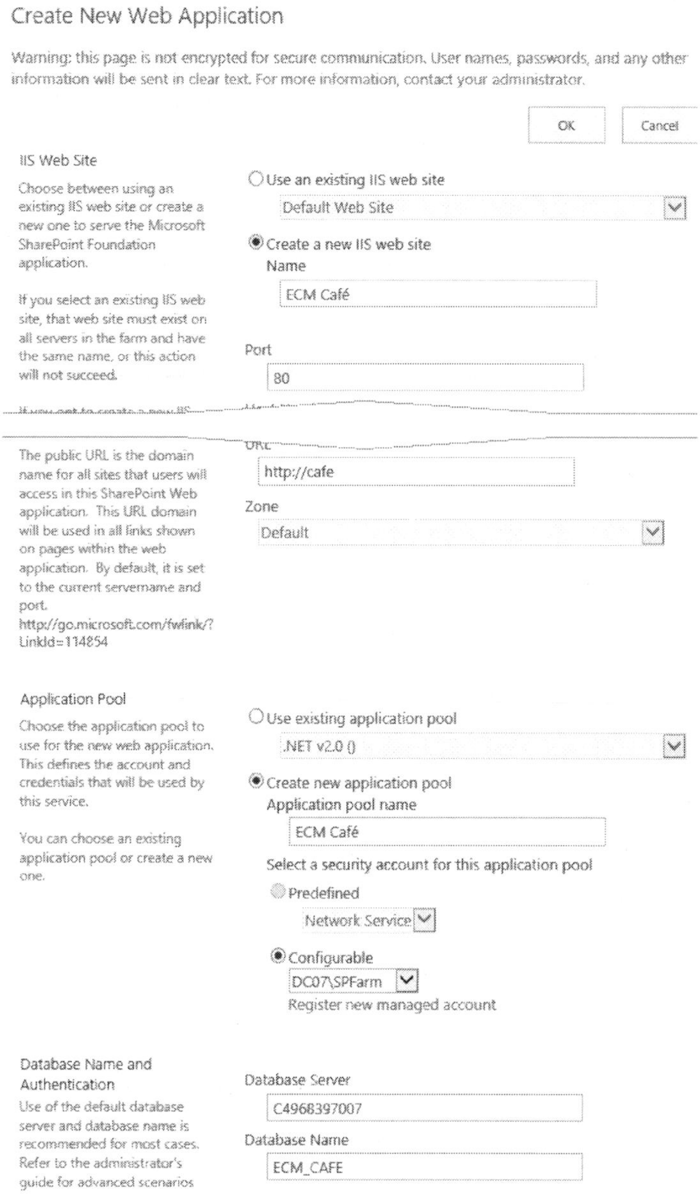

Create New Web Application

Warning: this page is not encrypted for secure communication. User names, passwords, and any other information will be sent in clear text. For more information, contact your administrator.

	OK	Cancel

IIS Web Site

Choose between using an existing IIS web site or create a new one to serve the Microsoft SharePoint Foundation application.

If you select an existing IIS web site, that web site must exist on all servers in the farm and have the same name, or this action will not succeed.

If you want to create a new IIS

○ Use an existing IIS web site

> Default Web Site ▾

● Create a new IIS web site
Name

> ECM Café

Port

> 80

The public URL is the domain name for all sites that users will access in this SharePoint Web application. This URL domain will be used in all links shown on pages within the web application. By default, it is set to the current servername and port.
http://go.microsoft.com/fwlink/?
LinkId=114854

URL

> http://cafe

Zone

> Default ▾

Application Pool

Choose the application pool to use for the new web application. This defines the account and credentials that will be used by this service.

You can choose an existing application pool or create a new one.

○ Use existing application pool

> .NET v2.0 () ▾

● Create new application pool
Application pool name

> ECM Café

Select a security account for this application pool

○ Predefined

> Network Service ▾

● Configurable

> DC07\SPFarm ▾

Register new managed account

Database Name and Authentication

Use of the default database server and database name is recommended for most cases. Refer to the administrator's guide for advanced scenarios

Database Server

> C4968397007

Database Name

> ECM_CAFE

FIGURE 4-3 New Web Application settings.

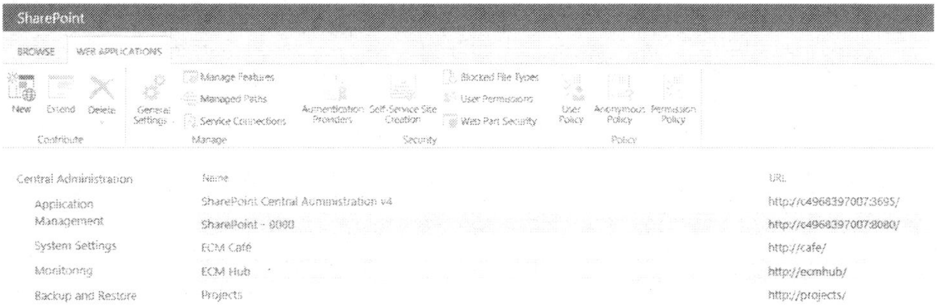

FIGURE 4-4 Web applications list.

As we will see soon, the ECM Café for the small-scale deployments will be the location of the entire ECM system, with the exception of team sites. And in the large-scale deployments, it will simply be a navigational web application that will be a landing page for the entire ECM system.

After we have created the three base web applications, we need to add a root site collection for each. To do this, you will need to navigate back to the Central Administration dashboard. Under the Site Collections heading, click Create Site Collections. At this point, as shown in Figure 4-5, you will need to select the web application that you are creating a site collection for, provide a title, and for these first three site collections, they will all be in the root of the web application. With the exception of the Projects web application, the template we will select for the root sites is Document Center, on the Enterprise tab. For Projects, we will use the Team Site template.

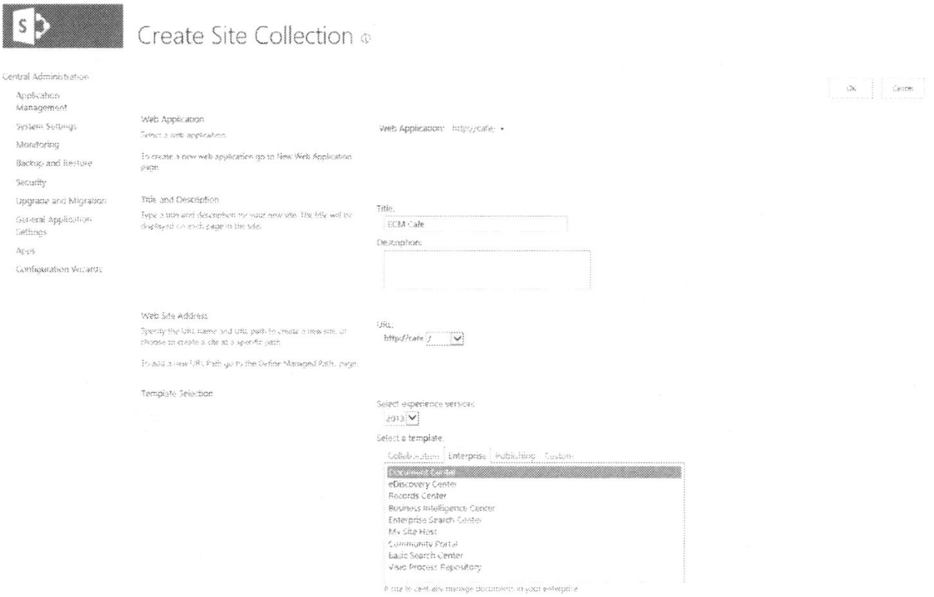

FIGURE 4-5 Create Site Collection page.

All other new web applications and site collections will be created in the same fashion as above, with the exception of the application name, site collection name, and content database name.

> **Note** You will need to refer back to this section when we create additional web applications for the large-scale and LOB deployments.

Now we can start establishing the first part of IA, components that are shared between both types of configuration, taxonomies with the managed metadata service, and content types used by all site collections in the SharePoint ECM solution.

The order of operation in the early stages of deploying your SharePoint ECM Solution is critical. If you get configurations out of order, you will find a lot of rework to be done. For example, if you configure your content types before you configure your managed metadata term sets for columns that the content type will use, you might cause problems with content type syndication. We recommend that you use the following steps to complete a proper baseline configuration:

1. Create web applications.

2. Create root site collections.

3. Create content type hub creation.

4. Manage metadata term store creation.

5. Create content types with retention periods and columns.

6. Enable syndication.

7. Create IA with sites and enable consumption of content types.

8. Create libraries.

9. Add content types to document libraries.

Managed metadata—taxonomy

Organizations typically have only three types of taxonomies: functional, regional, and period based. Functional is the most common and often the only one used. It refers to the departments or workgroups an organization has and the types of documents each of those departments consumes. Regional taxonomies are very common in organizations that are regionally diverse, such as retail companies or companies with field, branch, or remote offices.

Period-of-time–based taxonomies are the least common and should be used sparingly. They are used for seasonal business or components of a business where documents with set time periods are established—for example, meeting minutes for the Q4 2012 board meeting. Here the time period is relevant to the meaning of the document, not when it was created. The meeting minutes for the

Q4 2012 board meeting will always be about the board meeting that took place Q4 2012 and no other time period. The risk of period-based taxonomies is that time periods often change. If this is the case, a time-based taxonomy should not be used. Coho Winery is going to leverage all of these taxonomies in the example deployment so that we can cover each.

> **Important** Your organization's taxonomy might differ from the one presented in the book. As you follow along in the chapter, take note of the things that are optional and then adjust your configuration plans accordingly.

The process of building these taxonomies can be painful. This is especially true for functional taxonomies. To facilitate design, we will use the prescribed .csv (comma separated values) format that will allow for import into the managed metadata service. There will be a separate .csv file per taxonomy. While there are third-party tools and Windows PowerShell scripts for importing and exporting taxonomies to and from SharePoint, the only out-of-the-box feature is importing. For this reason, we will want to design all our taxonomies first in CSV and use this as a master record of the taxonomies and leave them unchanged. You can use an Excel spreadsheet to create your taxonomies structure and keep each type on separate tabs to keep them organized in one file. Then save the file as a .csv when you're ready to import them to the managed metadata service.

> **Important** After we import this taxonomy, it's set in stone. This concept of unchanged taxonomies might be uncomfortable for some. If it is for you, we would suggest that maybe taxonomy is not the right thing for your organization, because the purpose of taxonomies is a strict dialect. But also realize that flexibility is built into taxonomies, using synonyms on terms, which can be updated, and 90 percent of the time this is enough.

The real power of taxonomies comes from its rigid dialect. When you click on the term *contracts*, you want to be able to trust the system to produce all contracts. There are legal and adoption implications to this that we will discuss in later chapters. For this reason, terms must remain static. To support flexibility, we can introduce additional terms as synonyms. If taxonomy changes over time, it loses its accuracy and familiarity with users. If your organization does not want or need this level of precision, consider user-generated folksonomies.

Folksonomies and taxonomies look, feel, and are implemented the same way. The key difference is that folksonomies are user generated, so they are more flexible, where taxonomies are static values that we configure up front to force certain standard descriptions and language. Our recommendation is to stick with taxonomies, but folksonomies can be useful to smaller teams working on short-term projects or organization of personal content not related to a large or historical audience. The biggest risk of folksonomies is getting sprawling term sets where you have every variation and misspelling of every possible term. This ultimately makes the tool useless. Thus, a strict process of adding terms or maintaining them is required. We have outlined the CSV format in Table 4-1, along with the descriptions of each for your review.

TABLE 4-1 Taxonomy outline for a .csv file

Term Set Name	Term Set Description	LCID	Available for Tagging	Term Description	Level 1 Term	Level 2 Term	Level 3 Term

- **Term Set Name** This is where we will give the broad name or type of the taxonomy we are working on—that is, functional, regional, or period.

- **Term Set Description** This is a note to all administrators about what is contained in this set and how it's used.

- **LCID** This is the language code and is used only in SharePoint farms leveraging multilingual user interface (MUI). We will ignore this field for this application and use the code for English, which is 1033, but the column must be present for proper import.

- **Available for Tagging** This allows the term to be used in places where tagging is enabled. Because we want only to encourage adoption of the taxonomy and we want to be sure content is tagged, we will leave this as "TRUE" for all terms. If your organization leverages a folksonomy as well, you might want to set this to "FALSE" for all tags.

- **Level 1-3 Term** These are the actual terms we have decided to use for Coho Winery.

It's very important that if a term has a child term that the parent field not be left blank. This is one of the most common issues when importing .csv files. For example, if I have level 1 term of Contract and two level 2 terms for Contract (Signed and Not-Signed), I will have to list Contract twice. See Table 4-2 for the correct format. In this case, you can see that Contract is listed three times.

TABLE 4-2 Taxonomy outline for "Contract" taxonomy .csv file

Term Set Name	Term Set Description	LCID	Available for Tagging	Term Description	Level 1 Term	Level 2 Term
Legal Terms	Term set for all legal termi-nology to be applied to all legal documents	1033	TRUE	Contracts signed or draft format	Contract	
		1033	TRUE	Signed Contracts	Contract	Signed
		1033	TRUE	Contracts in Draft	Contract	Not-Signed

Note A very common and time-consuming mistake is having rogue term fields in the CSV. If SharePoint discovers one row with incomplete data, the import will fail. Make sure to test your imports regularly on a test MMS term set.

Starting with the simpler region taxonomy in Table 4-3 and the period taxonomy in Table 4-4, we outline the first 10 rows of each.

TABLE 4-3 Region taxonomy outline .csv file

Term Set Name	Term Set Description	LCID	Available for Tagging	Term Description	Level 1 Term	Level 2 Term
Region	Region	1033	TRUE	Tasting Room		
		1033	TRUE	Tasting Room	Livermore	
		1033	TRUE	Tasting Room	Livermore	Downtown
		1033	TRUE	Tasting Room	Livermore	Mines R.
		1033	TRUE	Tasting Room		
		1033	TRUE	Tasting Room	Napa	
		1033	TRUE	Tasting Room	Napa	City Center
		1033	TRUE	Tasting Room	Napa	Wine Trail
		1033	TRUE	Tasting Room	Napa	Sonoma Hills
		1033	TRUE	Production		
		1033	TRUE	Production	Napa	
		1033	TRUE	Production	Napa	Wine Trail

TABLE 4-4 Period taxonomy outline .csv file

Term Set Name	Term Set Description	LCID	Available for Tagging	Term Description	Level 1 Term	Level 2 Term
Period	Period	1033	TRUE	Financial Quarter	Quarter	
		1033	TRUE	Financial Quarter	Quarter	Q1
		1033	TRUE	Financial Quarter	Quarter	Q2
		1033	TRUE	Financial Quarter	Quarter	Q3
		1033	TRUE	Financial Quarter	Quarter	Q4
		1033	TRUE	Crush season	Crush	
		1033	TRUE	Crush season	Crush	2012
		1033	TRUE	Crush season	Crush	2013
		1033	TRUE	Crush season	Crush	2014
		1033	TRUE	Crush season	Crush	2015
		1033	TRUE	Bottle vintage	Vintage	
		1033	TRUE	Bottle vintage	Vintage	2005
		1033	TRUE	Bottle vintage	Vintage	2006
		1033	TRUE	Financial Quarter	Quarter	Q2

We started with these two taxonomies, because their terms are straightforward. However, the functional taxonomy takes substantially more effort.

The functional taxonomy will represent the documents organization-wide, but the taxonomies are defined on the department level. There are several ways to approach building your functional taxonomy. The approach we will use is to design taxonomies for each individual department and then reconcile them all at the end. We have outlined the following key principles to keep in mind when building your taxonomy:

- Do not user "Other" or miscellaneous terms. These terms are a catchall that will be used more often than you will like. People see "Other" and they quickly store an item without looking for the appropriate name.

- Do not use any transient terms. Terms like dates that will soon be invalid might be applied to a document and then never updated, so they become inaccurate. Dates and versions are the most commonly misused transient terms.

- Do not use plural forms of terms.

- Repetition is fine. Repetition in child terms will happen; this is common and expected. It's the entire path of a term that matters.

- Focus your terms on root concepts, and avoid being overly detailed. You can use synonyms for more detail.

- Do not create term depth further than 4 terms. Users will tend to stop applying terms at the third level.

- Do not use terms that are abbreviations, but use abbreviations in extended form for terms and synonyms.

The final taxonomy should be between 150–1,000 terms. We are outlining the beginnings of a taxonomy structure but by no means are these to be considered complete. Your organization is unique, and you will have to structure a taxonomy outline that meets your specific use case and requirements.

TABLE 4-5 Functional taxonomy outline .csv file

Term Set Name	Term Set Description	LCID	Available for Tagging	Term Description	Level 1 Term	Level 2 Term	Level 3 Term
Functional Taxonomy	Functional Taxonomy	1033	TRUE	Accounting and Finance	Accounting		
-		1033	TRUE	Accounting and Finance	Accounting	Policies	
		1033	TRUE	Human Resources and Staff Development	Human Resources		
Functional Taxonomy	Functional Taxonomy	1033	TRUE	Accounting and Finance	Accounting		

	1033	TRUE	Accounting and Finance	Accounting	Policies	
	1033	TRUE	Human Resources and Staff Development	Human Resources		
	1033	TRUE	Human Resources and Staff Development	Human Resources	Annual Employee Reviews	
1033	TRUE	Human Resources and Staff Development	Human Resources	Time Sheets		1033
1033	TRUE	Facility and IT Operations	Operations			1033
1033	TRUE	Facility and IT Operations	Operations	Communications		1033
	1033	TRUE	Facility and IT Operations	Operations	Communications	Telephone
	1033	TRUE	Legal and Risk	Legal		
	1033	TRUE	Legal and Risk	Legal	Contracts	
	1033	TRUE	Legal and Risk	Legal	Contracts	Employment Agreements
	1033	TRUE	Sales, Marketing, Promotional	Sales & Marketing		
	1033	TRUE	Sales, Marketing, Promotional	Sales & Marketing	Advertising	
	1033	TRUE	Sales, Marketing, Promotional	Sales & Marketing	Advertising	Print

When building functional taxonomies, it's important to realize that if the users do not relate or are not comfortable with the terms, the taxonomy will not be used. For this reason, it's very important to incorporate the different functional units in the development building process. We have outlined some guidelines that are commonly used when constructing a functional taxonomy.

Creating a taxonomy

1. List all departments and functions.

2. Take a screen capture of the shared folder structure for each function. The folder structure will be the starting point, not the result.

3. Create a list of representatives from each department or function that include project stakeholders or subject matter experts, and interview them by asking the following questions:

   a. What types of documents do you work with on a daily basis?

    b. How do you organize your documents?

    c. Do individuals organize by personal preference at a certain level?

4. Merge the terms from the folder structure with the comments made during your interviews.

5. After you have completed the taxonomy outline, review the functions taxonomy and terms with the project stakeholders in each department.

    At this point, you need to ask yourself the following questions:

    a. Does this structure make sense?

    b. Do the terms make sense?

    c. Is anything missing?

    d. Is there anything that can be omitted?

    e. Would you use this taxonomy on your documents?

6. Reconcile all functions into a single spreadsheet.

7. Compare all terms to the retention schedule. All retention schedule documents should be represented at some level.

8. Normalize overlap between departments. In some organizations, this means isolating common terms into one portion of the taxonomy for all to use.

9. Test the final taxonomy, within a staging environment with the easy and difficult departments' representatives.

As you are defining your taxonomy, it's important to remember to balance the details about the rules of a standard process instead of the exceptions. You will want to build your taxonomies around standard language and operational use cases and be careful not to overanalyze your taxonomies. You will need to fine-tune them as you conduct reviews with stakeholders, so leave some room for modifications in the process of constructing your taxonomies. Eventually, you will need to complete this effort and publish your terms.

Note Because of the way that SharePoint uses the managed metadata service and content types, publishing term sets for each department or function can become a burden from a configuration and maintenance standpoint. While it would be a best practice to separate taxonomies per function, it makes it very difficult to consume terms from one department in another. It also makes it difficult to reconcile with retention schedules. For this reason, and for SharePoint ECM only, we would recommend putting all functional taxonomy terms for all departments into the same term set. The benefit is easier maintenance. The downside is more terms shown to users than needed.

From the field

Inevitably, there are certain departments in an organization that are easier to work with than others. It's a good idea to find one of these and build out a taxonomy outline with them first, one that you can show to other departmental stakeholders and subject matter experts. It always helps to give an example of a result and show the value of keeping things simple and concise. - Chris

After we design our taxonomies, we must create these terms stores so that they are available to content types. We won't add the terms yet; we'll just create the store. Most organizations will be starting with a farm that already has a managed metadata service running, but we will create a new one called ECM_MMS. From your browser, navigate to the SharePoint Central Administration dashboard illustrated in Figure 4-6, and then click Manage Service Applications.

FIGURE 4-6 Central Administration.

Then click the New drop-down button and select Managed Metadata Service as illustrated in Figure 4-7.

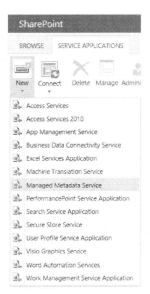

FIGURE 4-7 Select Managed Metadata Service.

A new dialog will appear, where you will give the new MMS Service a name. We will use ECM_MMS, to separate this managed metadata service from others used in the farm. We will use that name for the database name and application pool shown in Figure 4-8. For the last and very important setting, give the URL of the site collection used for the content type hub—either *http://ECMHub* or its internal name.

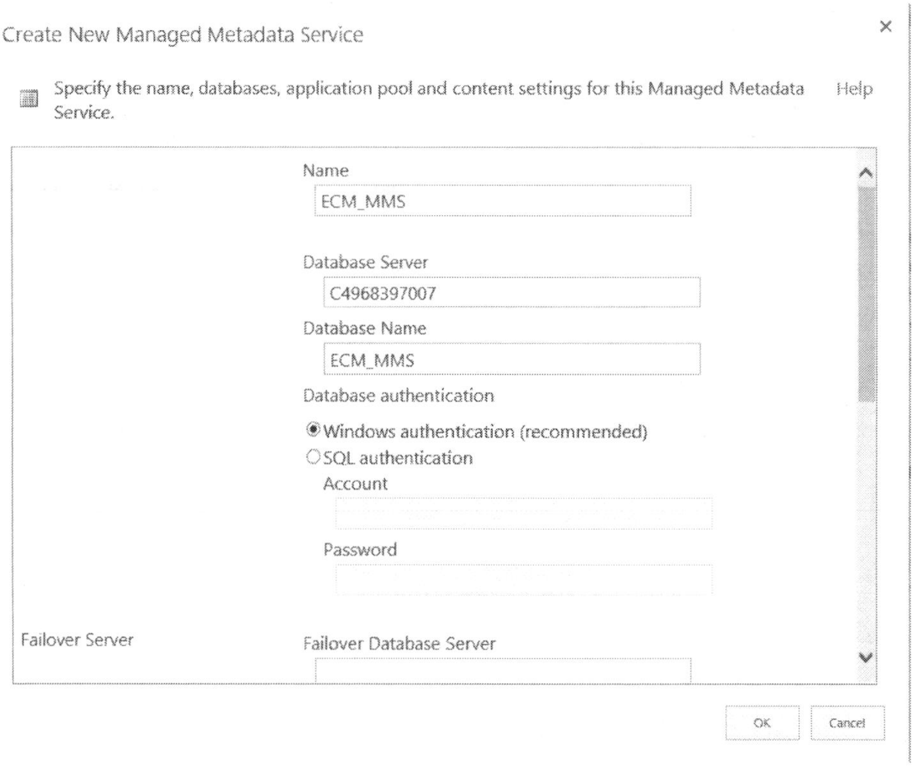

Create New Managed Metadata Service   ✕

Specify the name, databases, application pool and content settings for this Managed Metadata Service.   Help

Name

ECM_MMS

Database Server

C4968397007

Database Name

ECM_MMS

Database authentication

◉ Windows authentication (recommended)
○ SQL authentication
    Account

    Password

Failover Server   Failover Database Server

OK   Cancel

FIGURE 4-8 Create New Managed Metadata Service dialog.

When you click OK, the service application will be created and started. Before we can use it, we need to grant ourselves access. This is done in two places. First, as shown in Figure 4-9, click to the right of your new MMS service application so that the row is highlighted.

FIGURE 4-9 Highlighted ECM_MMS service.

Note Clicking the service application name will cause it to open the MMS management page. This is not what you want at this point.

Next, click the Permissions button on the ribbon. A new dialog will open, as shown in Figure 4-10. Add your user account, and because we want to create and edit taxonomies, give your user full control.

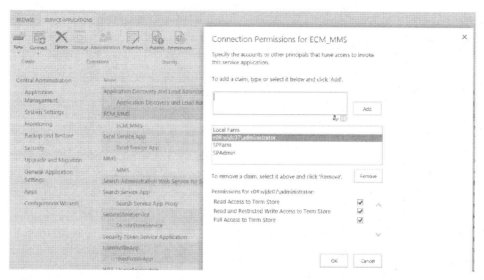

FIGURE 4-10 Setting user permissions for full control of ECM_MMS service.

We will need to do this in one other location, as shown in Figure 4-11. Click OK, and then click the Administrators button on the ribbon. This will open a new dialog box where you will also add your user and grant full control.

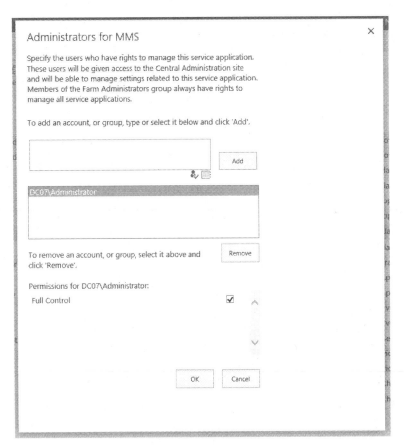

FIGURE 4-11 Setting administrator permissions for full control of ECM_MMS.

Below each service application is at least one service connection. We need to make sure that this connection is linked to the content type hub, as shown in Figure 4-12. To accomplish this, use a right-click and select to the right of the service connection name. In this case, it's MMS, listed just below ECM_MMS, and then click Properties.

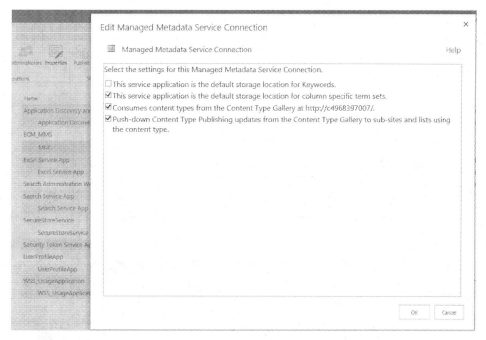

FIGURE 4-12 Link service connection to content type hub.

By default, the option Consumes Content Types From The Content Type Gallery at *http://ECMHub/* will be unchecked. Make sure that this option is checked. Also, because on this farm we are doing only ECM and only leveraging MMS in the ECM site collections, we will make this the default service application.

From the field

Initial configuration of MMS and content type syndication can be very challenging and require carefully following each step. There are many moving parts and functional dependencies at the SharePoint farm level. I don't believe I've ever gotten it right at first chance in the field. Some of the gotchas are making sure that MMS service is running, that your application pools are configured correctly, and that the MMS application you created has access to the application pool you set it to use. Work with your farm administrator when configuring this piece. After it's set up, configuration happens at the site collection level, and it's much easier. - Chris

Now that we have created, started, and granted access to the managed metadata service application, we can access it in our //ECMHub site. As shown in Figure 4-13, you need to navigate to your ECMHub and browse to Site Settings, and under Site Administration, you can then select Term Store Management.

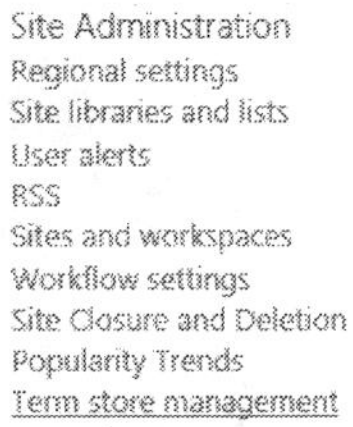

Site Administration
Regional settings
Site libraries and lists
User alerts
RSS
Sites and workspaces
Workflow settings
Site Closure and Deletion
Popularity Trends
Term store management

FIGURE 4-13 Term Store Management menu.

For now, we are going to create the base group and the three term sets we will use for Coho Winery. When you get into the Term Store Management Tool, you will see an existing group called "system." This is the group that will be used for SharePoint for managing hashtags and keywords for sites and MySites. We will not do anything with this group. Instead, as shown in Figure 4-14, click the drop-down arrow to the right of the term store name.

SharePoint
Site Settings › Term Store Management Tool
SEARCH
TAXONOMY TERM STORE
English
New Group
MMS
GENERAL
Available Service Applications
Sample Import
View a sample import file
Term Store Administrators

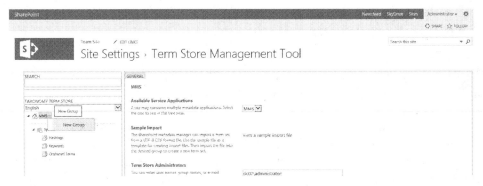

FIGURE 4-14 Term Store Management Tool.

Select the New Group option, and type the name of the group. In this case, we will use ECM Terms. Groups are a logical way to break up term sets and are usually tied to the use cases for which they are used, so name them accordingly. In this case, it's ECM. Rarely will you need to create new groups because of the size of term sets. Also, we consider keeping term sets to 800 or less to be a best practice for your SharePoint ECM solution. The primary purpose of the group is just having an easy way to organize MMS term sets when used for several use cases. We will call our Group ECM Terms. Now click the drop-down arrow to the right of ECM Terms, and you will be given options to create a term set.

On the new group, there will be a drop-down called Import Terms, as shown in Figure 4-15. Select your CSV file and select OK. Repeat this for the three different taxonomies we outlined earlier in the chapter—region, period, and functional, respectively.

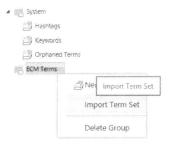

FIGURE 4-15 MMS term store groups.

The result, based on the preceding samples, should resemble the terms outlined in Figure 4-16 and show all three term sets.

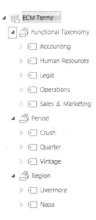

FIGURE 4-16 ECM term set results.

You have now successfully created and imported your taxonomies. These will be used in the columns for your content types. These steps we have outlined for creating taxonomies are applicable to the most commonly accepted procedures and best practices for building a SharePoint ECM solution. You should be able to apply these to your specific organization and use case.

Content types

Because both the large-scale and small-scale implementations will share the same content types and because the methods for managing content types use content type publishing and the content type hub we named *http://ECMHub*, we will not spend time setting up the content types and hub for both.

If you remember from the IA sections in Chapter 2, "ECM stack: content in," your content types are a single but important component of IA. Many organizations will tend to create content types for every document type imaginable, and they will use content types in lieu of other IA tools, namely taxonomies. We want you to remember that there is a balance. Our approach with Coho Winery is to use a predefined retention schedule that has been approved by the Legal department. This will be the foundation of our content type hub.

From the field

During a recent project that involved migrating content from a legacy ECM system to SharePoint, we encountered well over 200 separate and distinct document types. The document types had names with over 50 characters and in many cases were duplicated items that had been named differently by distinct departments and workgroups; they just grew organically over time. This made searching for documents difficult, and users found it hard to rely on the results. Our first plan of action was to complete a Records Policy and Retention File Plan based on the rules and regulations required. After the Legal department completed the policy, the Board of Directors adopted it and each department was briefed on the new policy and file retention plan. The total number of document types after this effort was reduced to under 100, and the names were kept to a common set of terms that would be used by all employees, regardless of which department they worked in. - Shad

---

Regulated and large companies all have retention schedules, but as we said previously, an organization of any size should create a retention schedule as a key tool in planning out an ECM system. It lists the types of documents the organization uses and how long a document should be kept. If you do not have a retention schedule, we have outlined the process of creating one for you to follow. It will be an interview process of each department and function to determine what types of documents the organization has and what impact they have on the business. It sounds simple, but it tends to be a time-consuming effort that requires subject matter experts in each department to perform a records inventory.

Documents that do not participate in specific LOB activities, or documents that are not risky from a compliance and legal perspective can be omitted from the file type listing. The benefit of this is greater ease of management, but the downside could be that those documents are either not used in ECM or used in a very general way, which could encourage free-form content storage and ultimately lead to bad adoption of the SharePoint ECM solution. If possible, we recommended taking the approach that if a particular type of document is neither relevant to a specific LOB system nor to ECM, it should be removed from any system and users asked to keep it in personal storage.

Next we need to determine the likelihood that these documents will be stored in the SharePoint ECM solution. In general, your goal should be to get all business-related content stored in ECM. In terms of eDiscovery and procedures such as legal holds for email and related content, it's not what you get correctly identified and stored and managed in ECM that hurts you; it's more likely the content that you don't control, file, or properly identify.

When this is done for each department and operational function, the types can be reconciled for the entire organization. We will want to eliminate redundant document types and terms and merge them to create a final list for the content types to be produced. This will be your content type list. For purposes of this implementation, we will use a subset of a retention schedule of only 10 document types that are typical for any organization. It is recommended that your organization try its best to consolidate document types by retention periods.

Note We will also build all content types based on the base Document content type, unless you have rich media such as audio and video, and then special document types are needed.

We have outlined our initial document type sets in Table 4-6. You will notice, just as with our taxonomy .csv files, that we plan everything in table form, including the columns we want to have prior to doing any setup in SharePoint. Remember that SharePoint is a tool to implement methodologies, not the other way around. Content types are a component of the IA methodology we have discussed; these are for organization of content. Do not expect SharePoint to give you the answer on how to organize or classify your content; it will do exactly what you tell it to do, so be diligent about your planning and documentation.

TABLE 4-6 Document types and retention period

Document Type	Description	Retention Period
Agreements	Includes leases, equipment, services, or supplies	AT + 2 years
Bids and proposals	Project bid submissions, including RFP, quotes, and so forth for projects from vendors	CYE + 2 years
Correspondence files	Various categories per department and/or type (that is, upper lateral letters)	CYE + 2 years
Minutes	Board and other meeting minutes	Permanent
Photographs	Historic, aerial, and other	US + 2
Deposits, cash receipts, worksheets	Checks, coins, currency, and credit card transactions	CYE + 10 years
Salary records	Deduction authorization, beneficiary designation, unemployment claims, garnishments	AT + 2 years
Employee time sheets	Signed by employee for audit and FEMA reports	CYE + 10 years
Purchase orders	Submitted purchase orders	2 years

Note Content type publishing is a powerful yet sensitive tool. It is imperative that the content type hub and publishing be enabled before any other site collections or sites can be created. If organizations mistakenly do this out of order, the connection between the hub and the consuming site will be broken. Correcting such an issue is non-trivial.

We need to cover the terminology that is used in retention schedules. In the retention period column, there is usually an abbreviation plus a time period. With the exception of permanent, which are records that should never be deleted (these should be rare), everything has a period after which it should be disposed of or archived. In Figure 4-17, we illustrate the relationship between content types, retention schedule, and document types.

- AT stands for *after termination* date. Agreements will be deleted five years after termination.

- CYE stands for *current year end*. On close of business of the current year, purge these records plus a certain amount of previous years.

- US stands for *until superseded*. These documents are replaced when or some period after there is a newer version of the document that is more current.

- CL stands for *close* or *completion*. These records are deleted when the project or activity has completed, plus some time.

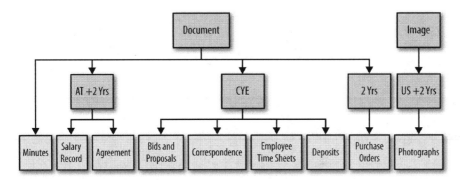

FIGURE 4-17 Retention schedule hierarchy.

> **Note** Some organizations might have some modifications to these abbreviation meanings, while other organizations do not use abbreviations but full text to describe retention.

The Document and Image content types already exist as a part of the base content types, so you do not need to create these. All of the boxes in the bottom row represent new content types that need to be created; we have outlined nine in total. We could create a content type just for retention periods; however, this would not provide friendly names for your users. Instead, we go ahead and create a content type for each known document type mentioned in the retention schedule.

Now that we know what the content types we need to create are, we need to know what sorts of metadata we need for each type.

Metadata is key for a lot of aspects of deploying a good SharePoint ECM solution. The results of applying an effective metadata structure are better findability, compliance, browsing, and consumption of content. However, too much metadata can be overwhelming. When deciding what types of metadata columns to add to each content type, you need to find balance. The proper balance allows you to use the most common search terms; don't be too narrow or overly broad in an attempt to cover every possible variable or exception. The following questions should be evaluated to provide general document search and satisfy records management functions:

- What metadata would be nice to have as search refiners when you search for documents?

- What metadata is needed for sorting document libraries?

- What metadata is needed to enable retention?

 Important Metadata is subjective to your specific needs. We caution you not to overproduce columns to satisfy every possible variable. It's a common mistake to create too many metadata columns.

Remember the content type's primary purpose is to be a container for metadata and enable retention schedules. We will also be using managed metadata, discussed in the next section, to make our content more powerful. We should allow MMS to take on the bulk of organization and IA. The number of columns you have in a content type should be the standard built-in types: *name, title, modified by,* and *modified date*. In addition to these, we suggest no more than four additional columns that you know will be used regularly. We modified Table 4-7 to outline the list of content types to include those columns we thought we would need for Coho Winery.

TABLE 4-7 Additional metadata columns

Document Type	Retention Period	Additional Columns
Agreements	AT + 2 years	Parties, Termination Data
Bids and proposals	CYE + 2 years	Vendor, Project
Correspondence files	CYE + 2 years	
Minutes	Permanent	Meeting Date
Photographs	US + 2	Superseded Date
Deposits, cash receipts, worksheets	CYE + 10 years	Transaction Date
Salary records	AT + 2 years	Pay Period
Employee time sheets	CYE + 10 years	Pay Period
Purchase orders	2 years	Issued Date, Amount, Status

For organizations with more content types, you might find that some types can be reconciled to be the same based on additional columns and retention. However, this should be considered as counterintuitive to a general user's ability to understand the name of content types.

In addition to the unique columns for individual new content types, all content types will have the following three new columns of type MMS that we defined in the taxonomy section previously:

- Function

- Region

- Period

We will require that the functional taxonomy be required and used on all content and that the regional and period be optional. The name of these taxonomies will be unique per organization but still the three most common types of taxonomies used for Coho Winery's SharePoint ECM solution.

We will begin by adding these three columns to the base Document and Image content types. We start here because all other content types will use these additional columns. We recommend that you think ahead about the type of your column; this could have significant impact on how it's used in workflow and information management policies. For example, we have a new column, Termination Date, which should be a date type instead of plain text. Here we will also want to group all new columns for easier management of them.

Creating each content type

1. Browse to the content type hub *//ECMHub*.

2. Browse to site settings by selecting the gear graphic in the upper right and clicking Site Settings.

3. Select Site Content Types, the location of which will depend on your version of SharePoint 2010 or SharePoint 2013 and enabled features.

4. Click the Create button on the top left. The New Site Content Type dialog box appears, as shown in Figure 4-18.

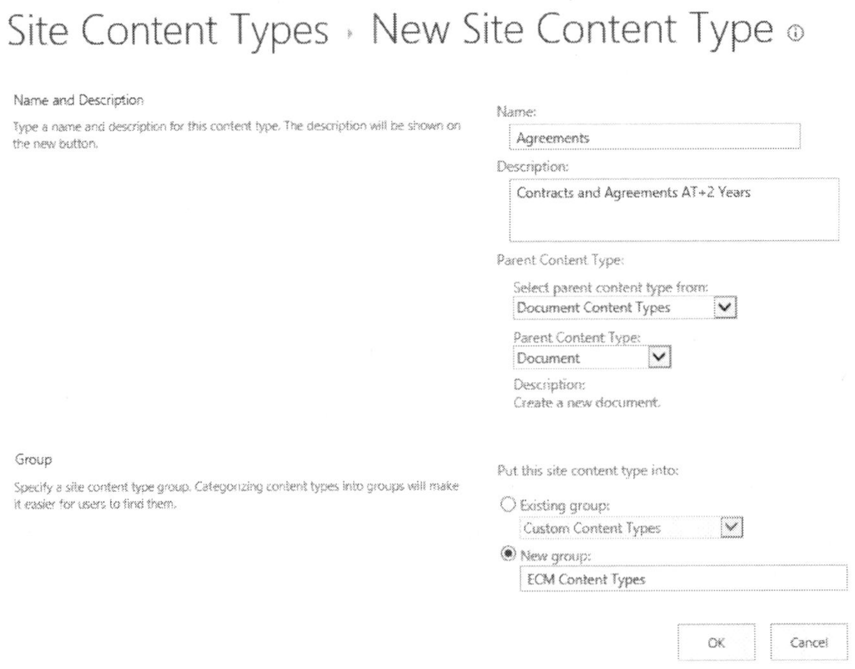

FIGURE 4-18 New Site Content Type dialog box.

5. Give the content type a name and description. Select whether it's based on Document Content Types, Document, or Document Content Types, Picture. It is a good idea to put new content types in a new group to avoid confusion. The first content type you create you will need to give the group a name, but for all others, you can browse to your group via the Existing Group drop-down. In this case, we will create a new group called ECM Content Types.

6. Click OK.

7. You are now taken to the Content Type Settings page shown in Figure 4-19. Here we will modify some settings and add columns.

8. Add all applicable columns. This content type has the unique columns Parties and Termination Date. Click Add From New Site Column.

9. Give your column a name, type, group, and make sure that the option Update All Content Types Inheriting From This Type? is set to Yes.

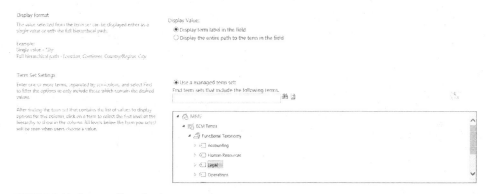

FIGURE 4-19 Content Type Settings page.

10. For columns Functional Terms, Period, Region, we will set these columns to type *Managed Metadata* and point them to the appropriate taxonomy. We will also select the Display Value option Display The Entire Path To The Term In The Field. The reason for this is that taxonomy terms are not only about their individual term; their relationship to parent terms is also important. Terms in taxonomy also repeat, but frequently with different parent terms. If you see only the selected term in a view, these two elements can cause problems in sorting and filtering. To make sure that there is no question, we show the entire path. Showing the entire path might be less aesthetic in views. The method for avoiding this is to hide this column unless it is absolutely required in the view. For taxonomies that are flat, where no term has a child term, you can leave this to the default. See the configuration options shown in Figure 4-20 for the Functional Terms column in the new Agreements content type.

11. Now that we have created the columns, we can apply the information management policies. On the Content Type Settings page, click Information Management Policy Settings. For the Agreement content type, disposition happens two years after the termination date of the contract. We will use the new Termination Date column to determine this.

Site Content Types › Edit Policy

Name and Administrative Description

The name and administrative description are shown to list managers when configuring policies on a list or content type.

Name:

Agreements

Administrative Description:

Deleted 2 years after termination

Policy Statement

The policy statement is displayed to end users when they open items subject to this policy. The policy statement can explain which policies apply to the content or indicate any special handling or information that users need to be aware of.

Policy Statement:

Deleted 2 years after termination

Retention

Schedule how content is managed and disposed by specifying a sequence of retention stages. If you specify multiple stages, each stage will occur one after the other in the order they appear on this page.

Note: If the Library and Folder Based Retention feature is active, list administrators can override content type policies with their own retention schedules. To prevent this, deactivate the feature on the site collection.

☑ Enable Retention

Specify how to manage retention:

Event	Action	Recurrence
Termination Date + 2 years	Send to the Disposition Library location	No
Add a retention stage...		

Auditing

Specify the events that should be audited for documents and items subject to this policy.

☑ Enable Auditing

Specify the events to audit:

☑ Opening or downloading documents, viewing items in lists, or viewing item properties
☑ Editing items
☑ Checking out or checking in items
☑ Moving or copying items to another location in the site
☑ Deleting or restoring items

Barcodes

Assigns a barcode to each document or item. Optionally, Microsoft Office applications can require users to insert these barcodes into documents.

☐ Enable Barcodes

Labels

You can add a label to a document to ensure that important information about the document is included when it is printed. To specify the label type the text you want to use in the "Label format" box. You can use any combination of fixed text or document properties, except calculated or built-in properties such as GUID or CreatedBy. To start a new line, use the \n character sequence.

☐ Enable Labels

OK   Cancel   Delete

FIGURE 4-20 Site Content Types–Edit Policy page.

12. Provide a policy statement and administrative description that are equal to the retention period. Click Enable Retention, and then click Add A Retention Stage. Here you will specify the stage based on a supported column and the action taken. For reasons we will explain in the records management and eDiscovery sections, we are choosing to move disposed documents to a new location. We will also enable auditing on all our new content types at this stage, on all particular events.

13. Our final step in creating the new content type is to enable content type publishing for it. Click Manage Publishing For This Content Type, select Publish, and click OK. Anytime you make changes to content types, it is good practice to publish or republish the changes. This should be very infrequent.

After you have built out all your content types, you are ready to build the IA for either the small-scale or the large-scale implementations.

The primary differences between the small-scale and large-scale deployments is the level at which the IA presents itself. Large-scale deployments are built for larger amounts of content; we plan for and configure them so that they are ready to grow. A small-scale deployment is built for ease of use and administration but not to support large growth or high volumes of content.

Shared Information Architecture

Let's first create the isolated site collections that have unique permissions and that will be used in both large-scale and small-scale deployments. These are Management, Legal, and Projects, respectively.

The Legal and Management sites have very strict security access and should not even be a part of the default navigation of any site. The Projects site should be accessible easily by anyone.

To create them, navigate to the Central Administration dashboard. Click Application Management, and then select Create Site Collections. Here you will give the site a Title and Type as shown in Figure 4-21. For Projects, we will select Team Site, and for Legal and Management, we will select Document Center.

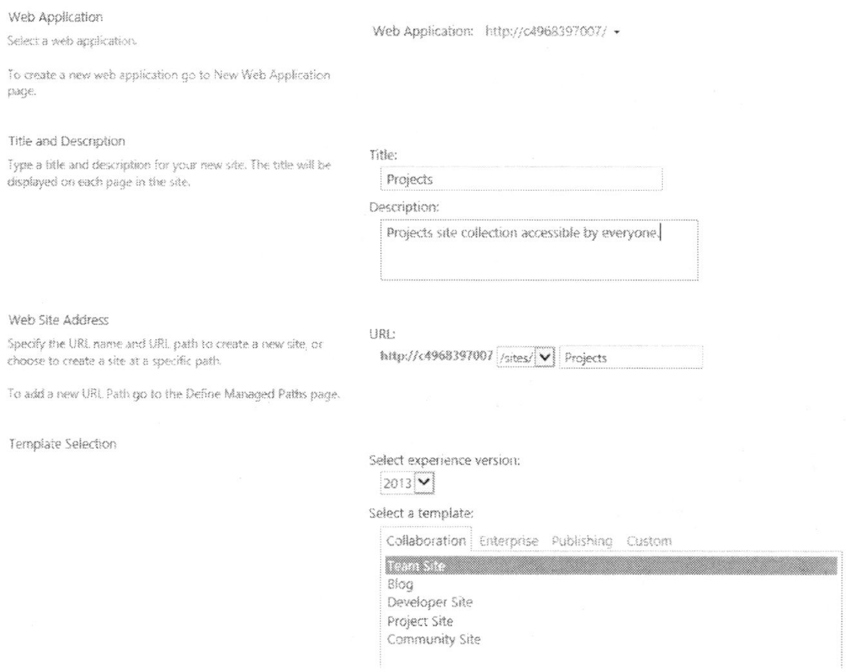

FIGURE 4-21 Create site collection.

For Administrators, we will select a super user, an IT user, and a records manager. You will recall that previously we recommended choosing three to five administrators who are trained and have good competency with SharePoint.

Repeat the steps for creating site collections for Legal and Management. When all three of the separate site collections have been created, we will assign special security to Legal and Management. For Projects, everyone in the organization will have access because projects serve as the location where all users from any function can work together. For Legal, we will make the entire site collection visible only to users in the Legal group. For Management, we will make the site collection accessible only to users in the Management security group. For the Legal and Management site collections, we can elect to not have any users from IT with access.

Browse to your new site collection—for example, //Café/sites/legal. Navigate to Site Settings, and select Site Permissions as shown in Figure 4-22. Here we will place the appropriate user groups in the right security level. For example, in Legal we will add the Legal user group to the Legal Owners group. You can do this by clicking Legal Owners.

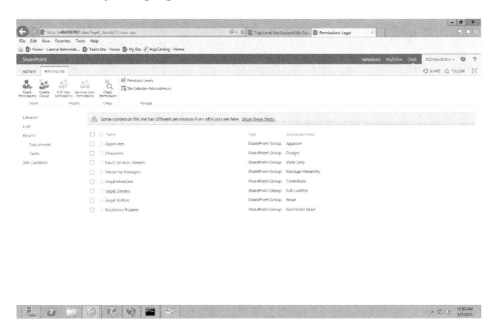

FIGURE 4-22 Site permissions for site collection.

Now click New on the top left, and select Add People To The Group, as shown in Figure 4-23. Type the name of the active directory security group Legal, and click Share.

FIGURE 4-23 Add users to group.

For Management and Legal, we will create the standard set of document libraries and rich media. Navigate to the root of one of these site collections—for example, //Café/sites/Legal. Select the Site Settings configuration menu item.

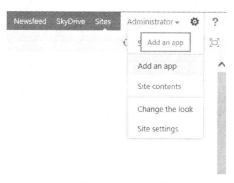

FIGURE 4-24 Adding a document library.

Select Document Library. We will create both a document library called Documents and a picture library called Rich Media. In most site templates, Documents is a default library that already exists. If it does, it does not need to be re-created.

For both of these libraries, we will want to use Advanced options and select to enable versions. The result should look like Figure 4-25.

Note The differences between the SharePoint 2010 and SharePoint 2013 user interfaces start to become obvious in the settings pages. In SharePoint 2013, new libraries and sites are types of apps, whereas in SharePoint 2010, creation of these can be performed from the Site Actions menu.

From the field

Are you scratching your head about the number of libraries we are creating? If you remember from our description of IA, the new approach is to be as flat as possible. In only one deployment was I able to fully utilize this approach, because the nature of most organizations and people are to overcomplicate the structure to account for every possible exception. We are showing you a new approach to content organization based on our experiences, both good and bad. We understand that you might have to make concessions for your organization and implement more libraries per site. - Chris

FIGURE 4-25 Legal site collection landing page.

 Note In SharePoint 2013, libraries do not automatically appear under the heading Libraries. New libraries appear under the Recent heading. You might have to navigate to Site Settings and modify Quick Launch navigation to get these libraries as static elements under the Libraries heading.

Before we are done, there are a few settings we will enable for all sites and libraries that we create from now on. This includes the sites and libraries created in the following sections:

- Document ID Service

- Custom Content Types

- Metadata Navigation

Because we want to make sure that we are tracking all documents as single immutable records, we want to enable the document ID service discussed before that will enable us to do this. To do so, navigate to your new site's site settings page and click Site Collection Features. Document IDs are a feature of the root site collection. As we see in Figure 4-26, we want to make sure that Document ID Service is selected.

FIGURE 4-26 Document ID Service option.

Navigate back to Site Settings, and select Document ID Settings. You should see the screen shown in Figure 4-27. Now you can assign a prefix used when IDs are applied.

FIGURE 4-27 Document ID settings.

Now we need to add the custom content types we created in our content type publishing hub //ECMHub. Navigate to each library, such as Documents, and add the appropriate content type for that site and library. For example, for the Legal site collection and the Documents library, we are going to add the Agreements content type. On the Library ribbon shown in Figure 4-28, click Library Settings.

FIGURE 4-28 Library ribbon.

The Settings screen for adding content types will be displayed, as shown in Figure 4-29. Click Add From Existing Site Content Types. Select the ECM Content Types group and Agreements. Click OK.

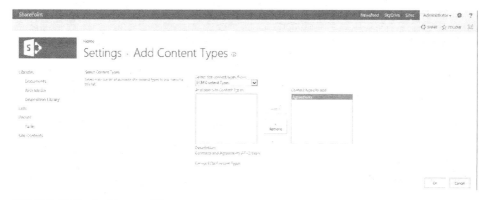

FIGURE 4-29 Content types settings.

Repeat this for all content types that are appropriate for that library. The content type will now appear as a type of document that can be uploaded and created in this library. It is now also a good time to modify the view of the library to show the columns that are relevant. At minimum, this should include the columns for functional, period, and region taxonomies as well as document ID. We see in Figure 4-30 that the Documents library in the Legal site has a sample agreement document uploaded and assigned to the Agreement syndicated content type.

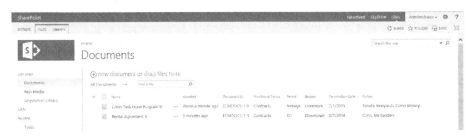

FIGURE 4-30 Legal site collection Document library.

Now that we have all the proper content types, columns, and features, we will enable metadata navigation with the taxonomies we have created so that we can improve browsing and filtering of documents, facilitating the flat IA. To do this, you can go back into library settings and select Metadata Navigation Settings. In this settings dialog, as shown in Figure 4-31, you will be able to pick folders, content types, and all available taxonomies. We do not recommend using folders. Instead, add the three default taxonomies we added previously for Functional Terms, Period, Region, and content types.

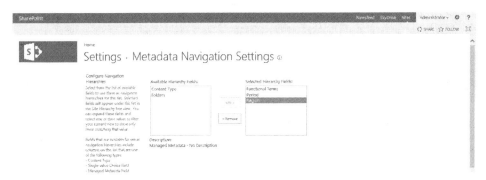

FIGURE 4-31 Metadata Navigation Settings page.

After you have done this, users will be able to navigate and filter libraries based any combination of types of documents and terms from the three taxonomies. This is a full representation of the power of a flat, well-defined IA, as shown in Figure 4-32. If you follow this structure, you will have an extremely easy to manage site collection and provide the superior search results that your users want and deserve.

FIGURE 4-32 Documents library search results.

You can now complete this process for all the libraries we have outlined. We encourage you to apply these best practices to the site collections that you create for your organization's SharePoint ECM solution.

In the Legal site collection, we will take one additional step and create a disposition library. This is the location where all information management policies will send content to have a final review by the Legal department before their manual and final deletion. *This is not just any library.* It is a special type of library called a Drop Off library. To create it, we first need to enable the Drop Off library feature, as shown in Figure 4-34. Go to the Settings menu, and select Site Settings. Then, under Site Actions, select Manage Site Features. Here you will see the Content Organizer feature; click Activate on this feature.

FIGURE 4-33 Site Settings–Site Features page.

Note Content organizer, document center, auditing, and so on are all features of the Enterprise Edition SKU of SharePoint. If you do not see these features, you might be logged in with a CAL without access to Enterprise features or have a non-Enterprise-enabled farm. For purposes of ECM Enterprise Edition, licensing of SharePoint is required.

This is automatically going to create a library called Drop Off Library. In SharePoint 2010, you will see this library under the Libraries heading; in SharePoint 2013, it is found under the Recent heading. Move the library so that it appears under the Libraries heading, and rename the library in Library Settings, as shown in Figure 4-34. We recommend that you provide a more recognizable name, such as **Disposition Library**; it's just more user friendly.

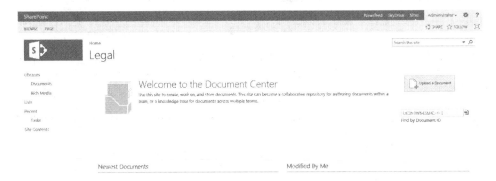

FIGURE 4-34 Legal site collection–disposition library.

Although we have created the Disposition Library, we will need to create a connection to it so that it can be used by the information management policies. The first step is to note the location of the Drop Off library. Go to Site Settings, and select Content Organizer Settings. At the bottom of this settings page, you will see a URL. Save this URL for reference later. It will look something like *http://c4968397007/sites/legal/_vti_bin/OfficialFile.asmx*.

Now browse to Central Administration. Under the General Application Settings, click Configure Sent To Connections. Here you will create a new connection, as shown in Figure 4-35. Give it a name, and pass in that URL that you noted before.

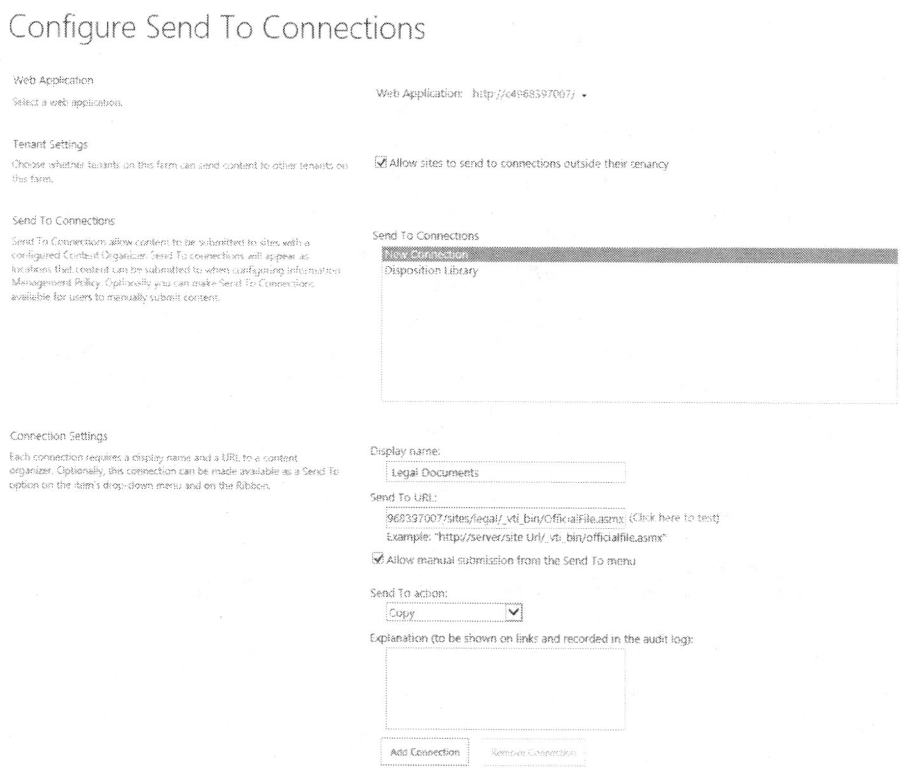

Configure Send To Connections

Web Application

Select a web application.

Web Application: http://c4968397007/ ▾

Tenant Settings

Choose whether tenants on this farm can send content to other tenants on this farm.

☑ Allow sites to send to connections outside their tenancy

Send To Connections

Send To Connections allow content to be submitted to sites with a configured Content Organizer. Send To connections will appear as locations that content can be submitted to when configuring Information Management Policy. Optionally you can make Send To Connections available for users to manually submit content.

Send To Connections

New Connection
Disposition Library

Connection Settings

Each connection requires a display name and a URL to a content organizer. Optionally, this connection can be made available as a Send To option on the item's drop-down menu and on the Ribbon.

Display name:

Legal Documents

Send To URL:

968397007/sites/legal/_vti_bin/OfficialFile.asmx (Click here to test)

Example: "http://server/site Url/_vti_bin/officialfile.asmx"

☑ Allow manual submission from the Send To menu

Send To action:

Copy ▾

Explanation (to be shown on links and recorded in the audit log):

[Add Connection] [Remove Connection]

FIGURE 4-35 Disposition Library Send To Connections page.

This new connection will create a send-to location that can now be used by all content types as a location for disposition.

We have dealt with the exception site collection where greater or unique security is required. We can now create the IA for the remaining functions. For Sales & Marketing, Human Resources, Operations, Accounting, and IT/Operations, we will create subsites under the root site collection //Café. Navigate to the Settings menu, and select Add An App.

Small scale

In the small-scale deployment, we will use the web application //Café as the root site collection and container for all subsites. We will create a site for each primary function in the organization: Sales & Marketing, Human Resources, Operations, Accounting, IT—with a separate site collection for Legal, Projects, and Management. The structure of the small-scale deployment, as shown in Figure 4-36, is based on the content types we created previously.

//Café	/	/	Documents	Document
//Legal	/	/	Documents	Agreement, Bids & Proposals
//Legal	/	/	Disposition Library	(All Custom)
//Management	/	/	Rich Media	Photo
//SalesMarketing	/	/	Rich Media	Photo
//HR	/	/	Rich Media	Photo
//Operations	/	/	Rich Media	Photo
//Accounting	/	/	Rich Media	Photo
//IT	/	/	Rich Media	Photo
//ECMHub	/	/		

FIGURE 4-36 Small-scale site structure.

As we build out the sites for the small deployment, we will allow them to be added to the top navigation. To create the subsites, as shown in Figure 4-37, navigate to the Settings menu and select Site Contents.

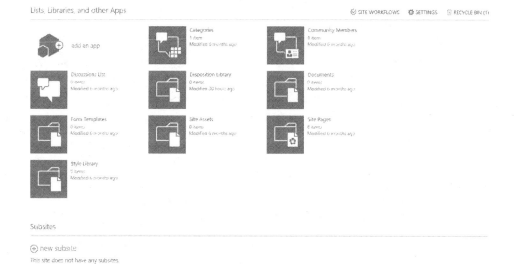

Lists, Libraries, and other Apps

Subsites

⊕ new subsite

This site does not have any subsites.

FIGURE 4-37 New subsite creation menu.

At the bottom of the page, click the New Subsite option. Give the site a friendly title, a URL name that should have no spaces. For all the subsites, we will use the Document Center template, as shown in Figure 4-38.

> ## From the field
>
> *If you have been working with SharePoint since 2007, you will remember this as a great tip when creating subsites. When creating subsites, remember to use names with no spaces. After the subsite has been created, you can go back and edit the name of the subsite and add the spaces back to accomplish a more general user-readable site name. - Shad*

Site Contents › New SharePoint Site

Title and Description

Title:

Sales and Marketing

Description:

Web Site Address

URL name:

http://c4968397007/ SalesAndMarketing

Template Selection

Select a template:

Collaboration | Enterprise

Document Center
Records Center
Business Intelligence Center
Enterprise Search Center
Basic Search Center
Visio Process Repository

A site to centrally manage documents in your enterprise.

Permissions

You can give permission to access your new site to the same users who have access to this parent site, or you can give permission to a unique set of users.

Note: If you select **Use same permissions as parent site**, one set of user permissions is shared by both sites. Consequently, you cannot change user permissions on your new site unless you are an administrator of this parent site.

User Permissions:

◉ Use same permissions as parent site
○ Use unique permissions

Navigation

Display this site on the Quick Launch of the parent site?

○ Yes   ◉ No

Display this site on the top link bar of the parent site?

◉ Yes   ○ No

Navigation Inheritance

Use the top link bar from the parent site?

○ Yes   ◉ No

[Create]   [Cancel]

FIGURE 4-38 New subsite configuration page.

The resulting site contents structure and top navigation will appear as shown in Figure 4-39, showing Accounting, Human Resources, Information Technology, and so on.

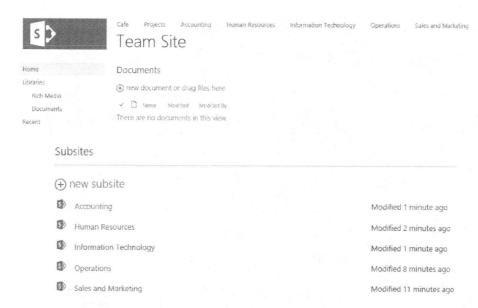

FIGURE 4-39 Subsite navigation.

After the sites are created, follow the procedures outlined at the beginning of this chapter for managed metadata, taxonomies, content type, and shared IA, as needed for each site collection:

1. Apply security groups.

2. Create the libraries.

3. Assign content types.

4. Modify views.

5. Enable metadata navigation.

When done, you will have the foundation for a small-scale farm with powerful SharePoint ECM solution functionality.

Large scale

Similar to small scale, with large scale we will start with the special site collections projects: Legal and Management. In this case, we will also create a web application for each function for ease of browsing. Therefore, instead of //Café/sites/legal, we will have //Legal. Additionally, Café will be used as a hub for all the other sites but not contain them. Figure 4-40 shows the structure of the IA for our large-scale deployment use case.

//Café	/	/	Documents	Document
//Café	/sites/Legal	/	Documents	Agreement, Bids & Proposals
//Café	/sites/Legal	/	Disposition Library	(All Custom)
//Café	/sites/Management	/	Rich Media	Photo
//Café	/	/SalesMarketing	Rich Media	Photo
//Café	/	/HR	Rich Media	Photo
//Café	/	/Operations	Rich Media	Photo
//Café	/	/Accounting	Rich Media	Photo
//Café	/	/IT	Rich Media	Photo
//ECMHub	/	/		

FIGURE 4-40 Large-scale site structure.

To create the web applications, we will follow the instructions we outlined at the beginning of the chapter when we created //Café, //Projects, and //ECMHub. Figure 4-41 shows the resulting Central Administration Manage Web Applications page.

Name↑	URL
Accounting	http://accounting/
Café	http://café/
ECM Hub	http://ecmhub/
Human Resources	http://hr/
Information Technology	http://it/
Legal	http://legal/
Management	http://management/
Operations	http://operations/
Projects	http://projects/
Sales and Marketing	http://salesmarketing/
SharePoint - 80	http://c4968397007/
SharePoint - 8080	http://c4968397007:8080/
SharePoint Central Administration v4	http://c4968397007:3695/

FIGURE 4-41 Manage Web Applications page.

In the large scale, we don't have the luxury of having the web applications and root sites appear in the top navigation automatically for café. We will want to add them manually by browsing to //Café and clicking the Edit Links button on the top navigation bar and clicking the + Link button to reconstruct the navigation shown in Figure 4-42.

FIGURE 4-42 Large-scale Team Site navigation.

Next steps

You have now successfully built out the base IA and features for an easy-to-use SharePoint ECM solution. If you have used SharePoint before, you can see the difference in the approach we are taking by using a flat structure. If you are new to SharePoint, you will have a great experience by following the best practices of IA outlined in this chapter. Now it's time to consider aspects of how to manage these deployments, build a team, and look at special functionality such as records management and eDiscovery.

CHAPTER 5

Building an ECM team

Your successful SharePoint ECM solution will have a large dependency on the ECM team that orchestrates its design and deployment. Up to this point, we have focused mainly on the structural and technical building blocks of the ECM solution. Equally, if not more importantly, the people who work together on the project will ultimately decide the heights of its success or the depths of its failure. If you can combine well-designed Information Architecture (IA) with solid teamwork and communication, you will be able to overcome any technical or operational change-management challenges that present themselves.

In this section, we will not only consider what it takes to make a great team but also the purpose of the team. Very often, organizations treat project teams as a checklist item on the long list of things you are "supposed to do" when executing a line-of-business application (LOB). When teams are used, they are also used more as a governance group rather than individuals looking for the best way to deploy an ECM solution. The project ends up being focused on getting SharePoint tilted up rather than the more important goals of building a solution that has longevity and is adopted readily by the user community.

Don't go it alone

We don't believe that ECM teams are uncommon, but their value and input on the project is commonly not what it could be. Therefore, we are suggesting that not only do you build a team, but you build one that is tactically involved in the entire implementation.

In most organizations, we encounter one of three possible scenarios that motivate ECM. The catalyst for ECM comes from IT, business users, or content managers. In some rare instances, the need for ECM is driven from the top down. In these cases, you are in a great position to achieve success. All too often, an ECM project is just another IT wish-list item and doesn't get the kind of early visibility and support it needs from the CXO suite. Leadership is key, and the Chief Officer positions can provide support and influence to help with budget and policy change and also make sure that the project is aligned with the organization's high-level goals and objectives. The Chief Officer should create an ECM Committee made up of key stakeholders and decision makers from the departments that will be adopting the ECM Solution. During the project the committee can address any escalation issues and operational decisions that will be needed from time to time. This takes the pressure off the core ECM Team whenever differing opinions or significant decisions are required. Often these issues center around budgetary, scheduling conflicts or operational changes that need to be addressed.

If IT has initiated the ECM project, it's usually driven by the concern that because content is not controlled, it poses a security risk to the organization, and because the vast majority of that content is digital, it is identified as an IT security issue. The good news about ECM projects starting this way is that it means IT is already involved. The bad news is that it's driven by a need to mitigate risk rather than better organization of content. The concepts and desire to secure content do not generally take into consideration the operational efficiencies that the business managers want or the ease of use that ultimately drives high rates of user adoption. Therefore, in most cases when this scenario is unchecked, it results in a partially built system with few ECM methodologies introduced and users that fight the system the whole way because it provides no real benefit to them. IT has a tendency to throw technology and features at the problem without considering how they interact with the user. They also tend to solve a problem and ignore what comes after the initial issue is resolved.

From the field

In nearly every casual conversation I have had with anyone about SharePoint, the same theme emerges: "We use SharePoint but no one seems to really like it." I believe this is largely due to organizations just rolling out SharePoint with too little planning and not nearly enough design and discussion about what the solution will solve in terms of operational inefficiencies. If you take the time to put together the right team and follow the concepts outlined in this book, your user community will have a much different conversation when asked about SharePoint. - Shad

If a business unit, usually Legal or Operations, mandates ECM, they do so from a need both of better content security and of process efficiency. The benefit of this is that there is greater emphasis given to how the system is used and the business needs that it should address. The problem is that, without IT, they are unable to align the theory of what they want with technology. Lack of IT buy-in makes it hard to get a project started and even more difficult to bridge the communication gap between the business needs and technology.

The last scenario, where the content managers drive the ECM project, can be the best from the implementation standpoint but almost as bad as IT when it comes to adoption. Content managers don't exist in all organizations. They are neither technology focused like the IT group nor are they engaging in the day-to-day LOB activities like the business users. However, they do share IT's strong need for content security, and they also have a strong desire to tie ECM to business operations. Content managers have a lot to lose with a system that does not work or is not used. And the ECM system certainly improves their ability to manage content. However, they do not always understand what motivates the end user to use the system.

Typically, when ECM projects come about it's one of the above personae (IT, content manager, or business user) that drives the project. And it's usually related to some event. For example, IT discovers that content has left the organization. Legal just dealt with a lawsuit where they did not have all the information until the very end. Or a business user is fed up because another lost document has caused lost efforts within their team or department.

It's great to have a strong motivation for ECM that is framed in problem/solution terms. However, because it's usually not incorporating disparate groups, things have already gone wrong, and this threatens the success of any enterprise or organization-wide project.

This is why we know it is so important to bring in other groups as soon as ECM is an idea being proposed for your organization. Not only does a team of individuals with different goals bring in ideas to improve the way the ECM system is deployed; it also lays out most if not all the problems up front.

From the field

An ECM project I was recently involved in made the mistake of not incorporating department managers. The organization insisted that the content manager and one IT person drive the entire ECM project. This is a good illustration of how critical a dynamic team is and where the mistake was made. The IT manager and content manager did interview a few users, but not enough, and the managers were not involved. I had the pleasure of sitting in on these meetings, and I made a note of how likely I felt the individuals being interviewed would adopt the ECM solution. I also noted that the managers were absent and that the focus was too narrow. Sure enough, four months after the system was deployed, the same managers that were not involved called a meeting and brought their whole department with them to protest that the system was not providing critical reporting features they needed. Had these department managers been engaged initially, this problem could have been avoided. - Chris

A team of individuals with differing goals and needs builds the most successful ECM solutions, small or large. The decision of building a team is a hard one for organizations for two reasons: time and conflict.

Time and conflict

Managers will indicate that time is a compelling reason not to allow individuals to participate in a team that distracts them from their daily responsibilities. There are many situations and ways to address this, and they are all tailored to fit the department or individual. It is important to be creative and key in on the psychology of the person or manager making the objection. For example, if a manager objects to committing resources to be involved in the project up front, you should ask them, "If you are not willing to put the time in to support the project now, are you willing to accept and use the system after it's implemented?" The results of not putting the time in up front will likely lead to an escalation meeting that outlines a laundry list of reasons why they will not use the ECM system.

Two excellent ways of dealing with this situation are to first identify another individual who does have time and who shares the desired objectives and goals of the project. Have them be a sort of emissary to discuss the project with their peers. Often a common set of issues can be identified and the proper resources can be assigned. Second, you can also spin the time complaint and have handy examples of how they are already wasting time because of operational inefficiencies due to lack of content control. You can point to broken processes, lost documents, and so on. Show them that by committing the resources and the time now, the future results of improved efficiencies will give them more time by utilizing their content properly.

The other reason ECM teams are avoided is conflict. This is a reason that might not be explicitly called out as clearly as the time utilization will be. It is that nagging fear of conflict that might cause project sponsors to hold back on bringing anyone else into the loop. This can be deeply rooted in office politics and bad previous experiences of working on IT-related projects that span the organization. We assure you that this quiet avoidance is just minuscule early on, and you should deal with it head on. After the system is deployed, the conflict will be tenfold, although it might not be as obvious. Users of the new system will express their anger either by being vocal (you can only hope) or by building animosity toward you and your team, which you will never spot but which will reduce your ability to do your job. In the worst case scenario, they will just refuse to use the system. Early conflict is good. Identifying where the problem areas are will allow you to move past them much more quickly and possibly even adjust the system to accommodate.

From the field

I have been in more than one ECM team meeting where users were visibly upset, sometimes even yelling, in protest of the new system. I paid close attention to those users and their issues, and I knew that this was an opportunity to mitigate future problems. It always amazes me how paternal users can feel about the organically adopted and flawed processes they have developed for managing content. In one case, I spoke with a department manager who openly admitted that their process for managing content was the use of folders and files on their desktop. On an annual basis, this individual basically started over every January by archiving everything to a shared drive and creating new folders on their desktop for the coming year. "IT will sort it out; I have a real job to do."
- Chris

Building a team will not be an easy task. There will be a time commitment, but the proper time spent will save loads of time for the entire organization after your ECM solution is in production. There will be conflict, and we encourage you to not only expect it but to embrace that conflict early on in the project. The results will be more ownership of the ECM solution by a broader audience, and it will mitigate the naysayers later on. Give everyone a chance to leave their mark, have their voices heard, and have their content management needs met. Now let's talk about how to pick your ECM team.

Team selection

You have, either on your own or with direction from someone else, identified a need for a new or improved ECM system. Perhaps you have a few peers who also see the dire need for improved content management, and you are excited to have them join forces with you. You have also identified that the need exists for a more established team. Here are the questions you need to answer:

1. How big should my team be?

2. Who should be on my team?

3. How often should my team meet?

4. What is the depth of participation of the team?

5. How should a meeting be conducted?

The size of the team is not exactly proportional to the size of your organization and deployment. We have found that between 5 and 7 members is the average size. However, we have seen successful teams as large as 12. The biggest problem that larger teams face is scheduling and time to value. We define *time to value* as the total number of calendar days you invest to complete the project before you start realizing positive results. In many cases, when you have too many people involved in the project, it is hard to form consensus and make decisions. This results in analysis paralysis, and the project never gets finished. We find that if you have too few people, say 3 or fewer, the results are more of corroboration between peers and can actually result in animosity developing inside the group due to one strong personality who tends to drive everything. This can also occur outside the group, by creating a perception that people are being left out of the loop. Who is on your team is the next important consideration.

The team should consist of many disparate groups of individuals. A good rule of thumb is to have two individuals representing the implementing group and one individual from each function, organizational unit, or department. In many organizations, this can be an individual who represents similar functions, such as sales and marketing, if they are separate departments, or operations and product. It's important to select team members who offer the path of least resistance and whom you already know will support the cause and project. We also encourage you to add some detractors at the very beginning. This can be a challenge, and most people avoid it, but it can greatly enhance the diversity of the team. Detractors tend to be pretty vocal, and they can undermine projects by spreading rumors and finding flaws. Put it this way: If you get at least one troublemaker to be a part of the ECM team, you can both resolve their concerns and get their trust. If you accomplish this, they can become a project's greatest advocate and have a positive impact on everyone else.

The more meetings the team has early in the project's life cycle the better. Most organizations have a standing weekly meeting on the ECM project. Some organizations set only monthly meetings, and this is not frequent enough. We generally find that these organizations are establishing a team just because they were told to, not because of the strength that frequent meetings can provide. We recommend biweekly or weekly meetings as the normal course of business, and as things progress, you can adjust for holidays and other organizational issues. The benefit of more meetings is that they tend to be easier to consume because they cover less content and therefore take less time. Be as consistent in your meeting schedules as possible, and send reminder emails with the previous week's meeting notes, noting all team members assigned action items from the previous week and the upcoming agenda or topics. This helps everyone maintain accountability and stay on track, especially in large projects with people who have multiple responsibilities. Other things to consider when scheduling meetings and planning the project are any planned leaves of absence due to vacation, family commitments, training, and so on.

As we said earlier, the team is not just a high-level strategy group; they should also be part of the technical implementation of the system. Implementers are the ones who do the configuration following the design of the system and IA to produce the final system from SharePoint. We know from this book that SharePoint is not an ECM system until its features are formed into one. It's these individuals who do the work. Implementers join practitioners, who are the heavy users of the system. This will definitely include your content management team, but it should also include heavy users in each individual function.

The reason that two to three of the team members should be a part of the implementation and practitioner groups is so that they can influence and guide practical applications in the team. Teams that discuss high-level concepts are good for getting theory down, but the team needs to quickly dive into both principle and technology details. The teams should be prepared to cover all the details outlined in the ECM stack found in Chapter 2, "ECM stack: content in," and Chapter 3, "ECM stack: content control," of this book. This means building the IA and designing taxonomies, but not the implementation cases in Chapter 4, "Cases in point." Give team members homework, and ask them to engage a subteam or key individuals in their department. Get tangible written results from your team members, and no matter how little feedback you receive, continue to encourage them to participate. We encourage you to offer rewards to encourage the right behavior and celebrate milestones, always giving credit where credit is due. We will cover this in more detail in the next chapter. This enables the team members to take ownership of a piece of the solution. For example, have each team member get a screen shot of his or her functional department's shared folder structure. Or ask the members to evangelize the concepts of why the system is being built in their department. The bottom line is this: We recommend that you use your team members for the important tactical work of gathering information, selling the benefits of the project, and showing the results of their efforts.

Every organization will have its own meeting style and structure. We strongly encourage organizations to embrace an adaptation to the scrum meeting methodologies. Because ECM teams are less tactical and task oriented than true development scrum, the approach does not work entirely. However, what scrum teaches us is focus and consistency. ECM meetings will be longer, they won't be held every day, and they will cover more vague and ambiguous topics than a typical scrum meeting. The adaptation we recommend is as follows:

1. Start with opening remarks by the implementation team and giving the current status of the project.

2. Share what each member did since the last meeting.

3. Share what they are doing before the next meeting.

4. Outline current impediments or issues.

You might elect to present these items as individual team members or have the project manager collect them and moderate each agenda item for the entire team. It's really a team decision as to how this is accomplished, but we do recommend allowing each team member to take some ownership of sharing his or her own agenda items.

The early meetings will take a different, more flexible, format as the team figures out how to work together and establishes early goals and timelines. But the meetings should quickly take a routine and standard format. Remember that you want to follow standard meeting protocol by setting defined time schedules and keeping the meeting focused, but you also want to balance the meeting with a standard of open and honest communication. Each member of the team has a responsibility to share issues without the fear of being ignored or penalized. Also, be careful not to let one person take over the meetings because people will become disinterested and the project will suffer.

From the field

One of my favorite strategies when kicking off a project with the ECM team is to lay all the messy stuff on the table right away—not just for the drama value, but because it's easier to rip off the bandage and get all the unfriendly items out in the open. This can include company politics, organizational changes, early objections to the project, or personal bias, and so on. During a recent meeting, one person shared that they had been involved in a SharePoint project at another company that had failed, and this caused them to be skeptical about the project. What's funnier is that they had been hired because they had SharePoint experience but they didn't necessarily share the details about the failed project during the interview process. Because we stressed open, honest conversation without consequence, they were comfortable sharing the experience. It ended up being a great asset to the team, because we then discussed all the reasons why the project failed.
- Chris

ECM team roles and responsibilities

For each member of the ECM team, it is important to clearly define each person's roles and responsibilities. We start by using a traditional organizational chart to illustrate a reporting and communication structure, as shown in Figure 5-1. Your existing organizational structure might be different, and we show only one department, Accounting, as the end user. You will include the appropriate number of end user resources as you begin your ECM solution design and planning. This will be true of every distinct operational unit in the organization, just substitute Accounting for the appropriate department.

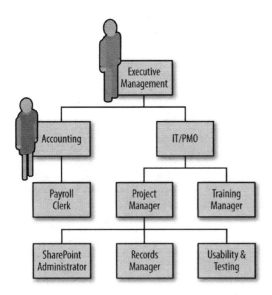

FIGURE 5-1 Project team org chart.

The most important point to get across here is that the Accounting business unit and the IT Department have equal influence and access to Executive Management. It is important that the project team has both business and technical stakeholders developing the final ECM solution design and IA. Equally important is personal chemistry between these leadership roles, and in the end, they will accomplish more if they have a good dose of mutual respect for one another.

Your initial project scope is most likely focused on the operational pain points in the business. These could be driven by a need to increase revenue or to cut costs around transactional inefficiencies. When evaluating the primary project roles, you should also consider who the people are that are best suited to adopt change and have a positive influence on the project team. SharePoint is usually a high-profile technology, so it's important to get a good track record for the platform in your organization. Consider other IT projects that have produced good results through strong teamwork. This might not be the greatest operational pain point but might be a great place to start your SharePoint ECM track record. If you can create a quick win and follow best practices for creating your IA and solution design, it will make it more attractive to other parts of the business that want to experience the same results.

Team culture

Establishing a team culture early in the project is very important. All organizations have a unique culture that helps establish a collective understanding of what the organization is chartered to strive toward and accomplish. Traditional methods of documenting an organizational culture include mission, vision, and belief statements that help people collect around a common ethos. Culture can also be promulgated less formally through direct leadership, strong personalities, and legacy business environments or specific industry norms.

Your project team will have its own culture, and it's important to define it in common terms so that everyone on the team can reference the definitions and use them as guidelines when making key decisions and communicating with other team members. As a baseline, you should incorporate the following three elements in writing to help define your project team culture:

- Project name, slogan, and logo

- Team objective in 25 words or less

- Team member agreement

Team communication

Open and frequent updates in a consistent format to each team member will help foster focus on the priority of the project and its overall status. Updates should be in the context of primary areas of interest for the whole team as well as specific to subject matter experts working on individual tasks and deliverables. We have outlined the following three common communication streams that you can use as a model for your communications plan:

- Project blog

- Deliverable status report

- Distribution list

Conversations should be strategic, when strategy is needed, usually early on in the project, and specific and tactical at all other times. This is important because when conversations mix strategy with tactical, they often frustrate one or more of the team members and result in confusion and wasted time. Strategy is good when talking governance and business needs of the system, including ROI. Tactical items are very specific elements of the system that need discussion and decisions. Mixing abstract concepts with these elements will delay action and results.

Project management

The primary responsibility for delivering a successful SharePoint ECM solution lies with each member of the core project team. Depending on the nature and scope of your ECM solution, you might have one or more Project Managers (PMs). If you are using a systems integrator or other third-party resources and have multiple PMs, it is important to create an escalation plan for issues that are not resolved between PMs. For the purposes of this book, we will assume that the project is being managed internally, with no outside project or resource management.

Standard project management practices are an important component to the success of your ECM solution. We recommend that formal practices of project management be followed, as outlined by the Project Management Institute (PMI) in its Project Management Book of Knowledge (PMBOK). PMI covers very broad uses and can be applied to everything from building bridges to IT projects, so it's important to utilize the tools and best practices that make sense for your organization's ECM project.

Not every aspect of the PMBOK will need to be used, but every team should incorporate the following key project management items:

- Scope of work and change control

- Detailed project schedule

- Deliverables-based acceptance criteria

- Training curriculum and resources

- Outstanding issues list

The scope of the project will need to be managed carefully so that key milestones can be met, the project budget can be managed, and any return on investment metrics are achieved. One of the critical elements of managing the scope is change due to feature or enhancement requests. It is also inevitable that operational needs will come up that were previously overlooked or unknown to the project team. You will need a method for managing the decision about whether or not to include these items. Our recommendation is to use change request documents early in the project life cycle. We talk more about this in the "Pre-Mortem" section, later in this chapter, in terms of feature sprawl and the ability to hit key milestones in the project. Momentum is very important to the CXO suite; if you hope to have their full support, you'd better have the documentation to support any schedule delays due to change requests or feature enhancements.

From the field

I advocate a process of conditioning the organization to the normalcy of formal written change request forms. Often in a project, I will take innocuous changes to scope and document them, have the key stakeholder sign off on the change, and then share with the team. As the project progresses, it is much easier to present and discuss a change that has real impact on budget, timeline, or ROI if they are already used to the process. If you wait until it's a big issue and you haven't already established a track record of managing change carefully, it can be a much more difficult conversation. - Shad

Subject matter expert

A *subject matter expert* (SME) is someone with training and experience in a specific functionality and topic area within SharePoint. They are the go-to person for their topic area. Later in the book, we will talk about super users. Super users and SMEs can be synonymous, but not always. A SME might specialize in a broader organization-wide topic, such as records management, whereas a super user is a more skilled SharePoint user in general.

For each specific element of the project, you will have SMEs responsible for managing task and deliverable completion. Their roles can be operational, technical, or project execution related. When delivering an IT-related project, you should have common roles for things like Testing/QA and

Training that are used on a regular basis for executing IT projects. The other SMEs will vary depending on the operational unit you are working with. The operational SME knows why things are done a certain way and can more easily represent and document the *as-is* state or the current way of doing things. The technical SME knows how software systems are configured and integrated to support the business. For example, the SMEs assigned to the Coho Winery ECM SharePoint project team are described in Table 5-1 and include a SharePoint Administrator, Records Manager, and Training Manager.

TABLE 5-1 Subject matter experts

SME	Skills	Responsibilities
SharePoint Administrator	An active listener and contributor. Understands all aspects of SharePoint, key LOB systems integrations, customizations, and third-party tools. Has general IT systems knowledge of network, operating system, database, web server and workstation software components.	SharePoint platform understanding, SharePoint site administration, user security, feature configuration, testing and validation of use cases based on SharePoint capabilities
Records Manager	Highly organized and understands the process of managing physical, electronic, and archived records. Has conducted a records inventory and completed a records file plan and retention schedule.	Taxonomy, file plan, records retention, records disposition, IA
Training Manager	Understands the varying degrees of operational and technical knowledge of users within the organization. Excellent written, verbal communication, and presentation skills.	Curriculum development, end user training, training materials, training schedule and FAQ publication
Super User	Knowledge worker in specific functions that will champion the usage of ECM in their department in the way the department can benefit from it the most. Encourages peers to use the system. This individual should also check frequently the quality of content and usage in their department and report this back to the ECM team.	Site manager, understanding of the functions IA, understanding of document and content types, departmental views

Technical team

The technical team will be responsible for managing all technical aspects of the project during both design and implementation and after the ECM solution is in production. This could vary slightly for larger organizations, where the technical team might not have access or information on the SharePoint farm level but on the site collection administration level only.

Each member of the team will have specific duties and bring key elements to the overall technical design and execution of the SharePoint IA. Usually, the people on the technical team will be included during key elements of the project and might not be involved in every aspect of the project. We recommend that at least one member of the technical team be the lead person responsible for delegating and managing technical issues and tasks to the correct IT resources throughout the project. This is most often assigned to the SharePoint Administrator we described in the previous section. Some key areas of consideration include the following:

- Datacenter and server management

- Application management

- Network communications

- Database management

- Workstation and Help Desk support

Quality control

Practice what you preach; quality control is everyone's responsibility. In most cases, there are focused testing procedures and quality control methods used during most IT projects. However, the more each team member is on the lookout for usability issues and system design flaws, the better. It's not always the software or technical SharePoint issues either; sometimes it's the quality of communication or documentation that is suffering. If you create a culture of quality from the beginning and each of the team members is committed to delivering a high quality of work, the results will speak for themselves. If you have a weak link and someone is not delivering at or above expectations, deal with it early. If shortcuts are taken, it will come out in the end and the ECM solution will not deliver the best possible user experience.

For SharePoint ECM, *quality control* refers to quality of the delivered application and quality of its usage.

Quality control and testing of the ECM application delivered on SharePoint should incorporate considerations such as the following:

- Does a SharePoint feature behave the way it's expected to?

- Do the users encounter error messages?

- How are the error messages recorded and acted upon?

- Do the desired interaction of features and workflows produce an acceptable result?

- How does someone request a change in a business process? (All processes will need to be changed eventually, so plan for it.)

- What is the change management strategy? (Change management is a critical element for quality and user adoption. You shouldn't confuse this with change control procedures that are used to document or minimize changes in scope, also known as *scope creep*.)

Some organizations appoint individuals to act as content organizers in the early stages of populating new sites and libraries. The content organizers populate libraries with metadata and initiate workflows so that the content is being routed with the proper metadata and is stored in the correct library. When the processes have been well tested and the libraries are populated with accurate content and metadata, it is easier for others to follow the same structure as they add new content.

Quality control of the usage of the system considers things such as the following:

- Are users using features, or are certain features abandoned? This includes checking site-level analytics to understand usage.

- Is content being contributed accurately with the right amount of metadata?

- Is the usage of metadata and IA accurate and consistent?

- Are content types being used properly, if at all? Content types should be used to control the metadata structure and models you're adopting and can help users when they are adding new content to SharePoint.

A good example of usage quality control would be to make sure the quality of metadata associated with a contract is always being filed in the right library with the right metadata. If you weren't using content types, users could file a contract in the wrong library and skip the step of adding the proper metadata.

Usage quality control is a big job and requires reviewing the body of documents on a regular basis during user testing and training. This should be a role taken on by content managers. If your organization does not have content managers, super users in individual departments who have a vested interest should take on this role.

Pre-mortem

Most everyone is aware of the post-mortem strategy where, upon completion of a project or portions of a project, you discuss what went well, what went wrong, and what can we learn from it so that we don't repeat the same mistakes. This is a great exercise to get in the habit of completing. If your organization is underwhelmed by the results of your IT projects, this can help you identify what you're missing. Remember that if your post-mortem is not done consistently, the next project can suffer from the same errors that you were experienced in previous projects. However, if the post-mortem doesn't happen, it does not benefit the current ECM project, and what is learned is often forgotten.

A strategy we use is *pre-mortem*. A pre-mortem is a projection of all the things that could and are expected to go wrong. Part of the exercise includes forecasting obvious scenarios, such as no adoption or an incomplete solution after a given date, as well as more subtle scenarios that are unique to the organization, such as inefficient business processes, lackadaisical content contribution, or projected organizational changes.

Note All too often, an ECM solution will incorporate manual business processes in an electronic form and not take into consideration that operations might need to change to make the most of the automation capabilities. Many have called the following statement the seven worst words in business: "*We have always done it this way.*" This is why it's important to have CXO involvement so that organizational changes can be adopted from the top down, and if necessary, adoption of the changes can become an organizational requirement.

To help you prepare for the most common issues that can negatively affect the ECM project and your team, we have compiled a list of items to be prepared for. You might not encounter the following issues, but they are fairly common:

- **Organizational changes** Changes in the organization most often cannot be forecasted. However, the team should be aware of what the impact could be if critical stakeholders in the ECM project are shifted around or leave the organization.

- **Feature sprawl** Feature sprawl can sneak up on the ECM project team, and it is a challenging problem because we all have the tendency to favor more and more features. The effects of feature sprawl can be widespread and not only impact delivery time but also could result in a convoluted implementation that negatively impacts user adoption.

- **Other prioritized projects** While many organizations give the ECM project a clear runway, there is sometimes a business need to give other competing projects a higher priority. This can cause cancellation of the ECM project or result in it not getting the attention it deserves.

- **Lack of internal support** Similar to feature sprawl, where requested features and demand on functionality goes up and down with newly discovered business needs and the internal awareness of the SharePoint platform, internal support of the ECM project can grow and shrink. The greatest cause of shrinking interest in the ECM project is not hitting critical milestones or not having something to show.

Organizations not experienced with this exercise of forecasting problems before they happen will find it hard to begin. However, after it gets rolling, you will be surprised at the items that will come up and how important they can be in guiding decision making for how the project proceeds.

Be a practitioner as well as an implementer

Have you ever heard the phrase, "Eat your own dog food"? It's critical that the team members responsible for implementing and launching the SharePoint ECM environment to the entire organization are also heavy users of the system. If you yourself are not regularly using the ECM system in the way prescribed by the ECM committee, you can't expect your users to either.

One of the most important aspects of the team is the undying support of the project and the results of the project. This means that, whenever possible, the team members should be evangelizing ECM in general before the solution is released, and after release, they should support the adoption actively.

An example of such influence is ensuring that when the ECM idea comes up the participants should ask their peers to begin practicing good organizational behavior. All team members should be working with non-team members to sell the project through good words and leading by example. Here are a few things to consider:

- Start by better organizing your own content.

- Think of file shares in terms of the infrastructure design elements you will need.

- Encourage the use of email as a transient communication tool and not as an ECM platform or document store.

- Encourage standard and repetitive file naming techniques.

- Encourage a single method of record for all documents saved.

All the principles covered earlier in the book can begin to be established even before the SharePoint farm stores a single document. Working on adoption from day one is a must.

During the planning stages of the project, the team should have ample opportunity to build a miniature ECM system (that is, a sandbox) where project-planning documents, IA plans, governance plans, and notes can be stored. You might even elect to use this miniature version of the broader ECM system as an example of how successful and helpful the platform can be. Because the ECM team can start eating their own dog food immediately, this also helps to encourage the quality control principles we outlined earlier. This should continue, and all members of the team should be supreme examples of ECM usage.

Earlier, we told you that we encourage you to bring naysayers on to the ECM team. During this practical use of the miniature ECM system, the tensions and challenges will become even more evident, and you will quickly learn as a team how to address them organization-wide.

Next steps

The ECM team can use the information in this chapter to establish a strong culture that will help them prepare for the difficult task of managing change and user adoption of the ECM solution. In the next chapter, we will discuss best practices for preparing your organization for the changes that will come with the implementation of your SharePoint ECM solution.

CHAPTER 6

User adoption

You can have all the right people on your ECM team, have support from the Executive suite and all your ECM components in place, but still fail to meet the goals that drove the decision to move forward with SharePoint in the first place. In this chapter, we will talk about how to maximize user adoption and sell the benefits of ECM throughout the project by having a clear understanding of the tangible and intangible aspects of having a community of users who love SharePoint.

Least common denominator

You are only as good as your least common denominator; in the case of your SharePoint ECM solution, the least common denominator is the user. To illustrate this point, we will use Coho Winery as an example. The project team has just finished implementing the ECM solution using SharePoint 2013. The team methodically built an Information Architecture (IA) plan, managed the project effectively, and utilized a detailed testing and quality assurance model. The ECM solution has all the functionality they require; it's easy to use and solves many business performance and legal issues. The primary driver for Coho was to have an ECM solution to help mitigate the legal risks of not having access to the documents they needed during the discovery phase of a potential lawsuit.

Two years after the ECM deployment, they get sued, and they now think that they are prepared, knowing that all of their content should be in the ECM system. Unfortunately, the content stored in SharePoint is incomplete due to low user adoption. The problem was that they did not focus enough on training and on user adoption. As users became frustrated, they quietly refused to use the system. They were not aware that content specific to the case was stored on local and shared network drives instead of SharePoint. In this example, the records needed to support a proper defense were not found until later discovery efforts uncovered the documents that would become the cornerstone of their defense. This caused increased legal fees, court penalties for not producing discoverable material in a timely manner, and time delays in getting the case settled.

You can illustrate similar examples where content either not stored or stored incorrectly in an ECM system that the organization assumes is being used can cause a lot of problems. But it does not have to be that extreme. Users engaging with SharePoint are where the return on investment for the system develops. Therefore, if they do not use it, the time and money put into the system is a waste.

To get user adoption you must achieve the following:

1. Create new habits.

2. Get users on your side.

3. Motivate users emotionally.

4. Give everyone a reason to visit SharePoint.

5. Create camaraderie and competition.

You can make mistakes in the initial deployment of the ECM system, and you can even omit functionality, but there is no wiggle room when it comes to effective user adoption.

From the field

I like to ask people who bring me in to review existing ECM deployments, "How many times have you tried to set up an ECM system?" Usually, they can count back to only a few years prior to their joining the organization. But almost always, the answer is more than three. Then I ask, "What was the problem with that one?" While I always get some technical excuse, the final response has always been "No one used it." - Chris

---

Preparing the organization

Working on your user adoption starts as soon as the ECM solution is an idea or concept that the organization is seriously considering. Because you are reading this book, we must assume that using SharePoint to build an ECM solution is more than just an idea and probably an actual project that has been approved. So if you have not already been working on your user adoption strategy, you have already fallen behind. That might sound ominous, but it's true, so let's start working on user adoption right now or, at the very least, as soon as you're done with this chapter.

Sometimes the language used to describe users and the tools used to increase adoption feel similar to the ways you might deal with children. Because users are already very busy, adverse to change, and not always welcoming of instruction, they can behave like toddlers at times. We do not mean to denigrate the intelligence of the user but to frame their initial impression of the system in an easy-to-consume way.

When you start introducing the solution into the organization, we recommend that you not talk right away about SharePoint or ECM. You should begin internal dialog with users by using business language to illustrate the problems of bad content storage and help identify with users about the inefficiencies and risk associated with the volume, findability, and duplication of content. Ask lots of questions and then actively listen; don't rush to solve the problem with SharePoint. Take notes and be patient, start building a story, and be cognizant of the terms and language each person uses to describe the challenges and chaos of poorly managed records and content.

Getting users to identify early on with the areas where productivity suffers as a result of looking for content and documents will help you when you begin to form a team and design an ECM solution that will address the problem. If you can help the users begin to identify with how nice it would be to solve some of these issues, it will help in the overall acceptance of best practices and culture shifts that are needed. In this way, SharePoint isn't being forced up on them; it is being crafted in their minds as their idea, which creates ownership. A successful best practice or method for you to engage in is performing content audits with various users in the organization. This can help identify key areas that can be used to focus users on the pain that they are experiencing but might not recognize. During a content audit, you will uncover ways to prove and help justify changes in content storage behavior. Here are some basic areas for consideration that most organizations uncover after a content audit:

- Users are searching for content but not finding it. Find out how much time the average user spends looking for documents.

- A large number of high-risk documents are stored in shared drives and lack proper security or backup.

- A number of documents have gone past the appropriate retention period and should be deleted, because when not deleted, they pose a potential liability or risk to the organization.

- The organization has a high quantity of nonbusiness related documents and content.

- The organization has a high quantity of duplicate records and content.

- A large number of business documents are saved in the average user's mailbox as email attachments.

We have listed these all as open-ended problems. Your goal should be that the users become conscious about their content and how much time they are wasting on just trying to find it, and occasionally duplicating tasks already completed by other users. This behavior will drive some chatter within departments about how bad the problem is, and users will make a self-motivated attempt to be better at content storage. If possible, it's best that this is done on a per-department level. When you have completed this effort, make sure to provide the results of the content audits to the managers of each department.

Crowd sourcing

The next step in getting users prepared for the concept of SharePoint and ECM is to crowd-source early change. Use the organization as a tool to begin the transition of content from the poor structure it currently resides in to the cleaner structure that the ECM team is establishing as part of the design process. It's important not to jump to ECM terminology too quickly. Try to use common terms that users are already familiar with. This will help build rapport and a common language without making people feel as if they have no idea what you are talking about. You do this by giving each department an idea of what their folder structure should look like. For organizations that are less resistant to change, you might be able to give them a folder structure that is derived from the IA that the ECM team develops. However, this usually is not the case, so instead you can pass on the principles you learned in the earlier chapters of this book to illustrate the general concepts on how they should treat the reorganization of their content.

This should be followed by a progress report as recommended changes based on the content audit are implemented. Be sure to call out specific actions and persons responsible for implementing the change and how this will benefit the organization. You can do this by using a comparison model to list all the items uncovered in the content audit, what the risk or ineffi-ciency was, and what's been done to eliminate risk and become more efficient. Be very careful to not deliver only bad news; if you are going to show a before and after, you must show results that have been achieved. If there are no results, your only argument can be that this department did not participate in the change but that others did—and give examples.

On a parallel track, start to introduce SharePoint to the organization. We will discuss this in more detail in the following sections.

The bottom line is that the ECM team should know where they are with user adoption at the point of project creation, when the initial blueprint of SharePoint is created, during implementation, and throughout deployment. We find that most often organizations consider adoption only after deploy-ment and, in most cases, as a reaction to poor user feedback.

Encourage behavior

The best way to get consistent and regular adoption of SharePoint is by creating good habits. To encourage proper behavior, you should offer more than just talk. For it to be taken seriously, it should be called out specifically in the project budget. As a part of your SharePoint implementation budget, there should be a line item for change management that includes user adoption activities and com-munications. This should make up 5 percent to 15 percent of the overall budget.

This budget can be spent on typical items such as formal training. But you should also consider other more unique programs and activities. Depending on the type of organization and employee policies, you should consider monthly gifts for the users who achieve the highest contribution and usage of the system. Incentivizing the user community works very well to build healthy competition and puts real value on good adoption of the ECM solution.

To do this successfully, you need to decide upfront the metrics to use and how to track them. Avoid making the measurement subjective. There are third-party tools that make this tracking very easy. If you do not have access to such tools, you will want to use individual site statistics and audit reports.

> **Note** We suggest the use of third-party tools occasionally in the book, and we will be outlining them in Chapter 10, "Extending SharePoint 2013 ECM solutions." This will include many useful links, including some of our favorite apps and administrative tools for metrics.

With a little effort, you can automate this reporting into a dashboard for easy reporting. Some organizations even take it one step further and publish a user leader board as a web part in all sites, putting it right in front of all users so that they know that other users in the organization are using the system in an active way.

From the field

A recent client I worked with held a competition to come up with a name for the ECM project. It was open to every employee and achieved 100 percent participation. The entries could consist of either a name or an acronym with a description of what made the entry unique and what the person hoped to get from the new ECM solution. The winner received a gift card, and the marketing department came up with a logo specifically based on the winning entry. The winning entry was selected by vote from all employees and was announced at a companywide meeting, along with runner up, most unique, and honorable mention. - Shad

Another way to encourage adoption, which is a soft motivation, is to find a way to get everyone involved. For example, create programs where users create new functionality, or suggest new functionality to the system. Or perhaps set up an employee-contributed forum where users get ranked for posting content to help the entire organization. For small companies, this could be as simple as users publishing and getting credit for SharePoint Tips and Tricks emails that can be sent out periodically. Do not underestimate the power of your users trying to improve their experience and get visibility for their contributions in the organization. If you can create a mindset that SharePoint will not only improve their productivity but their worth as a team member, you have done a great job.

Allowing users to suggest new functionality can be a tricky but very powerful game. This is easiest when it impacts web parts, branding, and user interface instead of core ECM features and IA. Make sure that you have a clear understanding of what you are trying to accomplish before you jump in, and if you do, you won't regret it.

In addition to incentives, the next best tool in a successful campaign to drive user adoption is to build an army of super users.

The super user

The *super user* can be defined as an individual who works with departments and individual functions within the organization to encourage better adoption of core content management best practices. This can be as simple as evangelizing a standard file naming convention to helping other users with frequently asked questions. We have compiled the following list of qualities that make an average user a super user:

- A super user must already have a clear picture of "why ECM?" and "why SharePoint?" They should have at the very least read the Introduction of this book.

- A super user must already know how to use SharePoint 2013 ECM functionality. We are not saying that they have to be technical, but they should be able to answer FAQs on usage.

- A super user should be self-motivated to using SharePoint for themselves.

- A super user should be self-motivated to help the ECM team. These individuals usually spot an opportunity to put something new on their resume and tend to look in the direction of technology.

- A super user is incentivized by positive career goals. Anytime you can tie the success of a project to future opportunities, people will generally put in extra effort.

From the field

I never had a problem finding super users in any of the projects I have participated in; I just had a challenge sometimes keeping them. Often the super users we identified had the goal of moving into a business analyst or technical role, so getting deep SharePoint experience helped them with that. As super users, they were fantastic at getting good adoption and helping with the overall goals, but eventually they were snatched up by other departments or they left the organization to become SharePoint experts! - Chris

After you have identified the super users, you need to make sure the organization knows who they are and that they are the first person to go to with any questions. It is good to formalize this group of super users with monthly meetings and some compensation incentives, such as a pay raise, bonuses, or even small perks such as tickets to a sporting event or a gift card.

The community

The broader world of super users is the SharePoint community. The SharePoint community, unlike any other enterprise-level platform, is extremely vocal and strong. They can be found on the web, at SharePoint Saturday events, and on social media sites. We have outlined these in greater detail and encourage you to engage with the community early and often. This will be your greatest asset as you strive to answer even the most difficult SharePoint challenges.

The web

Simple searches on the web will help you find a huge collection of articles and blogs on SharePoint. You will quickly identify who the leaders and influencers in the space are. You should encourage super users and end users to search for answers to their questions. There is no better accomplishment than solving a problem on your own. Of course, make sure that their user rights prevent them from breaking anything.

SharePoint Saturdays and SharePoint user groups

These local community events are one of the best ways to get real world information on how to use SharePoint, without spending a dime. Even if a user attends a user group session not related to ECM, they will have a better understanding of SharePoint in general and more enthusiasm for the platform. Encourage your users, or even mandate that they attend at least one of these events in a given time period. You should be able to find a SharePoint user group in your area. If not, you are always welcome to attend the SharePoint Saturday events.

Social media

As mentioned earlier, the SharePoint community is very strong. If users in your organization use Twitter, they can post a tweet using hash tag **#SPHelp**. This is a hash tag that the SharePoint experts monitor and respond to very regularly. Also, you can execute a simple **SharePoint user group** Bing search and find a huge set of experts who love to help individuals and organizations get better use of their SharePoint deployments. There are several LinkedIn groups dedicated to SharePoint that have very useful posts and legions of active users.

The experts

Unlike many platform experts who are hard to find, SharePoint experts find you. The leading experts in the SharePoint space carry with them the titles MCM and MVP. MCM is the Microsoft Certified Master. There are only a handful of these, and they have passed a series of very complex tests and labs to receive the designation. Many MCM individuals are also Most Valuable Professionals (MVPs). MVP is a status given by Microsoft to individuals it believes are valuable and influential in the SharePoint space to increase proper usage and adoption. Most MVPs specialize in one technical area or another, but they can always connect you with someone who can solve your problem. There are roughly 120 SharePoint MVPs at the point of writing this book.

When you have empowered your users with tools that are both internal and external of the organization, you have given them no excuse not to embrace the platform and become an expert themselves.

The change manager

We have talked about encouraging behaviors as a way to cement solid user adoption, and we suggested that, for this effort to be taken seriously, you should line-item budget for change management. This is often the most overlooked part of any SharePoint project. Even though it is implicitly stated for most SharePoint projects that the goal is to improve content accessibility, communication, and increase productivity, the changes required at an individual user level to accomplish adoption are rarely planned for.

Some organizations see this as a traditional role filled by a training department, but it is much more than just training users on what buttons to click and what functions to perform. If you don't already have a training department or manager responsible for user training, we suggest that you appoint a specific person to this task. A Change Manager will focus on all aspects of change and the effects that changes will have at the micro and macro levels of the organization. As part of the Change Manager role, consider the following items:

- Policy and procedure updates

- Forms and communication updates and standards

- Training materials development and FAQs

- Regular blog posts and/or video messages

- Quality and user acceptance testing

Each organization is unique, and the preceding items can be covered as part of several individual roles and responsibilities, so adjust your change management planning and assignments accordingly. Remember that people don't like change; that's a fact. The more you prepare people for the change, the less scary it is and the more likely you will be to achieve a high degree of satisfaction with the ECM solution.

But it can take more than all of this, and sometimes good adoption comes down to simple look and feel. How does the site make me feel, what emotions does it evoke, and how easy is it to navigate?

Branding

ECM is a somewhat plain vanilla type of business application. There is not a lot to get excited about. Unlike extranet, public websites, and intranets, there usually is not much thought put into the look and feel of the ECM sites. But it does matter, and it can make a huge difference if you put the time and effort into the branding aspect of the site(s).

To some users, if they feel like they are walking into a hospital with sanitary walls and boring décor, they can end up dreading the application all together. Adding a little flair to your environment will help with user adoption and the friendliness of the platform.

The trick with branding is to do the right amount. You can do too little, which is out-of-the-box look and feel. You can also go over the top by having too much branding. This can be distracting from regular usage, and even worse, it complicates the modification of any functionality and makes any future migration impossible. Also, too much branding that changes the way SharePoint behaves can actually work to cause problems in user adoption because the behavior of SharePoint ECM and other SharePoint applications will not be consistent. While no elements of branding are really tied to ECM functionality, you can do some simple things to make the look and feel more popular, such as the following:

- Web parts are the easiest way to change the look and feel of a site without impacting the core ECM functionality. Web parts can be added to any second-level site page. For example, the most useful web parts for ECM are content query web parts that show the latest content or that show the user leader board.

- Finding colors and small graphics to use as Favicons and in site root pages is a simple way to help the user feel more comfortable. No need to create custom style pages, but creating a custom theme is a good first step.

- Use naming conventions in site names, and use document library names that are less sterile and friendly. There is a reason that, in the IA section of this book, we called the hub for all the ECM sites the ECMCafe; this is an OK name that is not as sterile as ECM Home. But you can probably come up with something even be better and tie into a theme in your organization.

The look and feel of a site has a lot to do with how users perceive the usefulness of the site.

> ### From the field
>
> *I would say that about 80% of my clients who were in some nontechnical line of business branded their portal in some funny and very obvious ways, such as having stock tickers, weather widgets, and other gadgets on their pages. These tools, believe it or not, did make users feel more comfortable and gave them a reason to visit the sites. However, they also sometimes served as a distraction, and the HR ECM portal, for example, became only the place to get the current weather and stock trends. - Chris*

Gamification

Gamification is the process of creating a percentage of completion for things like rich profiles. It's important to encourage, if not require, users to complete their profile information with as much detailed information as possible. This helps to provide a personality for everyone who is engaged with using the SharePoint ECM solution. Like most things, it's important to have balance; don't go overboard with the profile information. If it's too onerous, users will avoid filling out the information. Start with the basics, and then later you can add additional elements and make it a fun contest or game to get additional useful information. There are several ways to encourage people to complete this basic task. There are third-party companies that provide more extensive feature sets for this particular feature, and SharePoint 2013 provides improvements in this area over previous versions.

You can gamify SharePoint by using features out of the box, such as reporting, and you can quantify contribution and consumption activities. Also, you can play with scoring users who show the greatest contribution and highlight popular items for consumption. Or you can look at the third-party tools mentioned earlier that allow gamification.

Bad for adoption

Because we have focused mainly on the items that we believe will help drive successful adoption of your ECM solution, we should also talk about the things that will hinder or destroy a user's successful adoption of SharePoint. Each organization is different, and some are just stuck due to immovable obstacles in the company culture that prevent change. If this is the case in your organization, you will just have to do the best you can or look for another opportunity elsewhere.

Bad habits

When you get to the root of most objections to using the platform, it comes down to habits. Users fear change. The worse thing to do in these cases is to try to accommodate. Rather than accommodating the users with features that they are comfortable with or allowing exceptions to the rule, repeat on a regular basis the reasons of why you are doing it and why it's better for them. The moment you give in to habits is when the system starts unraveling at a rapid rate.

Counter ECM features

There are several features in SharePoint that allow the user to contradict their ECM usage. They are Explorer view, Workspaces, email-enabled lists, and email-based libraries. Essentially, all these tools do is allow the user to live outside of SharePoint, thus preventing them from gaining any familiarity and comfort with the system and setup. Even worse, some of these tools, such as Explorer view and Workspaces, actually allow the user to contribute content to the ECM platform with no metadata, thereby bypassing all content type required elements. This will result only in bad habits and proliferation of bad content. Remember that it's not what you get right that hurts you; it's what you miss or contribute incorrectly that will lead into trouble both for the user and the organization.

> **Note** While these features encourage rapid addition of content, it's content that will later cause issues with the platform. There are third-party tools that give email-enabled libraries the features required to make them useful in ECM. It's important to be aware of possible problems, such as poor metadata that some features can create, and when evaluating third-party tools, make sure that these limitations do not exist.

Keywords and ratings

These features actually seem like they are useful for ECM. In the case of keywords, they are only useful if you also impose the strict taxonomies mentioned in the IA portion of the book. They are a useful way for users to use their own tags and dialect to provide metadata to documents. However, problems can arise if you use it without a mandated taxonomy, because users will default to keywords as an easy way to just get content into SharePoint. This will result in every possible keyword and spelling of keywords to be entered, and no consistent behavior in using search and browsing.

Ratings are another feature that seems useful and beneficial for helping with user adoption, if it's accurate. The catch is that only a large organization of 5,000 users or more, with a lot of content being consumed and rated, can have enough of an impact on the ratings; in this case, it can be very useful. In these organizations, there is enough input to give a sense of the quality of documents so that you can sort and search on highly rated documents. Ratings can be effective only if there is a high enough frequency of honest ratings and a library where 70 percent or more of the documents have been rated in such a way.

> ### From the field
>
> *Would you rate your boss's project proposal with anything other than five stars? Unfortunately, in most organizations, keywords are not the objective measure of good content that we want them to be. I've seen many organizations where every single document is a five-star document. What value is that? - Chris*

MySites

You are probably surprised that at this point we have not yet mentioned MySites as a tool for increasing adoption. There are rare very well-controlled cases where this is true. But in our experience, it's more of a detractor and actually serves to confuse users. The fact is that MySites can also be used as a document repository; users can live in and store their content there instead of in the IA you have designed for them to use. MySites can help by adding some personality to the entire SharePoint experience and some identity to what is going on, but without making a specific project out of deploying it and how it's used, we have not seen success and have seen MySites counteract efforts in the ECM application.

Adoption is 20 percent functionality and 80 percent people. It's far easier to get the technology portion right, and really, there is no excuse not to. There are some features in SharePoint that both help and discourage adoption, so like anything else, it's a balancing act. At some point, dealing with the people element is a messy business, and sometimes there is no better answer then strict enforcement.

Enforcing the plan

Strictly enforcing ECM usage is a painful process at the beginning. Be prepared to make enemies. But as examples are made of a few bad outcomes based on not following the prescribed usage, it will become easier very fast, as long as you stick with it and remain consistent.

Setting up the rules, and plans for user adoption is tactical and has a clear beginning and end, and reinforcing those plans never ends. First and foremost, you and the ECM team must have been given the power to execute an enforcement plan with users who adopt poor usage of the system. This is not to say that we are going to punish people; instead, it would be beneficial to have these use cases highlighted with the appropriate method or solution so that others can learn and avoid the same mistakes. Also, we aren't trying to make an example of anyone's mistakes, so always illustrate the corrective action using a generic user name.

From the field

I've never seen a perfect scenario where everyone adopted the system correctly. But what I have seen is ECM solutions where those who do not do what they are trained, encouraged, and supposed to do receive the proper consequences so that the policies and plans set forth were not empty threats. - Chris

There will be times when not making it clear that the importance of using the ECM solution properly is not an option. Improper usage of the ECM solution should be treated as seriously as insubordination and poor performance. Your organization faces risk and legal ramifications for inappropriate or lackadaisical use of SharePoint, which will make ECM adoption of best practices more difficult. As we alluded to earlier, if your organization is not ready to take content management seriously, they most likely are not yet ready for a true ECM solution. This must be understood before you embark on your ECM SharePoint project.

From the field

I have been asked many times what the difference is between a successful ECM project and a failure. While there are many factors that can impact a project in a negative manner, the one common thread between the hundreds of ECM solutions that you could point to is the people. SharePoint works very well and so do the principles we outline in this book, but without a solid ECM team and a user community that has taken ownership of the project, you will miss the mark. Having a good dose of empathy can make all the difference in how you interact, both inside and outside the team. - Shad

Next steps

The organization will readily adopt a solution that is built with every user in mind. By systematically engaging the user community early and often, your ability to seamlessly roll out the ECM solution to enthusiastic users who fervently adopt SharePoint will be without equal. You will not encounter the kind of revolt or quiet disruption that often accompanies projects that are designed and implemented in a vacuum. In the next chapter, we will be providing you with a planning guide to use as a roadmap and checklist. We will incorporate everything we have covered in a concise and easy-to-follow format.

CHAPTER 7

ECM planning guide

We have discussed the importance of planning and best practices for your ECM Project. A lot of what we have covered has been methodology and the application of ECM principles in SharePoint. To put this information to good use, you will need to create a detailed set of documentation that lays out the Information Architecture (IA) and its associated components. This will be a pivotal component used for completing your detailed project planning documentation.

Documentation serves several purposes beyond simple planning. This includes keeping everyone informed about the details of the project and how it will be implemented. It's important that the documentation be crafted in a way that supports your ability to illustrate to others that the project team has done the due diligence to make the project successful. In addition, it creates a historical record of how and why you did what you did, a tool to help with future inevitable changes in the organization, and, sometimes, a record of mistakes made so that they are not repeated.

Documentation

The types of documentation and how you carve out the various elements will vary based on the size of the overall project and, to a degree, the capability and maturity of the organization. We recommend that organizations create an ECM roadmap that builds from the documentation of the business drivers, leading to the decision to implement the platform to how it will be structured and implemented. This can be very useful for people outside the core team as well, and it can provide both a look into the future of what is planned for SharePoint in your organization and how the team will arrive at its destination during any given point of the journey.

It is important to document why the organization is implementing SharePoint and what the key business drivers are. This lets everyone know the thought process behind the implementation. This should be written in common business terms and be readable to a nontechnical audience. Most often, your biggest supporters or detractors will be outside of IT, and you will need to communicate in a language that is familiar to them. This portion of the documentation should be drafted by the Business Analyst role we outlined in Chapter 5, "Building an ECM team."

To document how SharePoint will be implemented, the ECM project team will be focused more on the technical elements and the ECM principles that will be followed. This should cover the tactical implementation steps that will be used and the core ECM definitions, outlined in Chapter 1, "ECM defined," which you choose to be implemented as part of your project. This should be written in a format that provides the actual steps taken on your SharePoint farm to implement any given feature.

For example, we recommend that you include the exact steps you took to create a content type. As you build, be sure to include all the content types that you created and the field level details.

In addition, we recommend that you create a section in your documentation that defines the best practices used for things like taxonomy, file naming conventions, and site structure. A good example of best practices would be to establish that SharePoint will not have a taxonomy that is over 500 terms and more than four levels deep for any given parent term.

From the field

I've become very fond of short descriptions that allow others to see how my SharePoint farm implementations are structured, accompanied by a detailed screen shot at each step. It's best if you strive to make it habitual by taking a screen shot after every new configuration screen and using a naming convention that helps you remember the sequence of events. For example, if I'm implementing a taxonomy, I will start with the Central Administration screen shot, with the text "Click Manage Service applications," followed by a screen shot of the ServiceApplications.aspx page, and so on. You will find that after you become skilled at this, your documentation cycles will decrease and become a byproduct of your daily efforts instead of a separate activity. So far, I have not found a better method of creating this type of documentation. - Chris

Configuration blueprint

Many audiences will ask for documentation to help them understand how the various pieces of the SharePoint ECM solution will fit together. We have found that the best way to illustrate this is to create a kind of configuration blueprint in the format of tables and lists that are easily understood by a wide audience. The key to this is to see the interrelationship of items so that, for example, you can understand how the IA and content types relate to each other.

Governance is a widely used term that is often misunderstood or interpreted in various ways, depending on the subject. For purposes of your documentation, we define it as a nontechnical section that connects the features of SharePoint with their proper usage and company policy—in essence, a rulebook. Governance in this context refers to the usage and control of content in SharePoint. This covers how to use the platform, such as how to properly upload a document with proper metadata, and proper types of content per a retention schedule or other organizational policy.

Some organizations will also have an IT governance plan that includes security considerations. This document is very often owned by IT and is separate from the ECM governance document. The section on ECM governance can include references to the overall IT governance plan where appropriate, but we recommend that organizations keep them as separate documents.

Source of truth

The danger of documentation is that it can be a resource vacuum and become never ending. To help mitigate this problem, we recommend as few authors as necessary to complete the effort. By limiting the number of people involved in the documentation process, you will have a better understanding of the boundaries that they have used to prevent unneeded detail on certain subjects. This also creates a more focused effort on where the information came from and why it was written and organized in a particular way—that is, a singular source of truth.

Obviously, a peer review of the documentation is necessary for accuracy and to get joint ownership, but multiple authors sometimes cause unneeded focus in some areas and too little on others. The other danger is the belief that the documentation has to be 100 percent accurate. We are not advocating glossing over mistakes, especially the technical ones, but sections like governance and records management are very often a moving target and can change over time. It's better to publish a 90 percent accurate document and move forward with modifications than to never publish anything. The document should be a foundation of future growth and extension of the platform; this requires an end point to its creation.

Quick tips

Here are some quick tips to help you build solid documentation for your ECM solution:

- Start with an executive summary listing high-level goals, business drivers, and the results that will be achieved from the ECM solution.

- Begin documentation early in the process; 80 percent or more of your time should be spent planning. During this planning process, you should have artifacts that can easily turn into documentation. There should not be a period where all focus is on creating documentation prior to the deployment. By the time of the deployment, you should have key documents already prepared.

- Define the purpose of each section before you write it. For example, IA documentation will be used to navigate the entire platform and align the configuration with records management policy.

- Use URLs when describing locations of links and in diagrams and graphs. This is a very practical tool that will allow readers of the document to use the content they are reading to navigate to various areas and to understand naming conventions at a high level.

- Set a completion date that coincides with your go-live date or some limited time afterwards.

- Include a section on future goals, such those things on your wish list that you wanted to complete but could not, or thoughts about certain functionality that is missing or saved for a later project phase.

In the rest of this chapter, we are going to focus on the areas that you should include from this planning guide that will be critical for your ECM solution. This is meant as a resource for you to select the elements that work for your project. This is not a one size fits all. Every situation is unique, and we recommend that you exercise your own judgment to apply as many of these elements as you see fit for your organization and project.

Information Architecture

As we outlined in Chapter 4, "Cases in point," Information Architecture (IA) is the logical and physical storage of content. Many of the best practices we covered in Chapter 4 are complimented in the following sections; these should be used together so that you can be very clear about the logical component. This will be a map to where and how content is stored in the platform. Together, the configuration blueprint and this documentation will be used as the final documentation needed for implementation of the IA. You need to include URL names, which are a critical component in any SharePoint documentation. You need to include the following three core elements in this document:

- Site and library architecture

- Content types and their purpose

- Taxonomies and their purpose

Site and library architecture

The two primary ways to document the IA are either in a diagram or in table form. We recommend that organizations do both because the added effort of one over the other is nominal when one is already created. This also helps various audiences digest the documentation in the format that is most familiar to them. The site and library architecture should go from the site collection level, down through sites, to document libraries. In the IA section of Chapter 5, we mentioned that organizations planning for growth would create a site collection per business unit, whereas other organizations will do an individual site per business unit. The difference in the documentation is simply the depth. They will essentially look the same. Let's review in detail a real-world example of each documentation type.

The benefit of a diagram is that it puts all components and their relationships in one place. This is usually very easy for most people to digest. The only downside of diagrams is that they can get very large and hard to print. As shown in Figure 7-1, the center of the diagram is the farm. Typically, the configuration at the farm or platform level is up to the IT department, and that is not included in the diagram. For purposes of this section of your ECM documentation, you do not need to provide technical details at the farm level.

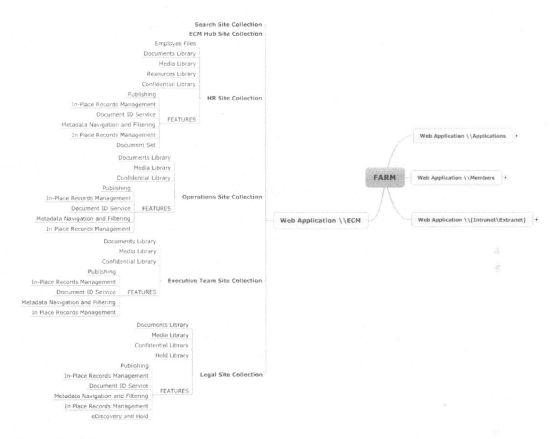

FIGURE 7-1 IA diagram.

Toward the right of the diagram, notice that we included three applications that will be used for other purposes outside of our ECM solution. These are listed as separate web application sites called Members, Applications, and Intranet. We list them here, even though they are separate uses of the SharePoint 2013 platform, because it's nice to have a full listing of root web applications for navigational purposes, and we might have a need to relate them to one another. For example, there might be a line-of-business application such as an employee or customer survey submission that creates a record in ECM, and we can easily document that relationship when they are all listed in one place. For purposes of this planning guide, we will not go into any deeper detail on these additional web applications.

Our focus is the ECM web application. In this diagram, we have taken the site collection approach per function. This could have been done for scaling or due to the size of content. Normally, if you take this approach, it means that you are also using more than one content database. If this is true, you should add the level at which content databases are chosen. For example, if you have a content database per site collection, note this as a parent of the site collection and the name of the content database used. This is important for IT support functions, such as planning backup configurations and disaster recovery procedures.

In this case, we are using a single content database per site collection. We are also using the root site of each site collection as the landing page of each function. As we mentioned in the IA section in Chapter 4, the trend is to have flatter architectures and leverage the power of metadata to improve browsing and search. This is a perfect example of that implementation trend and how to structure your IA.

Each site collection has a listing of libraries and features used. For every site collection, you can see that there are documents, media, and confidential libraries. The documents library is the largest in each site collection and will contain a listing of all content items such as documents, presentations, and text files for that business unit. The media library is used for rich media files, such as photos and videos, for each business unit. And finally, the confidential library is a location where managers of a business unit can store documents that are not visible to all the staff in that unit. For example, employee reviews can be stored here or in the HR library, depending on your organization's records plan.

These consistencies allow users to understand the navigation and structure of your ECM solution no matter what business unit or functional role they have in your organization. In the case of the HR and the Legal departments, there are some exceptions to this rule where some special libraries are called for. For Legal, there is a library for content holds. This will be used in any litigation scenario and is the location where content will be held during eDiscovery for legal review when preparing to respond to requests for production of documents during litigation. Because not all held content is visible to everyone, it's placed here for exclusive use by the Legal department.

In the HR department, you see special libraries for employee files and resources. Employee files also come with the special feature of "document sets." This library has legal implications due to the regulation around employee files and must be kept separate with appropriate security. However, the resources library is a location where the HR department might store content that they regularly provide to employees related to their employment.

You will also see site collections named Search and ECM Hub. These are special site collections with specific functions. Search will be the ECM-wide search application, and the ECM Hub will be the location that contains some testing for specific ECM functionality before and after it's deployed to the organization, as well as the official location for all content types that are published to all other site collections. These site collections don't have functional libraries. However, the ECM Hub might have libraries not for general consumption, to test out various features such as views and column setup.

Each site collection also has a listing of features that will be enabled. This is simply a listing rather than a detailed explanation of how each feature would be used. This should be included in the detailed screen shots we discussed in the documentation section of this chapter. This listing of each feature is a guide that lays out from a user perspective what features they will have access to.

As we recommended earlier, it might be helpful to organize this same documentation in the table format illustrated in Table 7-1.

TABLE 7-1 IA table

Web Application	Site Collection	Site	Library	Configuration
\\ECM	\Search	\	na	
	\ECMHub	\	na	
	\HR	\	\Employee Files	Publishing
			\Documents	In-Place Records
			\Media	Document ID
			\Resources	MMS Filtering
			\Confidential	Document Set
	\Operations	\	\Documents	Publishing
			\Media	In-Place Records
			\Confidential	Document ID MMS Filtering
	\ExecutiveTeam	\	\Documents	Publishing
			\Media	In-Place Records
			\Confidential	Document ID MMS Filtering
	\Legal	\	\Documents	Publishing
			\Media	In-Place Records
			\Confidential	Document ID
			\Hold	MMS Filtering eDiscovery and hold
\\Members				
\\Applications				
\\Intranet				

Most organizations' configuration will span, on average, 15 business units and be much larger than the four configurations shown in the preceding table. Table 7-2 outlines another format for a small city's IA. This structure uses a site per business unit instead of library.

TABLE 7-2 IA for a small city

Web Application	Content Database	Site Collection	Site	Library
	ECMDB_Hub	\ECMHub	\	na
	ECMDB_Attorney	\CityAttorney	\Documents	\Documents
				\Media
				\[HoldByDate]
	ECMDB_Manager	\CityManager	\Gis	\Documents
				\Media
			\Airport	\Documents
				\Media

Web Application	Content Database	Site Collection	Site	Library
\\ECM	ECMDB_Building	\DevelopmentServices	\Building	\Documents
				\Media
			\CodeEnforcement	\Documents
				\Media
			\Engineering	\Documents
				\Media
			\Housing	\Documents
				\Media
			\Planning	\Documents
				\Media
	ECMDB_Finance	\Finance	\Accounting	\Documents
				\Media
			\CustomerService	\Documents
				\Media
	ECMDB_Fire	\Fire	\	\Documents
				\Media
	ECMDB_IT	\IT	\	\Documents
				\Media
	ECMDB_Community	\CommunityService	\	\Documents
				\Media
	ECMDB_Police	\Police	\Records	\Documents
				\Media
			\Communications	\Documents
				\Media
			\ManagmentAnalysis	\Documents
				\Media
			\PoliceChief	\Documents
				\Media
			\Property	\Documents
	ECMDB_Works	\PublicWorks	\Administration	\Documents
				\Media
			\Environmental	\Documents
				\Media
			\WasteFacilities	\Documents
				\Media
\\Email	EMAILDB_[year]	\[year]	\[function]	\[user]

Web Application	Content Database	Site Collection	Site	Library
\\Projects	PROJECTDB_[projname]	\Projects	\[projectname]	
\\Search	SEARCHDB			

For simplicity, we have removed the Configuration column shown in Table 7-1, and we have added a Content Database column to Table 7-2. Because of added security requirements and larger amounts of content stored in SharePoint, the city needed to expand its deployment to many site collections and content databases. In contrast to the structure shown in Table 7.1, the small city has two layers of business units, which is still a very flat IA, where each business unit still has the standard library configuration of a documents library and a media library, with the exception of Legal. The other big difference is that you see the Projects web application where cross-functional projects are set up. Under Projects, there is a new site collection per project. You will also notice the email web application. As we mentioned before, email archival is a large project on its own. The city decided to implement an email retention policy that required all email older than 90 days to be deleted from their inbox and moved to the email web application for archive. The web application is visible only to the City Attorney's Office. Under the email web application is a content database for each year of archives.

For example, if this system were set up in 2008, there would be EMAILDB_2008, EMAILDB_2009, EMAILDB_2010, and so on up to the current year. The content database will store one site collection per year, with each site collection named per year. Within the site collection will be a site for each business unit, and under each business unit, there will be a site and a library per user in that business unit. This is the final resting place for all those users' emails. This configuration was required for the sheer volume of email, and for ease of browsing either in legal cases or to facilitate Public Disclosure and Freedom of Information Act requests.

Note The examples that we include are from real implementations done by the authors; they are not recommended examples for your environment, no matter how similar. All configurations are different, and these examples are used only to illustrate the methods and best practices described throughout this book.

When completed, both the diagram and the table could be used during training to help users get a high level overview of the farm and its configuration. During adoption, this is helpful because it allows users to see the big picture. In any case, each diagram and table should be preceded by an introductory paragraph that includes the assumptions made so that it is very clear to the organization why the IA was organized in such a way. In the beginning section of the IA document, you should include the following three elements:

- Describe the current state of document and records management. Reiterate why a need for reorganization using ECM is required.

- Include a high-level summary. This will be a general description of why you chose to structure the IA this way.

- Document the assumptions that were used. These are the boundaries that helped you formulate the requirements and limitations of your plan.

A good example to include in your explanations would be around scaling the ECM solution. List how much content you have now, what percent will go to SharePoint, and the growth rate. This is important in the decision of whether to do business units per site or per site collection. Include how the functions were determined and how the library names were selected. Anyplace you can anticipate inquiry, you should proactively describe the rationale behind the decisions that led to your IA.

When completed, the IA documentation should be a clear guide for how to navigate the entire ECM application in the SharePoint farm. But the logical storage of content does not stop there. Content types are not only part of where content is stored, but what is stored with it.

Content types

Earlier, we described the content type as the container for the content and its metadata. By the time most organizations reach the configuration of content types, they become weary and fail to go into much detail. They might elect to use out-of-the-box content types, which provide nominal value, or they might allow users to create their own content types, which results in content type sprawl similar to the issues surrounding a shared network drive.

The reason content types are so important is that they are the only way to embrace the future of flatter IA designs and a minimalist approach to document libraries. By using content types, you can leverage the power of documents-associated metadata to slice and dice information in numerous combinations. This allows users to browse more precisely, search faster, and make better decisions about the content in views.

The first part of documenting content types is providing a detailed summary of how content types are created, the thought process behind how they are used, and what policies were followed when creating them. The following four key areas need to be included when documenting your content types:

- **Content Type Location**   If you used this book as a guide for your ECM implementation, you already know that we recommend setting up content types in a single location for the entire farm. This is done by using the content type syndication feature. It allows for ease of administration of content types, and it allows the use of more advanced functionality when moving content around in the farm, without losing valuable information.

- **Standard and Custom**   Define the relationship of custom content types to standard SharePoint content types. For example, in Figure 7-2, we take the approach of extending all root content types with a layer of retention schedule content types, and then we include the user friendly name content types. This was done because the organization leveraged a retention schedule, which is a feature implemented at the content type level, and they wanted to have a content type for each objective type of document.

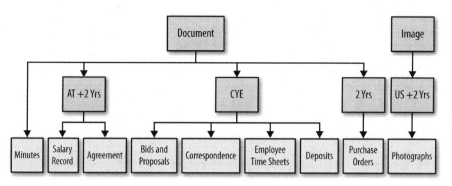

FIGURE 7-2 Content type relationships.

- **Content Type List**   First, describe how you chose the number and name of content types. This should be derived from an existing list of document types for the organization that support each business unit. The organization should be in a position to distinguish business-critical documents from those that are superfluous. ECM should be used only for business-critical content or content that has true value from a records or operational business perspective.

- **Usage Policy**   Here you will define how content types should be used. This will often include a guide for how to choose the proper content type, what metadata is required, and what is optional.

After you have given the high-level description of the methods used to create the organization's content type, you need to define what the final sets of content types are and how they are used. One of the big benefits, as shown in Figure 7-3, of the content type hub is that, at minimum, you can use screen shots of the content type hub and content type configuration page for this portion of your documentation.

Site Settings › Site Content Types

📷 Create

Site Content Type	Parent	Source
Business Intelligence		
Excel based Status Indicator	Common Indicator Columns	Team Site
Fixed Value based Status Indicator	Common Indicator Columns	Team Site
Report	Document	Team Site
SharePoint List based Status Indicator	Common Indicator Columns	Team Site
SQL Server Analysis Services based Status Indicator	Common Indicator Columns	Team Site
Web Part Page with Status List	Document	Team Site
Community Content Types		
Category	Item	Team Site
Community Member	Site Membership	Team Site
Site Membership	Item	Team Site
Digital Asset Content Types		
Audio	Rich Media Asset	Team Site
Image	Rich Media Asset	Team Site
Rich Media Asset	Document	Team Site
Video	System Media Collection	Team Site
Video Rendition	Rich Media Asset	Team Site
Display Template Content Types		
JavaScript Display Template	Document	Team Site
Document Content Types		
Basic Page	Document	Team Site
Document	Item	Team Site
Dublin Core Columns	Document	Team Site
Form	Document	Team Site
Link to a Document	Document	Team Site
List View Style	Document	Team Site
Master Page	Document	Team Site
Master Page Preview	Document	Team Site
Picture	Document	Team Site
Web Part Page	Basic Page	Team Site
Wiki Page	Document	Team Site

Document Set Content Types		
Document Set	Document Collection Folder	Team Site
Folder Content Types		
Discussion	Folder	Team Site
Folder	Item	Team Site
Summary Task	Folder	Team Site
Group Work Content Types		
Circulation	Item	Team Site
Holiday	Item	Team Site
New Word	Item	Team Site
Official Notice	Item	Team Site
Phone Call Memo	Item	Team Site
Resource	Item	Team Site
Resource Group	Item	Team Site
Timecard	Item	Team Site
Users	Item	Team Site
What's New Notification	Item	Team Site
List Content Types		
Announcement	Item	Team Site
Comment	Item	Team Site
Contact	Item	Team Site
East Asia Contact	Item	Team Site
Event	Item	Team Site
Issue	Item	Team Site
Item	System	Team Site
Link	Item	Team Site
Message	Item	Team Site
Post	Item	Team Site
Reservations	Event	Team Site
Schedule	Event	Team Site
Schedule and Reservations	Event	Team Site
Task	Item	Team Site
Workflow Task (SharePoint 2013)	Task	Team Site
Special Content Types		
Unknown Document Type	Document	Team Site

FIGURE 7-3 Content type hub.

As you can see, all content types are listed in one place. For the custom content type group, we recommend that you place all content types where they will be visible. The content type hub is a very nice tool for listing all content types in one place. In a pinch, this will suffice, but we recommend that you also create a separate table that includes more detailed information about content types, as shown in Table 7-3.

TABLE 7-3 Custom content types

| Friendly Name | Parent | Columns | | | Library Location |
		Name	Required	Type	
Medical Leave	Document\CYE+7	Created Date	X	Date	\\ECM\HR\Documents
		Modified Date	X	Date	
		Title	X	Text	
		Author	X	Text	
		Dept		MMS	
		Leave Date	X	Date	
Policy	Document\US+2	Created Date	X	Date	\\ECM\Operations\Documents
		Modified Date	X	Date	\\ECM\HR\Documents
		Title	X	Text	\\ECM\Legal\Documents
		Author	X	Text	\\ECM\Excutive\Documents
		Effective Date	X	Date	

In this example, we detail two documents of content types: Medical Leave and Policy. Both are created in the content type hub, and for this organization, both are derived from a base content type that is the retention schedule year.

Medical Leave is derived from the root content CYE+7, which is derived from the content type "Document," which means that this document will be deleted 7 years after the year it was created. It has the columns Created Date, Modified Date, Title, Author, Department and Leave Date. Department and Leave Date are unique content types.

Department is based on a managed metadata column that lists all departments, and Leave Date is simply a date field indicating the employees' last day of work prior to medical leave. Most of the columns in both content types are required. The organization should already have a predefined description of how they determine mandatory fields.

The Medical Leave content type is available in only one library, the documents library of the HR site or site collection, while the Policy content type is available in four sites or site collections: Operations, HR, Legal, and Executive.

When documenting these content types as outlined in Table 7-3, it's often easier to list only the columns that are unique to a content type. For example, in this case, the Leave Date column for the Medical Leave content type is unique across the board, whereas Created Date and Modified Date will be present in all content types.

One of the most common custom types of columns that we talk about in this book is managed metadata. This column links to the managed metadata service (MMS), where it pulls from a specific term set or from a subset of a term set. Frequently, content types will have more than one of these types of columns, and this is the location for all taxonomies, which is another piece of your IA that should be documented.

Taxonomy

The purpose of documenting your taxonomies is slightly different than for content types and the SharePoint farms IA down to the library level. Because of how taxonomies are implemented in SharePoint 2013, change control can be difficult. Properly designed taxonomies should not be updated frequently and should not be updated by the user because this is a quick path to sprawl and a return to the shared drive paradigm that quickly creates a digital dump of content and terms.

The individual taxonomies will be initially created in comma-separated value (CSV) files. We recommend that you have one file for each taxonomy that should be set up as shown in Table 7-4, in a strict format with no deviation.

TABLE 7-4 Comma-separated value placeholders

Term Set Name	Term Set Description	LCID	Available for Tagging	Term Description	Level 1 Term	Level 2 Term	Level 3 Term

These values are defined to support the following purposes:

- **Term Set Name** The broad name or type of the taxonomy we are working on—that is, Functional, Period, Regional.

- **Term Set Description** A note to all administrators about what is contained in this set and how it's used.

- **LCID** The language code, this used only in SharePoint farms leveraging multilingual user interface (MUI). We will ignore this field for this application and use the code for English, which is 1033, but the column must be present for proper import.

- **Available for Tagging** Allows the term to be used in places where tagging is enabled. Because we want to encourage adoption of the taxonomy and we want to be sure that content is tagged, we will leave this as true for all terms. If your organization leverages a folksonomy as well, you might want to set this to false for all tags.

- **Level 1-3 Term** The actual terms we have decided to use for Coho Winery.

When the taxonomy is completed, it will be uploaded to the MMS service application. While it is not available to be set up in a specific content type and used in the farm, it should be considered as read-only at this point. If you were to make edits to the taxonomy inside of the MMS service application, you would have no record of the change. When this happens once or twice, it's not a big deal, but over time, the collective amount of changes causes a problem for migration and understanding of setup. This is because you are unable to export taxonomies or merge them with the original CSV file in SharePoint.

This is why we recommend that all changes to taxonomy happen in the CSV file directly. To do this in an effective way, you need to track those changes. This is the primary purpose of documenting taxonomies, in addition to documenting the policies and principles that defined them.

In your taxonomy documentation, as with content types and IA, you should start with a description of why taxonomies are being used, how they will benefit the organization, and the high-level rationale that drove their creation.

It is very important to follow the rules that we outlined in the Chapter 4 examples:

1. Do not user "Other" or miscellaneous terms. These terms are a catchall that will be used more often than you will like. People see "Other," and they quickly store an item without looking for the appropriate name.

2. Do not use any transient terms. Terms such as dates that will soon be invalid can be applied to a document and then never updated, so they become inaccurate. Dates and versions are the most commonly misused transient terms.

3. Do not use plural forms of terms.

4. Repetition is fine. Repetition in child terms will happen; this is common and expected. It's the entire path of a term that matters.

5. Focus your terms on root concepts, and avoid being overly detailed. You can use synonyms for more detail.

6. Do not create term depth further than four terms. Users will tend to stop applying terms at the third level.

7. Do not use terms that are abbreviations, but you can use abbreviations in extended form for terms and synonyms.

8. No term set will be over 1,000 terms, including all child terms.

When creating your terms you want to follow the nine step process we have outlined:

1. List all departments, functions and/or business units to be included in the ECM project.

2. Take a screen capture of the shared folder structure for each. The folder structure will be the starting point, not the result.

3. Create a list of representatives from each group that includes project stakeholders or subject matter experts and interview them by asking the following questions:

    a. What types of documents do you work with on a daily basis?

    b. How do you organize your documents?

    c. Do individuals organize by personal preference at a certain level?

4. Merge the terms from the folder structure with the comments and feedback you collect during your interviews.

5. After you have completed the taxonomy outline, review the business unit taxonomy and terms with the project stakeholders in each department.

At this point, you need to ask yourself the following questions:

    a. Does this structure make sense?

    b. Do the terms make sense?

    c. Is anything missing?

    d. Is there anything that can be omitted?

    e. Would you use this taxonomy on your documents?

6. Reconcile all the collected information into a single spreadsheet for each department, business unit, and function.

7. Compare all terms to the retention schedule. All retention schedule documents should be represented at some level.

8. Normalize overlap between departments. In some organizations, this means isolating common terms into one portion of the taxonomy for all to use.

9. Test the final taxonomy, within a staging environment with the easy and difficult business unit and/or department representatives.

After you have documented how taxonomies were derived, you can list the taxonomies, their location, their last modification date, and history of changes, as shown in Table 7-5.

TABLE 7-5 Taxonomy list

Name	Type	Created Date	Modified Date	Location	Content Types used	History of Changes
Operations	Functional	8/1/2012	8/1/2012	\\ECM\ECMHub\Taxonomy	Policy Plan	
Departments	Listing	8/1/2012	1/5/2013	\\ECM\ECMHub\Taxonomy	Medical Leave	Added new departments
Human Resources	Functional	8/1/2012	8/1/2012	\\ECM\ECMHub\Taxonomy	Handbook Employee File	
Quarters Completed	Period	8/1/2012	3/5/2013	\\ECM\ECMHub\Taxonomy	Minuets	Added new quarters
IT	Functional	8/1/2012	9/1/2013	\\ECM\ECMHub\Taxonomy	Equipment Documentation	Added missing key terms "Server"
Legal	Functional	8/1/2012	9/1/2013	\\ECM\ECMHub\Taxonomy	Correspondence Action Letter	Added missing key terms "Risk"
Engineering	Functional	8/1/2012	8/1/2012	\\ECM\ECMHub\Taxonomy	Documentation	
Keywords	Folksonomy	8/1/2012	3/15/2013	\\ECM\ECMHub\Taxonomy	Keywords	Updated with user suggested terms
Office	Regional	8/1/2012	8/1/2012	\\ECM\ECMHub\Taxonomy	Office	

There are a few key elements to this table. First, we list the type of taxonomy. We explained earlier that there are limited numbers of types of taxonomy: functional, period, and regional. In this list, you will also see Folksonomy and Listing. Folksonomy is the flexible form of Taxonomy that is created and driven by the users. Therefore, it might not be something you track, but in any case, it is still something that we recommend against. Listing is a way to avoid using drop-down type menus to pick from a flat list of items. In this case, it's simply a list of the departments, as opposed to a standard taxonomy, which would normally indicate a term used to define the content's use in the organization. Some organizations might elect to continue to use the drop-down style column. The benefit of putting it in an MMS term store is having one place to manage all listings of content.

The other key element to this Table 7-5 is the location. As you can see, we are recommending that even your created and published taxonomies should be stored inside a library in SharePoint. This can be either the ECM Hub or a site collection or site belonging to the content managers and records managers. This gives the added benefit of tracking changes for you so that you do not have to include them in this tracking table.

Table 7-5 gives a minimal picture of where and when taxonomies were updated. The process of the update when updates are not frequent is to update both in the CSV file and in the MMS Service application term store. For frequent updates, we recommend that you consider third-party tools for synchronizing CSV files with SharePoint MMS.

Now that we have documented all components of the IA by creating a map of the entire SharePoint farm, we need to define how this configuration aligns with the content stored in SharePoint and the people who use the platform.

Content governance

Governance in the context of ECM is largely different from how most organizations consider governance. Organizations that are familiar with the term *governance* will put it in the category of IT governance that covers infrastructure and system security. There is no doubt that there is overlap with ECM as far as security is concerned, but usually the IT governance plan is a system of recording and controlling access security for discrete information systems, whereas the content governance plan is the system of record for security related to users' access to content, not entire systems.

The content governance plan is used to define the security of content, how content is stored, how it is used, and what constitutes good usage of the system. When creating your content governance plan, you can use the following principles as a guide for each element of the plan:

- Focuses on the ECM solution, not the individual features.

- Aligns ECM goals with budget and return on investment.

- Helps the system function well both today and five years down the road.

According to the IT Governance Institute, content governance consists of the leadership, organizational structures (policies), and processes that ensure that the organization's technology sustains and extends the organization's strategies and objectives. It is concerned with the risks, the costs, and the usefulness of the solution after it has been created.

The first part of a governance plan is an executive summary that defines what content governance means for your organization and the goals. The goals, at minimum, should include the following:

- Ensure that the investments in SharePoint generate business value.

- Mitigate the risks that are associated with SharePoint.

- Get users to adopt SharePoint and use it properly.

You should strive to be more qualitative and detailed when expanding these goals. For example, provide detail for an annual period, the number of users, and the amount of properly contributed content that you want to attain. We also encourage you to think of governance as a continuum in which you are striving to reach level four in the following progression:

1. No governance

2. Bargaining

3. Centralized–advisory

4. Centralized–empowered

A good way to illustrate the appropriate level of governance is shown in Figure 7-4.

You can have too high a capture cost and consumption effort so that ECM does not work. Similarly, you can have too much governance, where the users are so limited that adoption is essentially nil.

Obviously there is no excuse for having no governance, where each user is on their own and each business unit looks after their own interests. In such a scenario, the usage of SharePoint is no better than shared drives and often worse.

Bargained governance is where a few business units negotiate collectively a mutually acceptable solution. This seems reasonable, but content that was contributed prior to the negotiation becomes invalid after the negotiation and can later pose some serious problems and risk. Further, you cannot assume that the principles and methods used were generated by anything beyond efficiency and ease of use; users will seldom think in the best interest of the organization and from a strategic point of view.

In centralized and advisory governance, the ECM group works to come up with a governance plan and can give guidance, but they are empowered to enforce the policies that they create. Often in such systems, the governance works very well for a short period of time, often measured in months, after which users realize what they can get away with and quickly revert to bad habits.

Finally, there is the centralized and empowered governance, where the ECM committee has both the ability to create the policies and the authority to create compliance policy. This usually requires that, apart from building the committee we described, the team also incorporates Legal, Records Management, and the executive team. These members could be added after the implementation phase of the ECM project if needed.

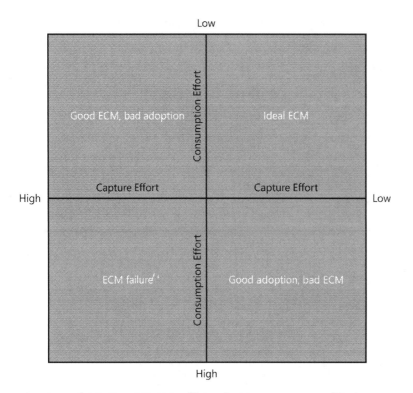

FIGURE 7-4 Capture and consumption.

Governance is a balancing act, and the challenge for IT organizations is to create an appropriate level of centralized control while at the same time avoiding any impact on the business benefits derived by placing power in the hands of end users. This is tricky and requires that the committee and organizations implement a system of introspection that looks at the benefit gained from policies versus the inconvenience and risk that is posed for user adoption.

When done prior to deployment, the tools used to implement governance can be done via technology or policy by using technology features that are implemented in such a way that users cannot bypass them with improper usage. The most common example is required fields in content types. With this method, a user cannot upload a document where the required fields are not completed. This is governance implemented through a function of the technology.

The same requirement could be implemented with a policy that dictates that all documents must have specific metadata entered in a specific way to be considered properly contributed content and that all users are expected to contribute content in a proper way.

Both approaches have their benefits. Technology is extremely easy to enforce, but when used excessively, users will simply stop contributing content because it is too onerous. Policy has the least impact on users but is extremely hard to track; you would have to impose a system of content audits per user, which is too large a task for most organizations.

In this case, there should be a balance between fields that are mandatory to ensure the functionality of the system and those that are implemented by policy.

This example holds true for all decisions about whether to manage governance with technology or policy, but some requirements, such as "do not use profanity," are easier to manage via policy.

As we mentioned earlier, SharePoint 2013 ECM projects seldom fail because of technology. If you use this book as a guide to your ECM implementation, your project most likely will not fail because you did not set up the platform correctly. It will fail due to poor adoption or excessive adoption in the wrong way, and governance is certainly part of this.

The planning for governance should start in conjunction with the design of the ECM system, before a single set of SharePoint configurations is implemented. The ECM team or a specialized governance team with a direct connection to the ECM team should be responsible for creating the content governance plan. It should build on the project's vision statement. A good starting point is to take the organization's existing policies and standards and link them to platform functionality.

While the governance plan is being created, similar to what was suggested with the ECM implementation, you should get started early in the project. Get your users familiar with the policies, and give them a voice to help shape both functional and policy-driven solutions. For example, early in Chapter 2, "ECM stack: content in," we indicated that you should get your users to start following the designed taxonomies even before SharePoint is set up. At the same time, get them used to the idea that there is good content and bad content.

Governance is not the thing you do after the system is implemented. If this were the case, it would likely be published and put away and rarely read. The document is only a record of the thought processes and decisions made regarding policy. More importantly, successful governance is about getting users involved.

As part of this, gently and over time, you need to convey the decisions made about policy and procedure and the reasoning behind it. Expect that users will react negatively to many of the decisions in the governance plan, but if you can get them to understand why and if you implement governance in a way that can be a habit and not interfere too much with their work, they will comply.

When you implement your governance plan, you must plan for updates and be flexible; things will change, and building a flowing structure into your committee will help embrace these changes and integrate them, when appropriate, into the plan.

The high-level goals of a governance plan should have the following characteristics:

- **Natural** Does it fit naturally into the operation of the business?

- **Trim** Does it contain just enough information that is measurable, precise, and time relevant?

- **Agile** Can it be adapted quickly to changing tactical requirements?

- **Safe** Does it satisfy the technical, legal, and operational requirements? (If it does not, it's doomed to failure.)

Each component of the plan should include its individual goal, when it should be completed, and who is responsible. It's important to understand that there is a cost associated with proper governance. Establishing a budget line item for this will help you make decisions that balance costs versus risk. If the reward for mitigating risk is outweighed by the available budget, you might have to plan alternative methods of governance. Outline what you are willing to spend, what you are willing to risk, and what is the opportunity cost of doing things a specific way based on that balance. A specific issue that arises out of poor governance could put the organization at risk; determining the potential fallout or costs of a specific issue or legal matter is difficult and varies greatly depending on the organization.

Balance is key in a good governance plan. This goes back to the team being introspective. Governance should not be the user community versus the ECM committee. The best way to achieve balance is by getting the users involved early and frequently. Try to balance consensus versus buy-in—that is, what you know the users will readily accept versus what you have no choice but to impose. In the spectrum of governance that we illustrate in Figure 7-5, you need to find that balance.

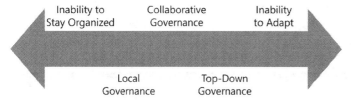

FIGURE 7-5 Governance and balance.

For most organizations, the objective is to be somewhere between collaborative governance and top-down governance. However, if you are in a highly regulated field, you have no choice but to rely heavily on top-down governance.

Another way to look at governance in SharePoint is from a feature/application perspective. In Figure 7-6, the diagram tracks upward from low governance (Social application with MySites) to the highest level of governance (Records Management with Records Center). Under each is a listing of common features unique to, but not complete or limited to, those applications.

Most of what we are proposing in this book is to combine records management and ECM. As you can see, these applications inherently demand more governance than others. They also are less innovative and change less than the lower-level applications. This immediately imposes more on the ECM/Governance committee, from both a governance and a rules perspective, and also requires the establishment of rules that should not change perspective.

Now that we have defined the nature and components of governance, let's turn to the document, which will be the published record of what you are going to do.

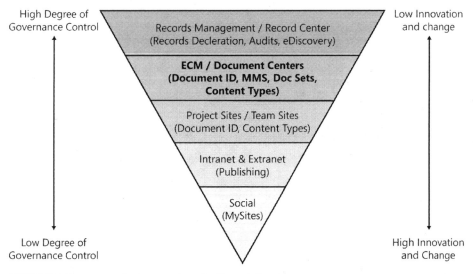

High Degree of
Governance Control

Low Innovation
and change

Records Management / Record Center
(Records Decleration, Audits, eDiscovery)

**ECM / Document Centers
(Document ID, MMS, Doc Sets,
Content Types)**

Project Sites / Team Sites
(Document ID, Content Types)

Intranet & Extranet
(Publishing)

Social
(MySites)

Low Degree of
Governance Control

High Innovation
and Change

FIGURE 7-6 Governance features and application relationships.

When we talk about content governance for SharePoint, we are careful with web searches on the term *governance* because they will tend to lead to content and diagrams for IT governance rather than content governance. While creating an IT governance plan is not bad, content governance requires some additional elements.

The document should start with strategic objectives and then become very tactical. The conceptual components that should be answered as part of the plan include the following:

- Strategy

  - Summary

  - Goals

  - The governance team

  - Future goals

- Tactical

  - Features and a proper usage description

  - Usage and adoption monitoring

  - How you track

  - Disciplinary action

The sidebar in this chapter entitled "Governance plan outline" provides an example of an outline for an actual governance plan.

Governance plan outline

1. Introduction

2. Executive Summary

3. Objectives

    a. Audience

    b. Scope

    c. Goals

    d. Risks / Concerns

4. Resources

    a. Team Roles and Responsibilities

    b. Individual Roles and Responsibilities

    c. Features

5. Governance Hierarchy

6. Operations Policies

    a. Application Usage Policies

    b. Conduct Statement

7. Communication and Training

8. Communication Plan

    a. Training Plan

    b. Support Plan

9. Definitions and Acronyms

10. References

The Introduction should describe the layout of the document and its purpose. After that, the Executive Summary should describe at a high level the purpose of the governance plan.

The Objectives section will include details about what the goals are of the published plan and the concepts derived from it. Identify the target audience of those who maintain and use the ECM platform, scoped to the platform itself, and a listing of the possible risks and concerns. These risks and concerns should include problems associated with noncompliance with the governance plan as well as things that might be missed and opportunity costs. Forward-thinking organizations might also want to detail the pain that will be incurred should certain components of the plan not work out.

The Resources section will detail the components of the system, including those who use it and work on it. It should first define the committee and their structure, including when they meet, how they make decisions, and when they will make changes to the plan. Then it should detail the types of users, including super users, what users have access to, what their process is for obtaining support, and what should be considered proper general usage of the system. This description should also include the policy for the continued or discontinued use of shared or local desktop drives.

The Features subsection under Resources should, in extreme detail, list the specific SharePoint 2013 Platform features used in the deployment, how they are set up, who has access to them, and what constitutes proper usage.

The Governance Hierarchy provides the details about who owns the configuration and management of SharePoint, to whom users should listen when it comes to proper usage, and how this aligns to executive management and business goals. It should be clear that there are ramifications of improper usage of the system, both operationally and materially.

The Operational Policies section takes the governance hierarchy into concrete details, such as what is the proper way to add a legal document and what are the ramifications of not doing it correctly.

The sidebar in this chapter entitled "Governance documents" provides examples of policies from a real governance document.

Governance documents

Content posting and editing policy example

- **Content Posting Cycle**   Remind users to delete content from its original source or collaboration environment when it is published to the official SharePoint repository (or use automated content disposition policies to make sure this happens routinely).

- **Content Editing**   Remind users to edit documents in place so that links from cross-site contributors are not broken.

- **Content Formats and Names**   Create file naming standards. Consider a policy for defining what types of content belong in your SharePoint solution and what types of content belong in other locations.

- **Content Types and Document Libraries**   Content types allow for the grouping of information and attachment to certain lists or libraries. In the [Company] system, two content types exist for the depiction of Case Documents and Discovery Documents. The user can select the content type when creating or uploading a new document to libraries. Upon doing so, they will be prompted to enter this associated metadata, which will then be tracked along with the document and made available to search.

- **Records Management**   Records management is the process by which an organization determines the types of information that should be considered records, how records should be managed while they are active, and for how long each type of record should be retained. Records management includes the performance of records-related tasks such as disposing of expired records, or locating and protecting records that are related to external events such as lawsuits.

- **Taxonomy and Managed Metadata**   Managed metadata is a hierarchical collection of centrally managed terms that you can define and then use as attributes for items in Microsoft SharePoint Server 2013. A user's role determines how the user can work with managed metadata. Users can see only global term sets and term sets that are local to the user's site collection. Local term sets are created within the context of a site collection. Global term sets are created outside the context of a site collection. If there are term sets that some users should be unable to view, assign these term sets to separate groups.

Application usage policies example

- **Site Provisioning**   Sites should be security-trimmed to specific SharePoint users. Employees will not be able to create their own sites or site collections. The assigned business site administrator is responsible for assigning further access to new sites.

- **Site Management**   To ensure that stale sites are removed and data storage is reclaimed, sites untouched for 90 days will be scheduled for automatic deletion. Site owners will be notified if their site is scheduled for deletion and provided with a mechanism to remove it from the automatic deletion list.

- **User Access**   All SharePoint administrators should review available training materials and complete a skills assessment prior to becoming an administrator.

- **Storage Quotas**   By default, SharePoint imposes a 50-MB limit on the size of a single document that can be uploaded into a document library.

    - Team Site administrators receive alerts when storage is at 90 percent of quota.

    - SharePoint administrators can override storage quota for site collections if necessary.

- **Document Management**

    - Allowed file types: .doc, .docx, .xls, .ppt, .pdf

    - Prohibited file types: .mp3, .avi, .mdb

        All portal content that reaches the portal site is created by a user and then deployed to the portal via a request to the appropriate content approver or site administrator to add or update the content on the portal. The administrator might be required to convert some of this content into a format more suitable for the portal prior to updating the portal site.

Content will be maintained by the appropriate business content owner—typically, the author of the content.

■ **Conduct Statement**   [Company] Employees or agents of [Company] using the [Company] SharePoint ECM environment are representing the Company. They are expected to conduct all business in a professional business manner.

The Operations Policy section will be the most controversial and most robust section of your entire governance plan. Each policy should be easily separated and published as a separate independent document from all others.

The Communication and Training section will detail the level of training users are expected to have and how they obtain the training. It will also detail and should include a directory of their first tier support, which should be super users in each function and how those users escalate support.

While the Communication and Training section details the goals, the plan will define concrete dates for when users will be training and how the training will be executed.

The Definitions and Resources section details the terms used to describe the environment and a list of resources, such as training videos and documentation, and even this book can be used to design the system and determine the governance.

Next steps

Governance can be, and is, an exhausting process. Starting right away is the easy way to decrease the exhaustion. The final document is rewarding in that it becomes a guide for the current system usage and future extensibility.

Here we have described how to create a blueprint with the IA documentation and how to describe proper usage with the governance documentation. But we left out a large component, and that is records management. While the governance recommendations in this chapter hold true for all organizations, only some organizations choose to embrace the processes and principles of records management, which we will discuss in the next chapter.

CHAPTER 8

Records management

In the context of SharePoint, we will define records management as the practice of maintaining electronic records in your organization from the point of their creation to their eventual disposal. A broader view of records management would include all business records, both physical and electronic, in any format. This could span paper, microform, backup media, and electronic records.

Principles and life cycle

In the context of SharePoint, a record is an electronic file or content that has been stamped at a specific time and place as a record of business. Stamping a document in SharePoint as a record consists of assigning a Document ID and, more importantly, declaring the document as a record. Content includes the body of all documents and its associated metadata, making it an immutable document that if modified either nullifies itself as a record or becomes a separate record from the original. The primary concern for management of these records is to provide evidence of an organization's business activity.

This definition, while relevant, does not contain the whole picture. How you achieve records management is just as important as what it is. Many organizations do not have the concept or formal practice of managing records. All organizations should explore the benefits derived from the principles of records management. These include but are not limited to the ability to dispose of records that no longer have a business benefit or purpose. Most organizations simply stockpile both physical and electronic records because they see the cost and risk of maintaining records beyond the appropriate retention period outweigh the costs and structure required to implement the procedures and system configurations needed. If your organization has intentionally established the structures for records management, it is in a good position to configure SharePoint to support the records management policies, retention schedule, and disposition practices.

In conjunction with the formal definition of records management, there are principles that are widely accepted for developing a records management program. We have outlined these principles to establish a baseline of understanding for your organization. You might find that referring back to these will be helpful when deciding how records management will best fit into your ECM project.

- **Accountability** There will be an individual or individuals responsible for all identified records, their content, and actions taken on that content.

- **Integrity**   Organizations will agree to a system for managing content and ensuring its integrity, authenticity, and reliability.

- **Protection**   Organizations will establish a system of record that protects records from alteration, unprivileged access, and business continuity.

- **Compliance**   Organizations will establish a system that allows them to comply with applicable laws and authorities in their industry.

- **Availability**   Organizations will establish a system that allows access to records in a reasonable time frame.

- **Retention**   Organizations will maintain records for a reasonable amount of time to satisfy legal, regulatory, fiscal, operational, and historical requirements.

- **Disposition**   Organizations shall securely and systematically dispose of records that are no longer relevant or required to maintain compliance with laws and organization policies.

- **Transparency**   The method of tracking, storing, and maintaining records will be transparent to authorities and authorized parties, and the practice should be verifiable and measurable.

Records management has a specific life cycle. As part of your records program, we recommend that you document and publish the life cycle outlined in Figure 8-1 as a formal process and policy that must be adhered to by the organization.

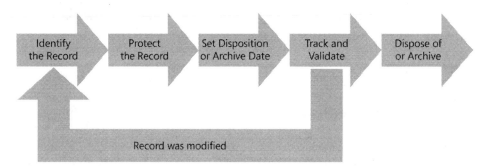

FIGURE 8-1 Records life cycle.

When you understand the principles behind establishing a formal records management program, you will want to start planning for the activities related to the practice of records management in your organization.

- **Determine a System of Record**   For the purposes of this book, the system of record is SharePoint 2013. It is the final storage point of the immutable record.

- **Establishing Policies**   Policies dictate how records are treated and who can access them. Where there is a physical version of a record, they also dictate how and when the physical version will be destroyed.

- **Retention Schedules** Building and maintaining retention schedules requires listing of all the pertinent documents for each department, including the history of compliance requirements of the organization. If the document type is not in the retention schedule, it should not be stored in the system of record nor should it be kept by the organization. In addition to the types of documents, the retention schedule will, at minimum, define the life of a document—for example, that a contract should be deleted five years after its termination date.

- **Usage Policies** One of the records management team responsibilities is to ensure that the system of record is used properly and the policies followed.

- **Auditing Content** Periodically, the records team will perform content audits to ensure that there are no discrepancies and to ensure proper use of the system and records.

- **Discovery and Holds** When matters arise, such as a critical legal or compliance-related event that requires the culling of content related to the topic of the matter, the records management team will issue notices to content owners, perform the hold, and, when the hold expires, ensure that content returns to its proper location and status.

- **Content Custodian** The records team is responsible for the integrity of content and can be called during a matter to testify that content is relevant, current, and properly managed. They might also have to document any discrepancies or incidents that might have occurred during the management of content.

From the field

During the first weeks of a project, I work to establish a records management program. The first step is to perform a records inventory. This can be a very time-consuming task, but it will provide the organization with many benefits. Our team will meet with each business unit to document the types, formats, and locations of all content, both physical and electronic. The information gleaned from these interviews can be used to help facilitate many of the elements we have covered in the book. This includes your Information Architecture and user adoption, and you might even find some good resources for the ECM team. - Shad

Business drivers

In most cases, the primary driver for establishing a records management program is an organization's need to comply with industry or regulatory-specific rules. These organizations are in an industry or field that has strict rules about how records are handled, and there is substantial risk associated with not properly taking care of their documents. Organizations not in a regulated field, or in a risky business, can also benefit from records management by achieving better organization and work habits related to content that would help to eliminate waste and inefficiencies.

There are two sides of the records management coin. The benefits for maintaining compliance and reducing the amount of records that are maintained can be counterbalanced with the amount of effort required to implement and maintain a proper records management program. This is often seen as slowing down business operations and not providing enough of a hard dollar return on investment. For smaller organizations, enterprise content management and records management can be one and the same. In theory, ECM is less strict, but in reality, 90 percent of properly established ECM systems incorporate records management as an integral part of the entire solution.

If you find yourself in the category of company that is smaller, in an unregulated business, and that does not have a compelling need for records management, this section is still useful to review and understand. The principles of records management correlate with proper uploading of content to SharePoint. We covered the process and benefits of establishing good content usage and practices in Chapter 6, "User adoption." For the user community that will be working with SharePoint, the organizational habits of records management can be a fantastic driver for change management. At a minimum, you should consider a subset of the functionality that might be useful for your business, especially when considering legal risk.

Documents created by the organization are not only an asset, but they also pose a potential risk. Some organizations feel that the historical value of documents outweighs the benefit of destroying records that have no real business value or functional purpose. There is no sentimentality in records management; either you need the records for compliance or you don't. More often than not, records that are kept beyond a specifically needed period of time become a liability. They could be leaked to your competition, causing your organization to lose valuable intellectual property (or cause embarrassment). It could be content that an employee created that is destructive to the organization. In the opposite risk case, problems could arise because you did not properly manage your records and did not keep critical business documents that were later required.

> **Note** Some organizations have established a formal records manager position, have implemented specific third-party records management tools, or use third-party records retention facilities. If this is the case at your organization, there is probably someone who is familiar with either AIIM International or ARMA International. Both of these independent associations provide specific records and information management resources, best practices, and guidelines.

In some organizations, all documents are records; in others, only a very specific handful of documents are considered records. In either case, calling a document a record implies very specific storage, security, handling, and life span, whereas all nonrecord documents should be disposed of immediately after their transient value is obtained.

SharePoint 2013 and its predecessor, SharePoint 2010, have a lot of functionality around records management and offer tremendous flexibility for how the platform can be used in a hybrid ECM and records management system, in strictly a records center, or where records management principles are utilized as just a subset of ECM.

In SharePoint, we talk about records management from the perspective of records management features and functionality, followed by processes and procedures. In the remaining portions of this chapter, we will take a look at both of these elements and apply them to the features in SharePoint that make them possible, and we will look at how the processes are executed with those features. But first, we will go into some detail about the power and detail of a retention schedule.

Retention schedule

A retention schedule is a detailed listing of the organization's critical operational, historical, or compliance-related content. In many regulated industries, the retention schedule is determined in advance and modified on a biannual or less frequent basis.

The beauty of a retention schedule is that it can be used to determine the following:

- Some level of Information Architecture (IA)
- Content types
- Metadata model
- Information management policies
- Security

From the field

Most organizations get shy when they tell me they have a retention schedule. Because it's a pretty dry subject and not a predominant technical feature, people assume it's not valuable. What they don't realize is that they just made our job as SharePoint ECM consultants much easier. When you have a retention schedule working with a new SharePoint deployment, planning, design, and implementation become so much easier than without. - Chris

Because organizations that have a retention schedule tend to be driven by strict compliance, there is no deviating from the retention schedule, which means that SharePoint should be set up to be consistent with the retention schedules already established.

A typical retention schedule will be segmented into a records series. Each document or content item will be associated with a unique alphanumeric identifier that can be used to categorize documents by retention period. The retention schedule should also include, at a minimum, the type of document, specific records status, and what department they are associated with. Pay attention to this because it can be used as an indication of IA already at work in the organization. If the retention schedule also includes the metadata that each record should have, this can be leveraged as an indication of content types and the columns in each content type. The document life cycle or retention period can be used to determine the information management policies set on each content type. If the content is identified as vital or privileged, this can help you as you establish your content security model. Unless the organization has internal security policies—for example, for management—the retention schedules security criteria can be used as the only security required for the records and your ECM solution.

As you can see, this defines 90 percent of what is done in ECM implementations; therefore, the retention schedule, when identified up front, is a huge help. However, if the retention schedule is not observed until later, this can also cause big issues during SharePoint deployment and usually results in project delay or a restart.

Because of its power, we recommend that organizations take on the practice of creating a retention schedule for themselves, whether or not they are in a regulated industry. The following considerations can help your organization decide whether to build out a records management program:

- Understanding of content relevance for retention

- Possession of confidential or proprietary documents and content

- Documents or content posing a litigation or liability risk

- Overall volume and diversity of content that is not purged

- Defining document types on an organizational level, not just by business unit

- Defining metadata models and a common language organization-wide, not just in functions or business units

Not only will an organization that goes through this exercise have a better sense of its content, it will have a large portion of the ECM planning done. Much of the heavy lifting will be done, and the organization will have already established the right state of mind that comes from properly managing and organizing content.

To help you visualize what a retention schedule looks like, we have included an example from a municipal government, as illustrated in Table 8-1. This is meant as a resource for you to see what other organizations have done. This is not a one size fits all. Although any retention schedule should contain familiar elements, all situations are unique and we recommend that you exercise your own judgment to prepare a retention schedule that meets your requirements.

 Note Permanent records are relevant only for documents that have operational long-term impact, such as bylaws or operational procedures. In Table 8-1's code legend, the retention codes S, T, and EL are unique to municipal governments.

TABLE 8-1 Retention schedule

Department	Content	Retention	Vital/Historical/Confidential	Authority
City Attorney	Court Decisions, Briefs, Research	CL+3yr	V,H	CCP 583.320(a)
City Attorney	Correspondence	CU+2yr	H	GC34090(d)
City Attorney	Legal Services Request	CU+2yr	H	GC34090
City Manager/GIS	GIS Documents	CU+3yr	V	GC34090
City Manager/ Airport	Gate Access Application	CL+2yr	C	GC34090(d)
Development/ Building	Inspection Record	P	V,H	CCP 337.15
Development/ Building	Construction Drawing	P	V,H	H&S 19850
Development/Code	Case Files (Citations)	CL+5yr	H,C	GC34090(d)
Development/ Engineering	Submittals	CL+7yr	V,H	CCP337.15
Environmental	Incident Reports	CL+7yr	V	29 CFR 1904.2

CODE LEGEND

Retention Codes:

> AR = Annual Review
> CL = Closed/Completed
> CU = Current year
> EL = Election Date
> P = Permanent
> S = Superseded
> T = Termination

Citation Codes:

OSHA = Occupational Safety & Health Administration

> CCP = Code of Civil Procedures
> CFR = Code of Federal Regulations
> VC = State Vehicle Code
> GC = State Government Code
> H&S = Health and Safety Code
> PC = Penal Code
> USC = United States Code

If you look at the City Attorney item in Table 8-1, you can see from this retention schedule that they will have five content types for legal services requests, correspondence, briefs, research, and court decisions. Correspondence and Legal Services Requests will have management information policies that will be set to dispose of these documents two years after their declaration as a record. Court Decisions, Briefs, and Research will have an information management policy that will be set to dispose of the documents three years after the matter close date, which means that they will need a custom column of the matter close date as a date field (in their SharePoint 2013 system). All the documents for the City Attorney appear to be historical, which might affect the IA of their site collection or site.

In the case of the City Manager/Airport department, the Gate Access Application is set to be a confidential document, which means that in the site collection security for the Airport, we should consider tighter security for these documents. This is a good example of the method we would use to leverage the retention schedule to help provide the details we need for IA, content types, retention schedule, and, possibly, site security.

We recommend that organizations start up front with a formal records management program and records inventory, all the way through to developing the retention schedule. After a retention schedule has been identified, planning of specific SharePoint functionality will follow suit and incorporate all the elements of this activity.

Records management features in SharePoint

We are assuming that all the standard ECM features that we have recommended are enabled for your SharePoint farm. In addition, there are additional sets of records management-specific features that can be used. These provide the functionality in SharePoint that allow you to perform core records management functions. We have outlined specific steps to follow, to enable the following features:

- Records center, as shown in Figure 8-2

- In-place records declaration

- Information management policies

- Content audit

- Content organizer

- Send-to locations

- Holds and discovery

- Site retention

The records center acts as a type of template or starting point. All documents saved in a site provisioned with this template are automatically declared as a record. No nonrecord documents will be stored in a records center. Usually, organizations will not have more than one records center, and they will provision more based only on size constraints, not security. This site is typically accessible only to content managers or records managers. After a records center site is created based on your IA, you will create libraries consistent with other sites. The libraries that can be unique could be hold libraries or libraries for very specific types of records, such as board, council, or executive team records.

In-place records declaration is usually the alternative to a records center, where instead of all documents in a site being declared a record automatically, the user or automated workflows decide when a document is a record, and nonrecords can live with records.

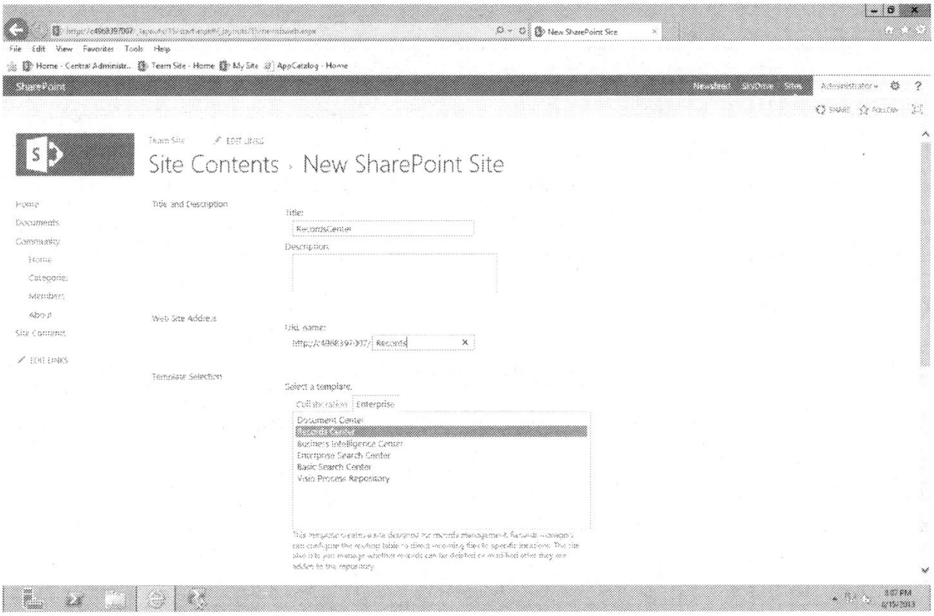

FIGURE 8-2 Records center site.

Follow the seven steps outlined and illustrated in Figures 8-3, 8-4, and 8-5, respectively, to enable in-place records management.

1. Navigate to site settings.

2. Click Site Collection Features.

> Site Collection Administration
> Recycle bin
> Search Result Sources
> Search Result Types
>
> Activate or deactivate features that provide additional Web Parts,
> pages, and other functionality to sites in this site collection. Some
> features may require activation at the Site Administration level.
>
> Search Configuration Export
> Site collection features
> Site hierarchy

FIGURE 8-3 Site Collection Features link.

FIGURE 8-4 Activate records center.

3. Click the Active button to the right of In Place Records Management. This will turn on the feature for the entire site collection.

Important Deactivating the records management feature after it has been used can be damaging to your content. Before considering such a change, it's recommended that you migrate content prior to deactivation to a temporary location, and then migrate back after deactivation. This will also inherently break the principles of records management; this is an extremely important concept to understand. As soon as you deactivate, you no longer have records as we have formally defined them and as a generally accepted practice of records management.

4. Even though the feature is activated, you need to choose which libraries you want the feature to be available in. Browse to a library where you want to allow in-place records management.

FIGURE 8-5 Library settings.

5. On the ribbon, click the Library tab, and then click Library Settings.

6. Click Record Declaration Settings. If you do not see this setting, it means that the feature was not successfully enabled in step 3.

7. As illustrated in Figure 8-6, select the Always Allow The Manual Declaration Of Records option. You will also notice a check box labeled Automatically Declare Items As Records When They Are Added To This List. This setting is essentially how the records center works. By default, all libraries in the records center template are enabled with this feature. For in-place records management, we will leave this unchecked because in this scenario we are allowing nonrecords to live with records.

Library Record Declaration Settings ⊙

Manual Record Declaration Availability

Specify whether this list should allow the manual declaration of records. When manual record declaration is unavailable, records can only be declared through a policy or workflow.

○ Use the site collection default setting:
   Do not allow the manual declaration of records
◉ Always allow the manual declaration of records
○ Never allow the manual declaration of records

Automatic Declaration

Specify whether all items should become records when added to this list.

☐ Automatically declare items as records when they are added to this list.

           [OK] [Cancel]

FIGURE 8-6 Library Record Declaration Settings dialog box.

You will have to repeat steps 5–7 on all libraries in the sites and site collection where you want the feature enabled. When enabled, when you select a document in a library, you will have the option to click the new Declare Record button on the File tab of the ribbon, as shown in Figure 8-7. When you do so, the document will be stamped with the time, location, and content. This means that it cannot be moved or edited unless it is undeclared as a record.

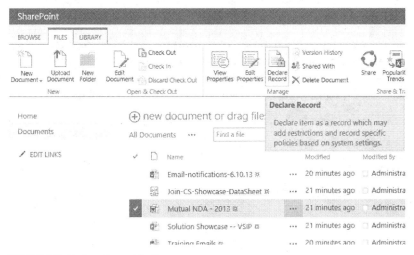

FIGURE 8-7 Declare Record button.

After a record is declared, users will notice a little lock symbol on the file icon, as shown in Figure 8-8. As you can see, this record is living with nonrecords.

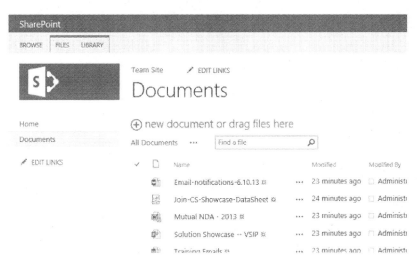

FIGURE 8-8 Records and nonrecords.

In-place records can also be declared via workflows or the content organizer feature in an automated fashion.

Based on existing metadata, usually a date, information management policies are the mechanism that decides when a document should be disposed of. For example, a disposition for a contract might be seven years after its termination date. In such a case, the content type will need to have an additional column for the termination date, and then it will need an information management policy created for it. When you built the content types in the ECM Hub, you established these information management policies on a content type level. Ad hoc creation of information management policies should not happen outside of this configuration.

Content audits allow content managers to review documents from a management perspective or if specific content is related to a matter. Content audits can happen on a document level, library level, or even a whole site level. Content audits will show, from the point that the document first arrived in SharePoint, all viewing, modifications, and automated actions taken on the content.

Follow the five steps outlined and illustrated in Figures 8-9, 8-10, and 8-11, respectively, to perform a content audit.

1. Browse to a library of existing content.

2. Select the "..." drop-down menu on the document.

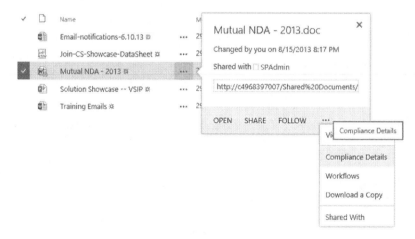

FIGURE 8-9 Compliance Details menu.

3. Click Compliance Details to open a new dialog box.

FIGURE 8-10 Compliance Details dialog box.

4. Click Generate Audit Log Report. This opens a window with various options for the types of audit logs as shown in Figure 8-11.

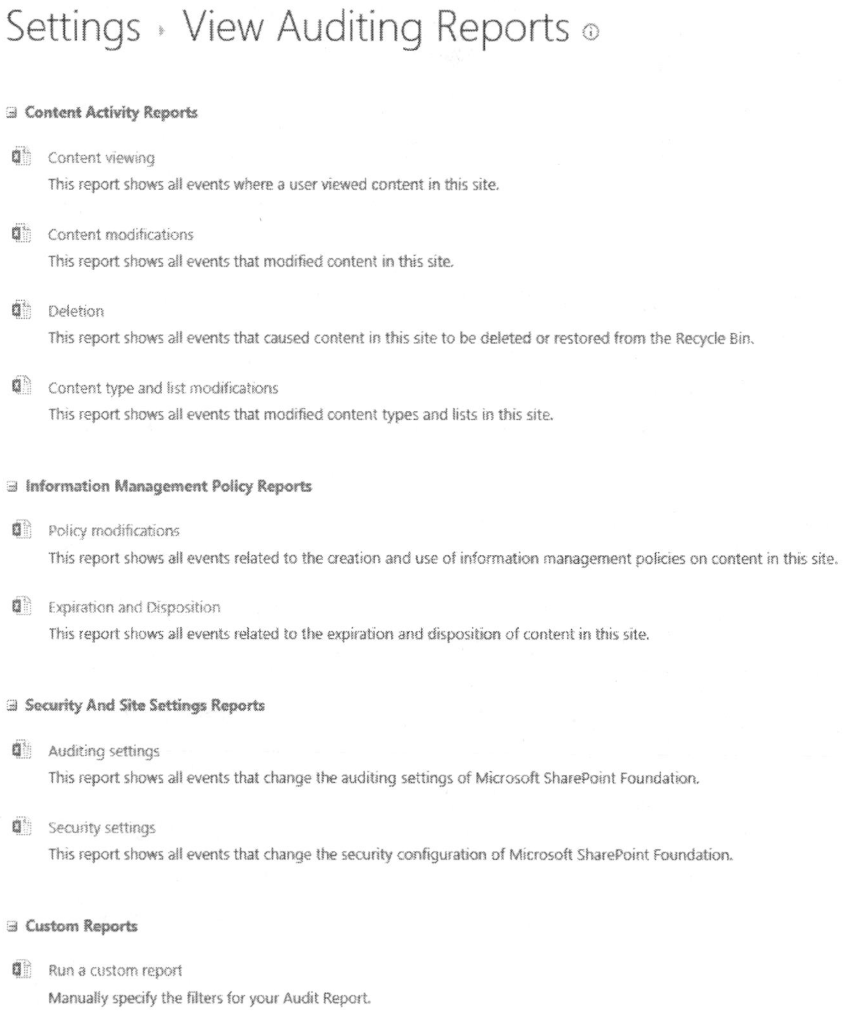

Settings › View Auditing Reports ⊙

⊟ Content Activity Reports

📄 Content viewing
This report shows all events where a user viewed content in this site.

📄 Content modifications
This report shows all events that modified content in this site.

📄 Deletion
This report shows all events that caused content in this site to be deleted or restored from the Recycle Bin.

📄 Content type and list modifications
This report shows all events that modified content types and lists in this site.

⊟ Information Management Policy Reports

📄 Policy modifications
This report shows all events related to the creation and use of information management policies on content in this site.

📄 Expiration and Disposition
This report shows all events related to the expiration and disposition of content in this site.

⊟ Security And Site Settings Reports

📄 Auditing settings
This report shows all events that change the auditing settings of Microsoft SharePoint Foundation.

📄 Security settings
This report shows all events that change the security configuration of Microsoft SharePoint Foundation.

⊟ Custom Reports

📄 Run a custom report
Manually specify the filters for your Audit Report.

FIGURE 8-11 Auditing Reports options.

5. Select the type of audit you want—for example, Content Modifications. You will be asked to browse to a location in the same site, where the resulting Excel file containing all audit data will be saved. At minimum, this should be a separate library from all other content, perhaps called the Audit library. Ideally, the content organizer is configured to take all audit content and route it to a centralized library specifically for records management to view audit documents. Mixing audit Excel files with live business content can confuse users and pose legal risks.

Note Audit log details are compiled by a SharePoint timer job, which means actions are not real-time. They could be every 15 minutes or even every day, depending on the platform configuration for the timer job operations.

The content organizer is a special type of library that can route or modify content uploaded to it based on metadata rules. Content Organizer is a site level feature, so you must select which sites you would like the content organizer to set up.

Follow the three steps outlined and illustrated in Figure 8-12 to enable the Content Organizer.

1. Navigate to the Site Settings page.

2. Select the Manage Site Features option.

3. To the right of the Content Organizer feature, click Activate.

FIGURE 8-12 Activate Content Organizer.

After the feature is enabled, you will immediately notice a new library called the Drop Off Library. We typically recommend that this library be renamed to a friendlier name for your organization, relevant to its function, but for now, we will leave it. Now you can create rules for this library to act on metadata when uploaded to it. First, before creating any rules, the ECM team must decide what the rules will be and document them. This feature can be useful to get users to do the right thing without even knowing it or to make sure that as content is contributed to ECM or Records Management, it goes through the proper processes.

Follow the four steps outlined and illustrated in Figures 8-13 and 8-14 to create a rule.

1. Navigate to the Site Settings page.

2. Select Content Organizer Rules under Site Administration. You will notice there is also a Content Organizer Settings section. For now, we are going to leave the defaults.

Site Administration
Regional settings
Site libraries and lists
User alerts
RSS
Sites and workspaces
Workflow settings
Content Organizer Settings
Content Organizer Rules
Site Closure and Deletion
Term store management
Popularity Trends

FIGURE 8-13 Site settings.

3. Click New Item.

4. Here you will have various settings for the rule. All rules will be given a name and a property status. You can select what types of content types this rule will run on. After you select this, you will be given all the columns available in the content type to build rules from. In the example illustrated in Figure 8-14, we are looking at the title of all incoming documents in the Drop Off Library. If the content is a Document content type, we then check the file name. If the file name contains "Confidential," we are automatically moving the document to the confidential document library.

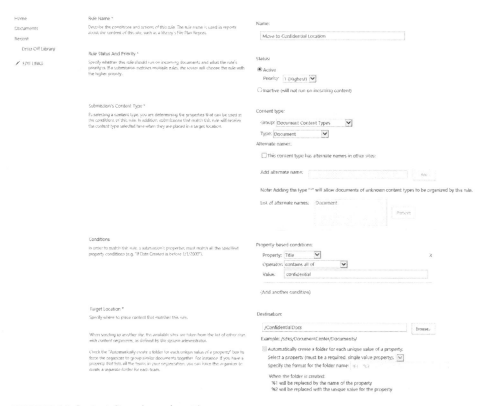

FIGURE 8-14 Content Organizer rule settings.

Now that this rule is created, all new documents that are confidential and uploaded to this library will be automatically routed to the proper document library.

From the field

Content Organizer is one of those features everyone wants. It's somewhere between creating workflows, which is more complex, and just setting up a document library, which is common for most SharePoint users. The problem with the feature is that it's so powerful that it can become one of those features that sprawl across your farm. Some clients I work with have just blindly started using it. They created rules without documentation and then later did not know what they meant, and eventually they completely lost sight of the value of the feature. Many of my clients would try to use Content Organizer as a shortcut for much more advanced things that should have been done with a workflow. I am embarrassed to say I've seen, on three separate occasions, content organizers sending items to other content organizers to complete a complex chain of content modification and relocation. Bottom line, it's one of those features that you need to plan for up front and decide its purpose, determine how it will be used, and (most important) fully document how it will be implemented before you even touch SharePoint. - Chris

Send To locations and Content Deployment paths are a mechanism in SharePoint to move content from one location to another in the farm. The reason this feature is so critical for records management is that content that needs to be administered by a records manager often does not originate as a record in the final location. Many organizations elect to have transient and living content in a less regulated area, but at some point, that content becomes either invalid and disposed of, or it is moved to ECM and/or records management sites for proper management. Send To locations also allow using features such as Content Organizer to its full capacity. The trick with Send To locations and Content Deployment paths is that they require configuration in Central Administration, which should not be open to everyone, and strategically placed drop-off libraries, which end up being the send-to URLs. Therefore, someone with access to Central Administration will have to participate in the set up. In the case of content deployment paths, not only does the path setup happen in Central Administration but so do the scheduled jobs.

For purposes of ECM, we are going to recommend using only Send To locations because they are the most available to the user, the most flexible when it comes to moving a batch of documents or a single one, and they fit nicely with the other features we talk about.

One of the most powerful new features of SharePoint 2013 is the ability to drag documents from one location to another. Now, moving a document from one library to another is as easy as dragging the file from one location into the desired library. This is a small enhancement but one that has huge impact as it relates to other methods of moving content. There are many cases in SharePoint 2010 where you would use Send-to connections or Content deployment paths to move content. Now with SharePoint 2013, you have an additional method; however, it's important to use the right method for each situation.

Consider the use case of moving content. If it's simply for the purpose of organization and not records management processes, you can consider allowing just the dragging feature within sites. If you need to move content across sites, related to some business process or enhancement in content contribution, use the Send-to connections. And finally, if you need to move large amounts of content based on a date or other action criteria on a semi-periodic basis, use Content deployment paths.

To set up a Send To location, you must first enable the Content Organizer feature in the various locations where you want to accept content. After you have enabled the Content Organizer feature, follow the nine steps we have outlined and illustrated in Figures 8-15 and 8-16.

1. Navigate to the Site Settings page.

2. Click Content Organizer Settings under Site Administration.

3. In the Content Organizer Settings window at the bottom of the page, you will notice a unique URL. This is the send-to URL for this particular content organizer. There will be one per content organizer, per site. The URL will look something like this: *http://c4968397007/_vti_bin /OfficialFile.asmx*. Copy this URL to a temporary location.

4. Now that you know the destination of content, navigate to Central Administration.

5. Click General Application Settings.

6. Click Configure Send To Connections.

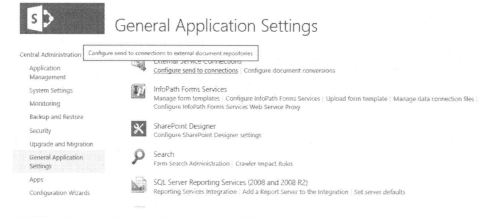

FIGURE 8-15 The Configure Send To Connections link.

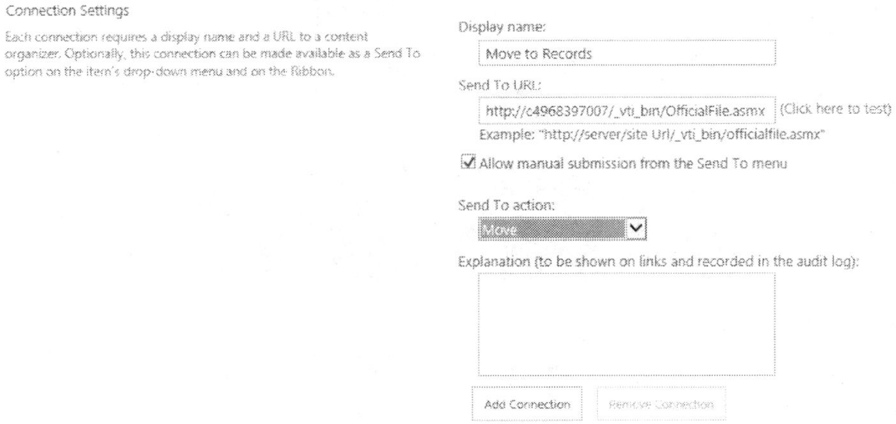

FIGURE 8-16 Send To Connection Settings page.

7. In the Send To configuration settings, give the location an action-oriented name. This will make users understand the purpose more clearly. Set an action type such as copy, move, or move with link. We recommend that you not use the Copy action type because this method causes duplicate documents in ECM and records management, which goes against the core principles we have outlined in the book.

8. Click the Click Here To Test link to verify that the Send To location works. It is not uncommon for security errors to occur. Verify that the Send To location has rights to all possible groups that might contribute content to it.

9. Click OK, and the Send To location will be added to the farm.

We recommend creating send-to locations for the following purposes:

- Send to archive

- Send to records

- Method for forcing proper content submission without imposing strict rules

- Method for sending content to locations that some users might not have access to

After you have configured your Send To location, you will have a new option on the ribbon, as shown in Figure 8-17, for send-to locations that can be used on individual documents, multiple documents, and even workflows.

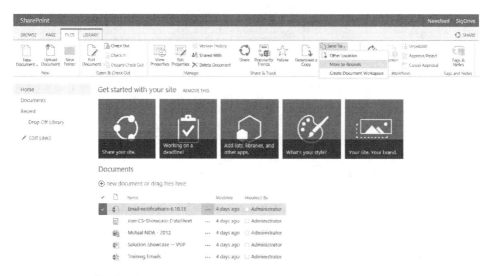

FIGURE 8-17 Send To locations menu.

Note The user experience of Send To locations is greatly impacted by the performance of the farm. If the farm is not high performance, users will get confused because content will not to appear to move for as long as 30 seconds. We recommend that you test and optimize the performance of this with your IT team.

Another major component of records management is the process of holds and eDiscovery. These features will be covered in detail in Chapter 9, "eDiscovery." We mention them here because in some organizations, even without the need for eDiscovery, holds are a tool used by records managers to audit and review content. The feature and mechanism for doing a hold and for using eDiscovery are the same but can have different purposes.

Site disposition is a brand-new feature of SharePoint 2013, and just like the ability to use information management policies to purge content on specific time frames based on metadata, site disposition behaves the same. This is an incredibly powerful tool to prevent sprawl on team and project sites. It would be extremely uncommon to have the core IA of either the records management sites or the ECM sites disposed, because these sites are not transient. However, a records manager's job is also to prevent sprawl. If you consider project sites and team sites individually as a document, their existence can produce content that ends up in ECM, but ultimately, when the project ends, the site should be removed.

We have provided an outline of the nine steps you will need to follow for setting up site disposition. This happens in two stages: first the creation of site policies, as illustrated in Figure 8-18, and then the setting of the site disposition date, as illustrated in Figure 8-19.

Site Policies are created at the site collection level, as shown in the following steps:

1. Navigate to the site settings of the root site for the site collection where you want to enable site disposition. For example, you could navigate to the root site collection of team sites where all the sites for each individual project will be created.

2. Under Site Collection Administration, click Site Policies.

FIGURE 8-18 Site Policies link.

3. Click the Create button.

4. Give the policy a name—for example, **Team Project Deletion**.

FIGURE 8-19 Site policy configuration.

5. Select one of the following options: Do Not Close Or Delete Site Automatically, Delete Sites Automatically, or Close And Delete Sites Automatically.

6. Select whether the deletion is based on the site creation or close date, and how long after—for example, 12 months after the project is created.

7. Select whether you want notification sent to site owners in advance of deletion and, if so, how far in advance.

8. Decide whether you will allow site owners to postpone deletion.

9. Select whether or not to make the site read only.

> **Note** The user interface indicates Site Collection only. However, disposition can be applied to individual sites.

Let's step through the decision process regarding what settings to choose over others. There are many approaches that you can take with site disposition. Each situation is unique, and we encourage you to build and configure your site disposition based on your requirements. Following are the positions an organization can take, along with their associated disposition configurations:

- Hard line

  - Site closure type: Delete sites automatically

  - Deleted event criteria: site created date

  - Allow owners to postpone: No

  - Site is read-only: n/a

- Bargained hard line

  - Site closure type: Delete sites automatically

  - Deleted event criteria: site created date

  - Allow owners to postpone: Yes

  - Site is read-only: n/a

- Empowered owner

  - Site closure type: Delete sites automatically

  - Deleted event criteria: site closed date

  - Allow owners to postpone: Yes

  - Site is read-only: n/a

- Empowered owner with flexibility

  - Site closure type: Close and delete sites automatically

  - Deleted event criteria: site closed date

  - Allow owners to postpone: Yes

  - Site is read-only: Yes

- Archive

  - Site closure type: Do not close or delete site automatically

  - Deleted event criteria: n/a

  - Allow owners to postpone: n/a

  - Site is read-only: Yes

The site closure type of "Do not close or delete site automatically" will become read-only if a site owner closes a site using this option. The benefit of such an option is realized if an organization chooses to archive all sites and maintain them for the indefinite future. This will essentially declare the site a record but still make it visible. The danger of this option is for areas where site creation is done rapidly, because this will result in empty and nonsense sites being kept forever.

We advise that taking the flexible or empowered owner approach is essentially the same as using no policies at all. Owners of sites will always be inclined to keep a site open "just in case." Even if they have the intention of closing the site when it's time, our experience indicates that they neglect to do so. This results in site sprawl and in a small portion of the sites being treated correctly where another portion is not. In our experience with ECM solutions and records management, it's not what you get right that hurts you but what you miss, so we are recommending these options be avoided.

The bargained hard line setting has the same problem of the site owner's ability to postpone, but you can limit the amount of time in days, months, years that a postpone will happen, and because the site closure is set to delete, there is no going back, so the bargained hard line setting works for a well-trained and conscientious site owner. A hard line is the recommended option, and we suggest that all organizations start with this option until it's a problem. It's easier to give the users choices than to take them away. For example, in the hard line, the organization must make it very clear how long sites will last for *all* new project sites and publicize this everywhere. We even recommend that the organization create custom site templates that include this notice in the home page of the site.

In summary, the archive approach should be selectively used only if archive processes have been established and made clear. The empowered owner approaches should never be used. And organizations should start with the hard line approach but move to the bargained hard line if they need to.

From the field

Deleting information is very uncomfortable, but this remains the biggest legal risk for organizations. In the case of SharePoint and site disposition, it also impacts the performance of the farm and the ability to later migrate. Without any control on site creation and deletion, sprawl is a huge problem that has plagued the vast majority of organizations using SharePoint, causing disruptions to normal business operations and the overall success of the platform. - Chris

Now that the policy is created, we need to apply it. Navigate to the site you want to apply the disposition to, and perform the folllowing three steps as outlined and as illustrated in Figure 8-20. If enabled, this is where the site owner can manually close the site.

1. Navigate to the Site Settings page.

2. Under Site Administration, click Site Closure And Deletion.Select the policy you want in the drop-down list, and click OK.

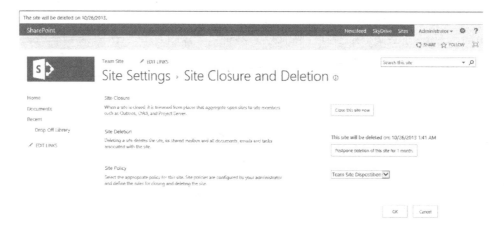

FIGURE 8-20 Site disposition settings.

After you click OK, this page will be updated with the deletion date. This is a good reference for records managers and site owners to keep track of.

After a policy is applied, owners will be able to close the site manually and see the disposition date. If they have been given the option to postpone, they can do so here. If a site has been closed and the retention date has been reached, but the policy allows for it to be read only, it will remain visible in the IA, but new content cannot be added and edits to existing content cannot occur.

Arguably, all features of SharePoint ECM are also features of records management. Content types, MMS, and the metadata model in general are critically important to the records management processes. However, the features we have covered and the steps to configure them are specifically used for records management in SharePoint.

The subtle difference between ECM with records management and ECM without records management is that ECM accommodates living documents as well as documents that will no longer be edited and will be used for reference and consumption only. We have found that this subtle difference has caused a lot of confusion and failure to act on SharePoint ECM projects. The root of the confusion seems to be the records center.

> **Note** If you are trying to determine whether or not to use a records center or in-place records management, remember that it is more of an organizational readiness and policy question than it is a SharePoint feature decision.

Records center vs. in-place records management

Prior to SharePoint 2010, the ability to lock down individual documents as immutable content with a stamp in time, location, content, and metadata was possible only with a special type of template called the records center.

In the records center, all documents were declared records. This gave a single location for records managers to manage their records, and it walled off records from nonrecords. But this created a problem because it did not provide flexibility and, ultimately, limited the domain of the records and Legal department to only this subset of documents. This created a large opportunity (and risk) for large chunks of content to remain in a digital dump without proper records management.

Starting with SharePoint 2010, a new feature of in-place records management was provided so that you could declare a document as a record and allow it to live with nonrecords. This increased the flexibility, allowing organizations to have records management principles across all ECM components in the farm. But it also begs the question, "When do I use records center over in-place records management?"

This seems like a technology and feature question, but it is not. It is a business question, and it has as much to do with the structure of your organization as it does with how it is implemented. As we showed earlier, any library in any site can essentially be converted to a mini records center where all documents sent there are automatically converted to a record, so it's not really a one-or-the-other option.

However, if you do commit to the records center, you are locked into a practice that must be maintained and that presents some risk and complexity if you want to undo or remove the features.

To help the organization make the decision about which method to use, here are some of the questions that you should ask the ECM team:

- Is it feasible to have nonrecords mixed with records?

- Can the curators of a record see the record after it is established as one?

- Do you have a dedicated records manager?

- Is the dedicated records manager responsible for all content or only for a particular subset of content?

- Are living documents excluded from the legal process of the organization?

- Is everything considered a record?

Table 8-2 provides the answers to these questions in the context of the records management system types.

TABLE 8-2 Records management decision matrix

Question	Response	In-Place Records Only	Records Center Only	Hybrid
Is it feasible to have nonrecords mixed with records?	Yes	X	-	X
Can the curators of a record see the record after it is established as one?	Yes	X	-	X
Do you have a dedicated records manager?	Yes	X	X	X
Is the dedicated records manager responsible for all content, or only for a particular subset of content?	Yes	-	X	-
Are living documents excluded from the legal process of the organization?	Yes	-	X	-
Is everything considered a record?	Yes	-	-	-

The matrix in Table 8-2 relates a positive response to the questions and what that implies in terms of features. You can see that a "yes" on only questions 3,4,5 has any implication to doing a records center, and only 4 and 5, which are rare scenarios, imply a clear need for using only a records center. If you have a records manager whose scope of influence or effort is only a small subset of highly critical documents, it's more convenient to remove those documents from the creators' eyes and put them in a single site collection or site where the records manager can operate. Similarly, if according to the organization's mandate, living documents are not considered records, it's important to isolate records from living documents to wall them off.

Most the time, we see that organizations find it hard to justify a records center only. We believe that a "yes" response to question 4 spells some serious problems for the organization, because limiting the scope of a records manager's manageable content is contrary to the purpose of the role of protecting the organization. And it's not common for organizations to not consider living documents as serious content.

Therefore, we find that most organizations have in-place records or a hybrid scenario. We would recommend starting with the in-place records management approach, and add hybrid later if needed.

In the hybrid approach, you establish a library in a site where the setting of the library is that all documents in this library are automatically declared as records. The biggest benefit of this feature is that the average users might not need to see documents declared as records on a regular basis, which prevents them from being inundated with a records declaration process or slowing interactions with content that is not considered a record. This can especially be true with our recommended approach of flatter IAs. By moving the documents to a separate library where they can be declared as records automatically but also allowing declaration of records in the spot where they live, the organization has the greatest flexibility.

The problem with the hybrid approach is that it requires thought and intention for some users who might not be familiar with the concepts outlined in this chapter. If it's a records manager, this is a part of their daily job, but if it is a knowledge worker, this will often be neglected and not followed, resulting in documents that should have been moved to a records library and declared a record.

Again, we recommend starting with the in-place records management approach until such time that declared records of a particular type become troublesome for day-to-day users.

We have covered in detail the features of records management in SharePoint, but what about their application? After all, this is one of the killer problems of SharePoint, where features are easy to throw out to the masses but usage of those features is not contained, nor is correct usage established. The processes themselves are as important as the features that make the processes possible.

Records management processes in SharePoint

In the last chapter, we talked about governance. With the records management portions of SharePoint, governance over features is key. Let's start with who manages this governance.

In larger organizations, there is no question of who is in charge of the accuracy, consistency, and management of the content. This individual is usually given the title Records Manager or Content Manager. They will be found in all regulated industries and in government.

Looking at smaller nonregulated organizations, the records management position is not common, and it's unfortunate. Having a role responsible for content shows intent to manage content in the correct way. Without the intent, contributors to the system are considering only their immediate goals with the system, such as uploading or searching for content. These actions add up, usually not in a positive way, to a collection of events that can pollute the content management system.

Our hope would be, even in small organizations that do not have the ability to hire a specific role for a records manager, to establish this as a duty of one of the existing roles. Making it the responsibility of an existing role that the organization does require will allow for some to take ownership of the records manager function. Without this, the organization is at high risk for being unsuccessful with the ECM solution, along with records management.

In addition to the oversight, the interaction and the abilities of users is also very important. SharePoint, with all its flexibility, opens many back doors to doing the wrong thing. For example, workspaces allow users to avoid metadata and records declaration, even if in a records center.

Not only is the organization responsible for planning out records management, the features, and how they will be used, it also, as we described in Chapter 7, "ECM planning guide," needs to plan how those features are governed. Records management done incorrectly is the equivalent of not doing it at all. Here are the top questions to consider when governing the records management features of SharePoint:

- **Who can declare a record?**   Can anyone declare records? If yes, all users need to be trained on what types of content should be declared a record, and when. If this can be automated at the content type level with information management policies, it should be. If everyone can't declare a record, users need to be aware that the feature exists but that they are not to use it.

- **Who can un-declare a record?**   We recommend that only legal and records mangers can un-declare records upon request from users. This should be an extremely rare occurrence. It is possible with a flexible security model, where users are all content owners, to determine which users can have the option to navigate to compliance details and un-declare a record. If so, they need to be aware of this feature, and a policy needs to be created telling them if they are not allowed to use it.

- **Who can run a content audit?**   For most organizations, this is not a concern, other than having more unneeded content that needs to be managed. Because all audits create a new Excel document, you do not want users blindly running the process. However, for the most part, you can allow all users to do so if they need to see the history of a document, but this is rare. For some organizations, there is a concern that users will see information about other users' contribution or viewing of content. Therefore, they might want to create a policy of not allowing users to run audits.

- **Where do audit documents live?**   We do not recommend leaving audit documents in the same location as the content being audited. Instead, we recommend setting up a content organizer drop-off library where all audit documents are placed. When put in this library, they should be routed to a central audit location visible only to certain users. If users can see audits, we recommend adding to your IA an audit library in each site where audit Excel files can be placed.

- **What are the site policies and disposition?**   It sounds funny, but you need to create a policy for site policies, or you need to strongly limit who can be site owners. It is possible for site owners in SharePoint to, at any point in time, set the site closure policy to "no site policy." If you want to allow site owners, such as in project sites, this is a real possibility. There needs to be a policy that is strictly enforced, telling site owners that they cannot remove site closure policies.

- **What do records managers have access to?**   Our hope and recommendation is that records managers have access to all content. The exception to this might be content managed by the executive team, or employee records for the managers and all other employees. Employee documents should never be part of ECM. The record manager should be a site owner on all sites, with the exception of the executive and employee record content, and should not have the ability to audit content, but have the ability to audit the IA and site dispo-sition policies.

- **What happens to physical records that have an electronic equivalent?** Depending on your organization's records management principles, you will have decided what the immuta-ble record is, whether the physical or the electronic. If you have decided that it is the physical record, the records management features in SharePoint should not be used, but there should be a policy that when that physical record is created, the electronic one is deleted completely. Usually the opposite is true, that the electronic document is considered the record. In such a case, the organization needs to be educated that printing a document is for temporary consumption only, and the document should be destroyed after its use is completed, meaning that no physical document should live for more than some period of time, hopefully less than a week. This is a very critical point, because any duplication, even in a different medium, is the equivalent of not doing records management at all.

From the field

I had a client who came to update me months after I had configured their ECM and records management system in SharePoint. The user told me, "Chris, you will be so proud of me, I do not keep any records in SharePoint, only living documents. What I do when a document is completed is I print it, put it in this file cabinet, and then delete from SharePoint." I was shocked. The problem was that SharePoint had been designated as the official system of record, but now the user had decided to make a separate system of record. This was not good practice, and when we explained why, the user understood, although it was still hard for the user to give up the physical documents. - Chris

Next steps

As you have seen, a common theme throughout this book has been that ECM and records manage-ment features in SharePoint are fantastic. However, the success of the system depends on how you plan for and implement the solution. As you start to understand the relationship of features to one another, the relationship of features to users, and how the system as a whole is governed, it becomes much clearer how you will achieve success. SharePoint projects fail most often because of unclear planning for how the ECM solution will be married to the operational business and functional require-ments. This leads to low user adoption and disappointment.

At this point in the book, you have a deep understanding of ECM methodologies, SharePoint ECM features, IA design, and now, records management. In the next chapter, we are going to discuss an extension to records management that we have touched on called *eDiscovery* and *holds*. Like records management, it's not found in all organizations, but the benefits and principles of eDiscovery and holds are useful and relevant to anyone planning an ECM solution in SharePoint.

eDiscovery

For most organizations, electronic discovery (eDiscovery) goes hand in hand with records management. In SharePoint, the two are used together to enable the gathering of content associated with a specific matter. A *matter* is a topic of interest related to compliance, legal, or audit activities.

The reason organizations initiate eDiscovery is to compile content that meets a specific criterion that can be associated with a matter for analysis. A wide scale audit or litigation can become very expensive. It all comes down to the ability to find the information that is required to support eDiscovery. Using SharePoint is a way to reduce the risk and costs associated with retrieving and culling content.

In this chapter, we will first cover in detail the reasoning and principles around eDiscovery and holds, and next we'll look at how these processes are used in SharePoint.

Note This chapter and Chapter 8, "Records management," cover topics of legal matters. All advice in these chapters is from the perspective of real-world applications and configurations of the farm. It is not legal or regulatory advice, and legal counsel should be consulted on the configuration and setup of all features and processes mentioned.

Holds

eDiscovery and holds are technically the same; the only difference is the implications. eDiscovery implies legal-related matters, and *holds* refer to internal or compliance-related audits. For example, someone will usually use the term *eDiscovery* to mean retrieval of content related to a litigation or petition. However, a records manager might use the term *hold* to refer to content being put on hold for audit purposes or related to compliance, such as the Freedom of Information Act or public disclosure in local government, where anyone can request documents related to a particular subject.

For purposes of this book, we will use eDiscovery to define the process, and we will use hold to define the mechanism. A hold is exactly the same as declaring a document a record and noting the hold by some name, such as the matter name, and having a process for releasing the hold. When a record manager refers to a hold, they will refer to it by some name. Often this is the date of the hold, the name of the matter, a code name, or some other relevant identification.

Only large organizations in compliance-driven spaces, often government, will have several holds going on at the same time. The following are three common reasons for using eDiscovery features in SharePoint:

- To bring an early discovery process in-house to reduce cost

- To have a better way to isolate content for audits

- To help justify SharePoint as a system of record in legal matters

Reduce the cost of eDiscovery

A commonly accepted range of $18,000 to $30,000 is used to calculate the cost per GB of data for eDiscovery. You can imagine a large Fortune 1000 organization that needs to manage terabytes of relevant data. The number will typically grow over time, and the requirements of managing that data can be quite daunting. The role of a records manager is to ensure that growth is managed by using retention and disposition so that when an eDiscovery event occurs, the process can be managed effectively. Organizations in the compliance space have little choice but to consider eDiscovery, but organizations that are not in the compliance space and choose not to think about it can be blindsided by tremendous costs. These costs break down into the following four categories:

- Time and labor to isolate and retrieve content related to a matter

- Equipment costs to retrieve and organize content

- Monthly hosting costs to temporarily store matter content in a separate location

- Legal costs to review final culled matter content

If you consider the categories and begin to calculate the costs based solely on labor and professional costs, you can see that the costs can add up quickly. This is the very reason why the technologies and principles around eDiscovery have been established. The legal review cost is the most expensive because the legal team might need to review gigabytes of information at an hourly rate. Providing more accurate and refined results by using SharePoint records management and eDiscovery can reduce the amount of time that the legal team spends reviewing content and thus reduce the costs associated with a matter.

Early case assessment is a term that is used to describe preparing for a matter as soon as possible. In early case assessment, the process of finding and culling content happens as soon as the topic of the matter has been identified, to prevent massive losses due to fines and sanctions related to a matter.

Previously, organizations would send 100 percent of their physical and electronic content to an organization specializing in eDiscovery. The service provider would then charge a per-page processing rate to convert the physical documents to electronic and review the results. After all content was converted to an electronic format, the service provider charged a processing fee per gigabyte to locate content by using search algorithms, predictive coding, and text analytics technology. There was also a substantial setup fee to configure the software tools for the particular job. This also included painstaking configuration of the document imaging hardware and capture software to support the highest image quality and accuracy.

It would not be unheard of for organizations to spend 1–2 million dollars on this process. If this sounds familiar, you know the costs and are preparing for the future. Because you are going down the path of ECM, this should greatly reduce the time spent with external service providers, or ideally, you won't need them at all.

The ECM system, in conjunction with eDiscovery, isolates a subset of content for discovery, and organizations well established in this process might need to contract with a third-party vendor only for validation processes, not the whole outsourced eDiscovery process.

Isolating content

Not only does eDiscovery substantially reduce the cost of matters; it is a tool to improve the way content managers and records teams can review content in bulk.

Let's take the example of a disgruntled employee leaving the organization. The executive team is nervous that the employee might have created improper or erroneous content in the ECM system just prior to leaving, or perhaps they suspect a claim or want to pursue legal action against the former employee.

At this point in time, it would be good to start thinking about what information this employee has interacted with or had access to. In the past, this would be a manual process of first listing all the locations and types of content the employee worked with, perhaps even identifying other coworkers. After each location is identified, a painstaking search of each location is performed to find the content, along with a final sweep of the entire system using a search tool. After all the content is found or discovered, you will want to isolate the content so that it is unalterable. Under normal circumstances, you would have to manually move the content and notify other users of this action.

Now, with the eDiscovery tools found in SharePoint 2013, you can perform a search or variations of search(es) from a single location and then isolate and move content, without poking around in different spots in the farm. This dramatically reduces the risk and effort on the part of those responsible for performing an eDiscovery role.

Litigation support

This new technology and approach to culling content has created a new opportunity as well. The savvy legal teams have realized that, with great technology behind them, they improve their chances of success with a legal matter. Very early on in cases, the legal team, empowered with technology, is introducing the system of record they used to manage content and that they can now also use to cull the content for the case.

They will present flow diagrams of how content is stored, the governance plans, the team established to run the system, the processes to ensure the content's authenticity, and finally, the approach taken to cull and analyze content. They will ask the judge essentially to validate and approve the system used to manage content in the organization, the ECM platform. They will then ask the judge to trust and accept the content that comes from the system of culling they have established.

This gives the legal team a leg up. By getting validation of the discovery procedures in advance, they are giving the judge confidence in the tools and the approach used to manage content, and thus in the validity and honesty of the content itself. The following list of legal standards includes just a few that have made ECM, eDiscovery, and records management solutions a powerful litigation support tool:

- **ABA Rule 1.1 of Professional Conduct**   Lawyers will provide competent representation to a client. Meaning that the tools and system used to represent the client are vetted, stable, and validated.

- **FRCP Rule 37(e)**   Those participating in a matter have semi-safe harbor where destruction of content is carried out in a good faith and in the routine operation of an electronic system. (See Hynix Semiconductor, Inc. v. Rambus, Inc. and Micron Technology v. Rambus.)

- **FRCP Rule 37(f)**   All parties must participate in good faith in developing a proposed content discovery plan as required by 26(f)(3) (which indirectly implies that those with the better system of record have an upper hand in determining the system for obtaining content for the matter).

- **Common law duty**   The expectation to preserve responsive data during a matter. (See Stevenson v. Union Pacific R.R. and Zubulake IV.)

- **FRCP Rule 26(f)(3)(C)**   All parties must develop a discovery plan addressing subject matter, timeframes, and any documented issues which may have impacted content.

- **FRE 901(e)**   Evidence must be properly secured with supporting chain of custody documentation.

- **Seventh Circuit Principles Relating to the Discovery of Electronically Stored Information, Principle 1.02**   An attorney's zealous representation of a client is not compromised by conducting discovery in a cooperative manner. The failure of counsel or parties to cooperate in facilitating and reasonably limiting discovery requests and responses raises litigation costs and contributes to the risk of sanctions. (See also The Sedona Conference Cooperation Proclamation.) The purpose of this principle is to mitigate the risk of one side burdening and wearing down the other side with information requests that they know will be time consuming, delay the matter, and possibly impact the other side's ability to represent itself.

- **FRCP Rule 26(b)(s)**   Electronic information that is not reasonably accessible because of undue burden or costs need not be produced but party must identify source it does not intend to search or from which discovery will not be made. This standard in some ways implies that the easier it is for an organization to perform discovery, the more content they might be asked to produce. However, it does not look good on the side of the party who makes the claim at the beginning of the matter that a large portion of content is not obtainable and thus does not need to be discovered. It will also raise objections from the other side and risk the reputation of the party who claims it.

> **Note** All legal descriptions are from the perspective of real-world experiences involving litigation support and configurations of the farm. It is not legal or regulatory advice, and legal counsel should be consulted on the configuration and setup of all features and processes mentioned.

The only way an organization can take the new approach of proving the system is by having a well-architected, implemented, and governed ECM solution. After that is established, a clear, concise, and measurable eDiscovery process can be implemented using SharePoint features and written policies and procedures.

One of the issues that the legal team will raise will concern the content chain of custody. Chain of custody means there is a custodian. The custodian will include a records manager or content manager role and someone from the legal team or a legal representative. As we noted in Chapter 8, we recommend the assignment of this role to some individual even if it is not a dedicated or full-time position.

The chain of custody is the trail from the point of creation that proves the content was managed in a proper way. This includes being able to prove that it is a single version of truth, supporting omission and destruction of all duplicates and identification of the original content as a record. Additionally, the content has the proper audit tracking to prove who and what have touched the content, even as an automated process. If necessary, the organization will need to show that the content has complied with industry, legal, and internal regulations.

The biggest risk an organization faces is when they do not follow their own rules. Inconsistencies in managing content will imply that there are holes in the system where issues could have arisen. This is the purpose of good planning, governance plans, and a solid immutable Information Architecture (IA) and taxonomy.

eDiscovery processes

We have outlined the steps that are used to support an eDiscovery process. Each organization is unique; specific industries or jurisdictions can require additional steps, so make sure that you work with your legal team to identify any special circumstances or requirements that might differ from the following stages, outlined in Figure 9-1:

1. Content creation / chain of custody activated

2. Information management

3. Trigger of a matter

4. Content identification

5. Content preservation and collection

6. Content processing, review and analysis

7. Matter hearing and decision

8. Content release or archive

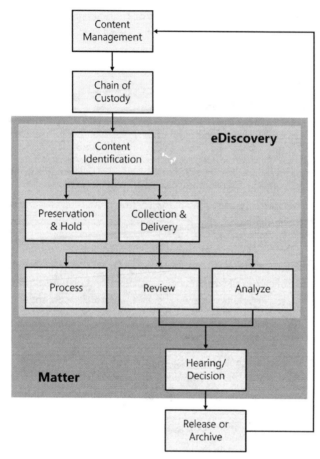

FIGURE 9-1 eDiscovery stages.

Steps 4 and 5 are the actual eDiscovery process as it relates to the ECM solution. And it is the hold process that identifies the content based on search criteria or other filters. The next step is to collect the content, by noting its location and associating it with the hold and, in some cases, moving it to another location. During a matter, which can take months or even years, the content associated with the matter is typically exempt during that time from any information management policies / retention. In addition, the content must be preserved as a record and not altered or spoiled in any way.

Content is then delivered to the tools or the people who will process it, reduce it to its most refined dataset, review and annotate, and finally analyze and make decisions about the content and its influence or impact on a matter.

Note Governance in the world of legal discovery has a slightly narrower focus then the governance topic outlined in Chapter 7, "ECM planning guide." If you speak to a lawyer, the purpose of governance is to protect content and prepare it for legal matters, whereas the governance we are encouraging the reader to embrace not only manages the ECM solution, but it also ensures good adoption and future extension.

The risks associated with not being prepared and not understanding eDiscovery are notable and should be clear. We have outlined the following key risk factors for your consideration:

- Inflated data volumes, which impose a burden if legal matters arise

- Inability in a legal matter to prepare for Rule 26, to meet and confer with all parties

- Advantages to opposing counsel because of inaccurate and incomplete collection of content

- Dramatically increased review costs

- Risk of producing privileged or sensitive information to opposing counsel that is not covered under a protective order

- Monetary sanctions by the court, including punitive damages and attorney's fees

- Negative inference and adverse effects on jury and judge

- Dismissal of case or summary in favor of opposing counsel

As the use of eDiscovery processes continues to mature, we would expect that more improved early case assessment is achieved by providing ECM as the system of record that can identify content related to a matter even before the matter happens. In essence, this means locating high-risk activities or content in advance, alerting records and content managers so that legal matters might be reduced or avoided all together.

Office 365 consideration

We cover Office 365 in Chapter 10, "Extending SharePoint 2013 ECM solutions," but until then, it's important to note a key eDiscovery consideration. One of the biggest challenges when it comes to using the cloud offering is that the amount of data that is stored in the cloud can grow very large as it is contributed or uploaded over a period of time. If that content has to be culled, there could be serious bandwidth costs and latency associated with the transport of content. If you are considering Office 365 but know you have to prepare for eDiscovery, make sure that you understand how eDiscovery will occur and the costs associated with it, especially in the cloud. The precedence here is not strong, but some organizations have claimed the FRCP Rule 26(b)(s) rule that cloud content was not reasonably accessible.

Now that we understand why we do eDiscovery and the principles behind it, let's get into the practice of how the eDiscovery principles can be aided by tools built into SharePoint.

Implementing eDiscovery in SharePoint

Most of the time, SharePoint is not going to be the only system of record. Discovery usually includes email, social media, backups, and archives. If your organization is new to ECM and does not have a solution of any kind, you can add to this list all the local and shared drives, legacy databases, and other physical media or paper records.

Prior to configuring SharePoint for eDiscovery, it's important to plan for the discovery process. This includes listing all electronic repositories that are used to store content, including the location for both electronic and physical records. Determine and document the process for notifying users in the organization that content has been put on hold. For specific users or groups involved in the review process, make sure that the process is well defined for how content will be accessed during the hold. If your organization is also using Exchange as a mail server, you will benefit tremendously from the recent additions in eDiscovery functionality for SharePoint 2013.

At minimum, your organization will have SharePoint and a mail server as locations where discoverable content can reside. The legal and records teams will, in conjunction with all parties in the matter, decide what *discoverable* means. Content most likely is discoverable if it is reasonably accessible, current, and not considered confidential. Confidential records can include documents that contain personally identifiable information such as Social Security numbers or healthcare records. In addition, there could be trade or intellectual property rights to consider. Most litigation processes will provide a protective order to prevent opposing parties from seeing sensitive content that could compromise competitive advantages; this content would be subject to attorneys' eyes only.

> **Note** All legal descriptions are from the perspective of real-world experiences involving litigation support and configurations of the farm. It is not legal or regulatory advice, and legal counsel should be consulted on the configuration and setup of all features and processes mentioned.

In an ideal scenario, you will have moved all your content to SharePoint, including archived email, although any email that is more recent is still discoverable in most cases.

After you have identified all the systems and physical content needed to satisfy discovery on the matter, you will need to define a process for collecting the information. This includes all steps in the discovery process from notifications and collection to release of holds. For each activity, you should list who does it, in what time frame, and where the results go.

Ultimately, all collected information is put in a central location for review. For most organizations, it becomes extremely complex to reconcile content from various systems. In some cases, it might be necessary to isolate a location in each system of record where collected content is stored during the hold period.

In SharePoint, you have two ways to hold content: You can hold it in-place, or you can hold and move. We recommend, unless your legal team advises otherwise, to hold and move the content in SharePoint 2010, and in SharePoint 2013, we recommend that you issue in-place content holds.

Holding the content in-place will keep the content where it originated and declare it as a record. The hold mechanism will then track pointers to the content's location. The reason that we recommend holding and moving the content in SharePoint 2010 is due to limitations in eDiscovery functionality. Discovery in SP2010 is more ad hoc in terms of the steps taken to process. In SharePoint 2013, eDiscovery is set up as more integrated and real-time process, with tracking and reporting. In-place holds are required to maintain the integrity of the content during the discovery process.

If your organization does choose to use the hold and move method, it needs to consider, as part of its IA planning, a location where content should be moved.

This will also include considerations and estimations about the size and the amount of content that will be a part of a typical hold. Most organizations include a specific library in each site collection that is accessible by records managers and legal. In some cases, a subsite is created where the content marked for hold is moved to.

Special consideration needs to be given to who can run eDiscovery and who can view collected content. Consult with your legal department to make sure that their requirements are met. We have found that in most organizations, records managers will have the ability to run eDiscovery and holds, but only legal will have the ability to review the content.

At this point, the differences between SharePoint 2010 and 2013 eDiscovery functionality are clearly illustrated. In SharePoint 2010, eDiscovery was a feature on the site collection level. It amounted to a combination of the search functionality in SharePoint and the ability to create holds based on search criteria. You could search for content and then hold in-place or move it to a different library in the farm.

In SharePoint 2013, many new features are introduced, including a new site collection called the eDiscovery Center, built specifically for eDiscovery. This gives the added benefit of centralized discovery. The site provides integration with Exchange mailboxes, the ability to run discovery on shared drives, support for exporting the results of a hold, and finally, an API for automating discovery with external applications or third-party discovery tools.

From here on, we will reference the functionality found in SharePoint 2013. To start using the eDiscovery functionality, a site collection must be created by using the following steps, outlined in Figure 9-2:

1. Go to Central Administration.

2. Under Application Management, click Create Site Collection.

3. On the Enterprise tab, select eDiscovery Center.

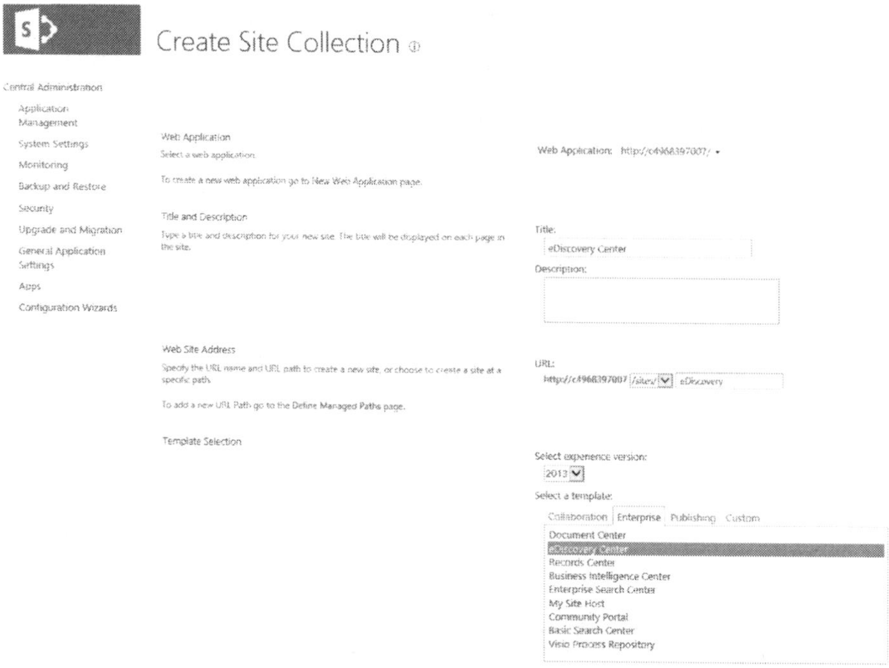

Create Site Collection ⓘ

Central Administration

Application Management

System Settings

Monitoring

Backup and Restore

Security

Upgrade and Migration

General Application Settings

Apps

Configuration Wizards

Web Application

Select a web application.

To create a new web application go to New Web Application page.

Web Application: http://c4968397007/ ▾

Title and Description

Type a title and description for your new site. The title will be displayed on each page in the site.

Title:

eDiscovery Center

Description:

Web Site Address

Specify the URL name and URL path to create a new site, or choose to create a site at a specific path.

To add a new URL Path go to the Define Managed Paths page.

URL:

http://c4968397007 /sites/ ▾ eDiscovery

Template Selection

Select experience version:

2013 ▾

Select a template:

Collaboration Enterprise Publishing Custom

Document Center
eDiscovery Center
Records Center
Business Intelligence Center
Enterprise Search Center
My Site Host
Community Portal
Basic Search Center
Visio Process Repository

FIGURE 9-2 eDiscovery site collection.

In the configuration of the site collection, make sure that the proper records managers and legal groups have access to the site collection. In most organizations, not even IT administrators are added to the security group of this site collection. This will be a one-time setup in conjunction with your IT team, and it should happen as a part of your core ECM deployment.

> **Note** You will not find the eDiscovery template when creating subsites. The eDiscovery Center must be built at the site collection level. This requires some additional planning for most organizations.

Having a separate site collection for eDiscovery allows for legal teams to organize multiple holds in a more comprehensive manner. This is a tremendous benefit because matters are broken into cases. A case technically is created as a subsite of the eDiscovery site collection created with the eDiscovery Case template. This will be the location of all held content associated with a matter. To create a case, on the root page of the eDiscovery Center site, click the Create New Case button shown in Figure 9-3, to the right of the welcome message.

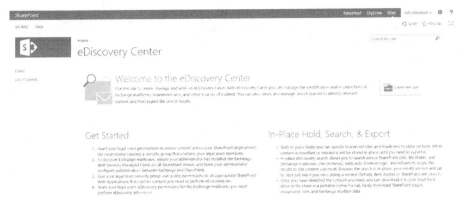

FIGURE 9-3 eDiscovery Center home page.

Next, provide a title, description, and website URL, and then select a template for the new case site, as shown in Figure 9-4.

FIGURE 9-4 New eDiscovery case site.

After you have created the site for the case site, you will have many options for acquiring content, as shown in Figure 9-5. You will have the ability to create eDiscovery sets, perform queries, identify sources, configure exports, review documents, and browse site contents.

FIGURE 9-5 New case home page.

We recommend not making any modifications to the configuration, to the look-and-feel of the eDiscovery Center template, or to the eDiscovery case templates after they are created. The eDiscovery functionality is tied closely to platform-level features such as search, and modifications to the configuration of these sites might impact their ability to function.

There are four custom lists in the eDiscovery case site template:

1. **eDiscovery Sets**   Allows you to specify the combination of locations and a broad criteria for content you want to collect.

2. **Queries**   Searches that are run on held content and used to determine what content, if any, to export from the eDiscovery Center.

3. **Export**   A custom list of all the exports run associated with the case, and the content contained in them.

4. **Sources**   All the locations where content can be pulled. You can also specify with sources the custodian of the content. Today this feature is available only via the discovery API.

While there are various ways to perform eDiscovery with the eDiscovery Center, we recommended the following process:

1. Create an eDiscovery set.

2. Add sources.

3. Create filters.

4. Pick a time period.

5. Preview results.

6. Refine if needed.

7. Save eDiscovery set.

8. Create a query.

9. Export the results of the query.

10. Export the eDiscovery report.

11. Spot-check content for holds.

To create an eDiscovery set, add sources, create filters, and preview results, use the following nine steps, also referring to Figures 9-6, 9-7, and 9-8.

1. In the new eDiscovery case, click the eDiscovery Set button. Here you can view the settings of existing sets, see their status, and even retry holds if necessary.

2. Click the list's New Item button.

3. Give the set a name.

4. Click Add & Manage Sources. This will launch a separate dialog box where you can add mailbox sources from your Exchange server, or location sources. For now, we will assume that all sources you are adding are on the SharePoint farm and thus a location source. Enter the complete URL of the site where content might be stored.

 Note Location might also include shared drives that are accessible by the SharePoint farm. It is recommended, for farm implementations with two levels of IA for site collections and sites, that you start broad and go narrow due to the propensity to create overwhelming result sets. If you start with root site collections, you will get all the content of subsites as well. In the event that the results are overwhelming, try limiting locations to a subset of the sites in that specific collection.

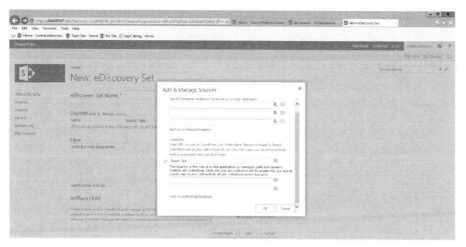

FIGURE 9-6 Add & Manage Sources dialog box for a new eDiscovery case.

Note Attempting to insert source URLs that are URLs for a library will work but they will resolve to the site that the library belongs to. However, URLs for Content Organizer libraries will error. To avoid errors when copying and pasting source URLs, try to stick to the site level URL instead of any page or library.

5. Enter the query for the search. There are lots of options for creating the query. Any search parameters you can use in SharePoint search you can also use for queries configured here, such as logical operators.

6. After you have built a query, remember to click the preview results option. In the Preview Results page, you will see a list of all the content, including the location. To limit content, here you are balancing being too inclusive with not being inclusive enough in your search. Therefore, carefully review the results of the preview as shown in Figure 9-7, to see whether you are getting satisfactory results. It will be the final page of results in the preview that will list potential documents.

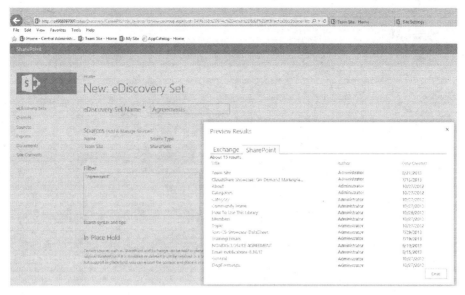

FIGURE 9-7 Preview query results.

When testing out query results, it is always helpful to have a list of trusted content, or those documents in the farm that you know belong to the matter, from manual identification. A listing of 20 documents in various locations in the farm where you have already manually verified that the content relates to the matter/case will help you judge the quality of your query results. If you are not noticing any of these documents in the preview, you have a problem. It could be that the result set is so large that the limited preview is not showing all documents, and therefore omitting those that you included in the manual list. Or it could be that your query is not including the documents that are most interesting to you. Either way, this needs to be addressed prior to completing your new case.

> **Note** When previewing the results and when you do not have mailbox discovery filters set, always make sure that you are on the SharePoint tab of the Preview Results window, as shown in Figure 9-7. It's easy to think that you have no results without clicking this tab, because the Exchange results tab is the default view.

7. You can also filter based on date ranges, authors, senders of emails, and specific domains from Exchange when working with mailboxes.

8. Select the Enable In-Place Hold option as shown in Figure 9-8. As we mentioned earlier, because eDiscovery is an integrated process in SharePoint 2013, you cannot do a hold and move, which is the recommended best practice for SharePoint 2010. Therefore, you will always want to enable in-place holds to protect the integrity and location of content during the case, because this is one of the legal standards imposed on custodians and the discovery process. This will ensure that content will not be altered or deleted during the case, changing its impact on the case or putting the organization at risk after the case.

FIGURE 9-8 Enable in-place hold.

9. After all settings are established, click Apply Filter and then click Save. This will add the eDiscovery set to the eDiscovery sets list.

Keep in mind that you can create multiple eDiscovery sets per case. There is no standard practice for when to choose to create multiple sets, but it will be directly related to the size of your farm, your IA, and the ability to easily create understandable queries that produce the desired results.

The larger the farm, the more likely it is that you will need to separate queries based on different sources so that validation of results is possible in the preview and so that you are validating information in smaller consumable chunks.

The more complex the IA is due to the number of site collections and sites, the easier it is to create an eDiscovery set per site collection. You might create a library per functional group or department, rather than trying to encompass all functions and departments in the same location. If you try to incorporate all site collections together, remember that the preview results will show predominantly locations instead of documents.

And finally, if your queries start to become complex, most notably if you have to use exclude logical operators, it could be a good opportunity to break your filters into separate eDiscovery sets, as shown in Figure 9-9.

FIGURE 9-9 Separating by eDiscovery sets.

The nice thing about this division of labor when it comes to the searches associated with the matter is that the lists provide you a complete guide on the places you have looked for information and the results you have found. This dashboard approach process is also useful when presenting the information and showing how it was discovered during litigation.

Exporting content

Now that you have the specific locations that you collect content from and their broad category of results, you will want to export the content. To perform the export of the content, you must first create a query. This can be confusing because you are essentially querying content twice: once for identification and hold, and then querying that subset for export. The reason this is done is because of the litigation and matter process; you might not want to expose all discoverable content all at once. So although you have identified and held all possible content related to a matter, what you want to export and expose at any given time is a subset of that content that is related to an even more specific topic or discovery request.

To create a query, you will follow the following four steps:

1. Navigate in the eDiscovery case site to the Queries custom list. Here you will see the history and details of all the queries you have already run. This includes the number of results and the size of the results. Click the list New Item button.

2. You can enter a search query here, as illustrated in Figure 9-10. You can limit by criteria including date periods, author, email sender, and now in SharePoint 2013, even the type of document. Before saving your query, click the Search button to see the results in the Query Statistics section and, below that, on the Exchange and SharePoint tabs.

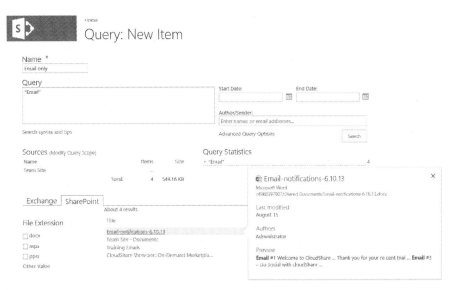

FIGURE 9-10 Creating a new custom query.

 Note In the query creation processes, you want to be as specific as possible and get broad only when needed. In contrast, when you are working with the filter creation process, you want to be as broad as possible and more specific when needed.

3. When you have finished creating your query and are satisfied with the results, you can initiate an export immediately, or you can save and close the query. If you choose to save and close, a new item will be created in the export custom list as a record of an export that is ready to be run.

4. If you choose to initiate export immediately, you will see a new dialog box with export options. We recommend always selecting the following options: Include Versions For SharePoint Documents and Include Items That Are Encrypted Or Have An Unrecognized Format. The export processes will copy the physical files and their metadata from its original location to the location specified in the export. This is done using an ActiveX control called the eDiscovery Download Manager. The results found will be exported to the file location specified in a folder structure that mimics the IA of where the content was found. It will also include a cache folder with system level information used for audits and chain of custody, a reports folder including specific reports, a summary file for the results of the export, and a manifest XML file. This XML file is in the standard Electronic Data Reference Model (EDRM) load file format, which is a standard format for eDiscovery systems. This shows how important the governance of whom, why, and where exported content can be placed is so critical.

A progress bar in the eDiscovery Download Manager dialog box is displayed after you initiate an export, as illustrated in Figure 9-11.

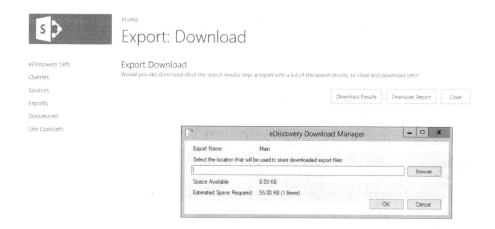

FIGURE 9-11 eDiscovery Download Manager dialog box.

Security

Before any export can happen, the organization must decide the location of exported content and who can run and view it after export. The exported content will take on the security of the location it is exported to; any item-level security or IA-level security will be ignored. This will expose the content to anyone or any workflow process that has access or is otherwise associated to the network share or content export destination location. This could be an immediate security risk for the organization. Most organizations will set up a special network share that is accessible only by legal counsel. This location could have a separate backup system and sometimes is performed using external or mobile drives.

In the exports library will be a history of all exports run and their status. It is easy to get confused between sources in the custom list and sources in eDiscovery sets. The custom list uses a special tracking mechanism for sources, where you can include additional metadata such as custodians and description. When added, you will be given status of the various sources, but they are different sources than in eDiscovery sets. A source added to an eDiscovery set will not show up in the sources custom list and vice versa. It is possible for an organization to never use the sources custom list.

Note The eDiscovery process is very reliant on proper search configuration for the farm. If your organization is facing any issue with SharePoint search, these should be addressed prior to configuring eDiscovery functionality.

The home page of the case site, as shown in Figure 9-12, will have a complete picture of the number of sets associated with the case, the current status of in-place holds and the amount of content associated with those holds, the status of exports, and finally, the queries used for the exports. Within 15-minute intervals, this dashboard should be accurate for the current status and should be a good indicator of how the content collection associated with a matter is being processed, how long it might take, and whether it is progressing as expected.

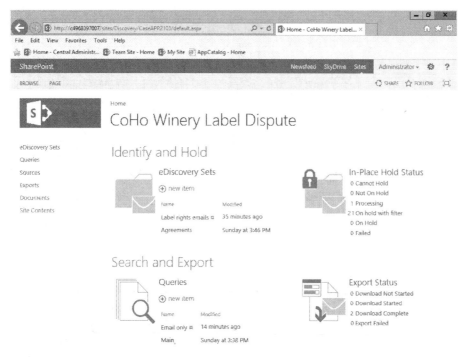

FIGURE 9-12 Case site home page.

The process can vary if the content of the matter is not clear or is in a state of flux. If so, this is an indicator that discovery and culling of content needs to happen in phases. Your legal counsel should make determinations about how eDiscovery will be run, given the functionality established in the various systems, prior to any matter arising.

Notification

While we have covered all the mechanisms and the principles around eDiscovery, there remains one large challenge for the organization, and that is the people.

When discovery happens across an organization, it can be very disruptive. As part of this process, there is a mandatory notification of all owners and consumers of the discoverable content that discovery is taking place. This is not an option that can be avoided. If notification does not occur, users of the content will be confused when they are unable to access content because it is held.

This type of notification can lead to questions and concerns from knowledge workers across the organization. It is compounded by the fact that most of the time the organization and legal team cannot fully disclose the subject of the matter or the status or implications of the case.

When preparing the notification of the matter to the knowledge workers, consider the following:

- Make it timely.

- Scope it correctly.

- Determine a policy for content modification.

- Give clear options for questions.

- Where possible, eliminate doubt.

Make sure that the notification goes out before any discovery has happened. If you have already held content in SharePoint or mailboxes, you are too late. Scope the notification to only the users whose content is affected. For example, if you know that discovery will happen only on the human resources site collection, send notifications only to those users who have access to this site collection.

In the event that a user needs to access or edit content that is related to their work but is being held, create a policy for these types of situations. Ideally, the policy will include the ability to have the content reviewed by legal counsel and, upon approval, have a duplicated editable version created that might be modified to exclude risky content or that is tagged appropriately so that it can be easily accessed if needed in the case.

The notification should not be closed off in its tone, and it should feel to the user that they have some avenue of getting information. We recommend making someone responsible as a single point of contact in the organization who can answer questions. More progressive organizations are building simple SharePoint sites with a FAQ about the matter and a location to submit a question. It can be tricky balancing a vague notification that produces too many requests with a notification that exposes too much about the matter. After the idea of the matter has settled in with the knowledge workers affected, the typical behavior will be to submit requests only for questions related to a particular piece of content a user might need to edit.

And finally, try your best to curb doubt. The last thing you want is to create a chain reaction of doubt in the system, or a fear of the ECM solution that results in poor user adoption. Do not draw attention to the process any more than needed, and do not make users feel that contribution to the system will hurt them. If possible, use the process as an example of how great user adoption is and how the use of ECM has put the organization in a good position with a process to support litigation in a simplified and organized manner.

For organizations in regulated industries, chances are your users have faced matters before, and it will not be too surprising. The element that could be surprising is the efficiency in which discovery can now happen by using SharePoint, yet the ability to lock content might be very discomforting. Users should be made aware that the lock down is also to their benefit and protects them from being more involved in the case than they might want to be.

Next steps

We have taken you across the spectrum of governance and control. From general Enterprise Content Management, through creation of governance policies for good user adoption and proper usage, to the stricter records management features and principles, and finally to what happens to content when it is associated with a legal or compliance matter.

Not all organizations will incorporate all components of these topics. In fact, the vast majority of organizations fail to take advantage of the general ECM features of SharePoint and, unfortunately, have to deal with eDiscovery from time to time. However, understanding all the features and principles is important to help your organization to understand what could be looming in the future, and things they should consider adopting to be better prepared, to increase efficiency, and to reduce cost if these issues arise.

In an ideal world, all SharePoint farms will have the beginnings of all the functionality we mentioned, but we know this is not the case. For the sake of taking a step forward, if your organization does not fully adopt the records management and eDiscovery functionality of SharePoint 2013, make sure to document in your governance plans the options for these components and at which point in time you will consider taking them on.

CHAPTER 10

Extending SharePoint 2013 ECM solutions

As we explained in Chapter 1, "ECM defined," SharePoint is a platform. The platform contains a collection of features that can be configured to provide an ECM solution, and it provides many other application solutions that an organization can leverage for specific-use cases.

Because it is a platform, it has more flexibility than other industry-specific ECM products provide. This chapter will first cover the unique ways that SharePoint can be extended or used in varying capacities, by exploring SharePoint in the cloud with Office 365. We will then discuss the strong ecosystem of integrators and third-party tools that are available to extend and enhance SharePoint ECM solutions.

Some of the material we will cover in this chapter is forward-looking and somewhat speculative, based on the best available information at the time. We do not advocate or include any specific marketing or positioning of third-party software vendors or integrators; instead, we have outlined functional areas and features in SharePoint that companies have focused on to provide extensibility by use of these third-party products.

Office 365

Up until the last two years, SharePoint has been installed primarily as an on-premise solution. We use the term *on-premise* to mean that all software bits and configurations are installed on the organization's servers within their firewall and domain infrastructure. While some companies have offered hosted versions of SharePoint, the vast majority of deployments are on-premise, and we generally include in our definition any hosted instances of SharePoint that belong to a single organization.

For purposes of this chapter, we determine that it is an on-premise solution or a cloud solution by asking: "*Who controls and has access to the servers hosting the farm?*" If the answer is a third-party service vendor, you are using SharePoint in the cloud; if the answer is your IT department, we consider it on-premise.

But even SharePoint in the cloud has evolved rapidly. As the cloud has become more popular, Microsoft has started to facilitate SharePoint running in the cloud. First they introduced the concept of multitenant farms, where various organizations could share the same farm but have completely separate and walled-off instances of SharePoint.

This gave rise to hosting vendors who offered shared instances of SharePoint. Microsoft itself had a hosted SharePoint offering called Business Productivity Online Standard, or BPOS, which was renamed to Office 365.

With the rename came big advantages from a user experience standpoint. The primary benefit was that SharePoint in Office 365 was no longer just a hosted version of SharePoint on Microsoft's servers; it also provides a fully integrated version of Office web applications for Word, Excel, and PowerPoint as an independent product and service offering.

SharePoint in Office 365 became less connected to the on-premise solution and received its own frequent release cycles and product teams. This means that although the core of SharePoint 2013 on-premise and SharePoint in Office 365 are the same, they are on different development paths, with a shared road map.

On-premise SharePoint continues to receive regular service pack releases every three to six months, while Office 365 follows a more agile release process, with releases every month and in some cases weekly.

The other huge difference is that SharePoint is referred to as a component of Office 365 and usually not called out as a specific functionality. It joins email and Office Productivity applications to become a whole suite.

With Office 365's agile release processes and fully integrated approach, it makes it more of a moving target and is harder to reference in terms of the Enterprise Content Management solutions.

Office 365 offers a complete solution of ECM-like functionality, with minimal effort to purchase, provision, and set up. Office 365 also expands to large organizations and soon will have virtual private instances, making it nearly indistinguishable from on-premise instances, with the exception of who manages the data center and physical/virtual server infrastructure.

 Note Throughout this chapter, we will refer to differences in functionality or options that you might have as they pertain to Office 365 and third-party software utilities and solutions. This information is relevant at the time of writing the book, during the first half of calendar year 2013.

Important comparisons

There are numerous user, administration, and architecture differences between on-premise SharePoint 2013 and Office 365. We will focus on the primary areas of comparison as they relates to the ECM topics covered in this book. At this point, Office 365 does not fully support content type and metadata navigation or remote BLOB storage, and there is no dedicated central administration. Now let's cover each of these in a little more detail:

- **Content type and metadata navigation**   This feature provides users the ability to browse and filter libraries based on their metadata. We suspect that the limitations on using content types and metadata for faceted navigation in libraries is a feature that will soon be part of the general Office 365 offering.

- **Remote BLOB storage**   Currently, Office 365 has a limitation in the ability to externally store binary large objects (BLOB) of content to secondary sources that are not directly managed by SharePoint. The purpose of this feature in on-premise SharePoint is to help increase performance when storing large files or to accommodate the archive requirements of ECM and records management. In the scenario of accommodating large files, an obvious reason for this limitation is bandwidth considerations. Office 365 has a current file size limit of 2 GB, which accommodates the vast majority of files. We speculate that there will be some remote BLOB storage functionality in the future that might include Azure BLOB storage with Office 365. Office 365 does not currently have a solution that would facilitate a records management archive. If your organization requires an archive and uses Office 365, we recommend adopting a procedure where archived content is moved from Office 365 to an on-premise instance of SharePoint. Office 365 is recommended for use of active content only.

- **Isolated central administration**   The biggest challenge of Office 365 as it relates to ECM functionality is not having isolated central administration access. Office 365 does provide each organization a management dashboard that is similar to central administration, but there are limitations to its functionality. This impacts those features specifically configured at the platform level, such as Publishing, Managed Metadata, SendTo locations, and your Information Architecture. The net result is that while you will have access to all these features, the amount of customization is limited. For example, you will not have the amount of granularity with your Information Architecture as you will with an on-premise instance of SharePoint. The same is true for content type publishing. We suspect that as the virtual private instances become publicly available to larger organizations, all functionality available in central administration will be available.

From its BPOS days to the most current release of Office 365, Microsoft has adapted very quickly and continues to make improvements toward offering all the required functionality you find in SharePoint on-premise. Just two years ago, the limitations for attempting to use ECM principles or build a solution with Office 365 were too great to attempt configuring a complete solution. Now, the greatest limitation for any organization is not features but rather content governance and connectivity or bandwidth limitations.

Data security

Because a cloud service provider, in this case Microsoft, can technically access the information stored in Office 365, each organization needs to consider this as part of their governance strategies. When considering security in the cloud, there are two primary threats: the threat of it being a cloud service, thus exposed to the public web, and the threat of the service provider employees accessing information.

Cloud service providers take very seriously the custody and security of data they store or process. There is nothing more critical to the backbone of establishing a trusted relationship with customers than security. Because of this, they take very seriously how they isolate content from other customers and how they prevent their staff from accessing customer data. We encourage you to review carefully all Microsoft policies currently in place to determine your organization's comfort level with the Office 365 policies in place at this time. The threat posed by a cloud service provider having a breach due to an employee accessing your content is somewhat unrealistic. The sheer volume of data and the steps necessary to crack encryption keys and breach the security architecture present a very low probability of success for a breach. Then you have to factor in the end game; ask yourself how far an employee would be willing to stick their neck out to make it worth their while to take this type of action. They could lose their job, face the possibility of litigation or criminal prosecution, and permanently damage their professional reputation. Typically, and in the case of most cloud service providers, they do require the need to access individual instances to provide support services based on your requests. In the case of Microsoft employees accessing individual instances of Office 365, they access configurations based only on your support requests. It is in the best interest of the organization to protect your content and your configurations. We believe the threat of a vendor damaging or accessing your information is no greater than the same threat from a disgruntled employee or from a visitor to an organization's private network, and thus should generally be disregarded as a threat. In the event your organization has confidential, highly sensitive, or proprietary information that will be stored in Office 365, our recommendation is that this subset of information be stored in an on-premise instance of SharePoint. The same recommendation should be made during the Information Architecture (IA) design for on-premise solutions where a handful of employees have access to this type of information.

The threat of the public Internet is the second consideration that we need to address. Public cloud service providers staff network operations centers (NOCs) 24 hours a day, 365 days a year. The professionals working in these NOCs are at the top of the IT world and specialize in network security. When comparing the security of Microsoft's NOC team to the typical organization's IT security team, they are far more secure and advanced because of the round-the-clock monitoring and access to tools most other organizations will not typically have. For this reason, 9 times out of 10 the security of information in Office 365 SharePoint is more secure than an organization that currently has a SharePoint instance open to the public web.

There might be circumstances that will prevent you from having any content in the cloud. These are usually related to your local government's content privacy acts or to specific regulations within your industry. These same regulations will prevent you from having a SharePoint 2013 on-premise instance with public web access. In these cases, you do not have an option, and you should consult all your government and industry-related compliance specialists or representatives prior to choosing an ECM solution.

Bandwidth and accessibility

The next challenge that organizations must consider, and often much more impactful then security, is that of accessibility. While there is limited offline access to Office 365 SharePoint, it is assumed that using the solution requires Internet access.

Accessibility to the Internet is becoming more ubiquitous every day, and performance improvements are constantly being made. The most common mistake organizations make when evaluating accessibility of Office 365 with on-premise SharePoint is not accurately identifying and diagnosing availability issues within their own network.

Every network, whether cloud or on-premise, will face accessibility issues from a user's point of view. These could be due to poor Virtual Private Network (VPN) connectivity, physical network infrastructure issues with switches or routers, poor wireless connectivity, or any number of other issues related to the network. In each of these cases, downtime is going to happen. Organizations need to compare their internal service-level agreement (SLA) over a period of a year or two with the current SLA of the cloud service provider. Many are surprised to discover that their internal availability has been less over the years than that of Office 365. Now add to that the ability of your users to access the public web, and you might have a slight degree in difference when comparing the availability of on-premise versus the cloud. This is especially true for organizations with large numbers of remote employees, but for the most part, organizations find the availability within the tolerable range of productivity, and this is improving every year.

Similar to availability of the public web, Office 365 does suffer from bandwidth limitations that users within the firewall using an on-premise SharePoint will not face. The transfer rates of the web will most likely impact users attempting to upload or download large documents. This is also an issue when bulk-loading large document sets or folders and performing the export scenarios we talked about in Chapter 9, "eDiscovery."

Actions demanding large amounts of bandwidth can be very challenging when working with any cloud solution. The frequency of these activities will help determine what type of solution is best for your situation.

As you can see, the arguments for moving to Office 365 are stronger than not in most cases, and this will be the general trend over the coming years. We also see a lot of interest in a hybrid approach, which could be useful in the following scenarios:

- Keeping records management on-premise and active content in Office 365

- Keeping archive on-premise and active content in Office 365

- Moving all collaboration to Office 365 and then moving final documents or records of business to on-premise SharePoint

The benefit of the last hybrid scenario is that it avoids all the issues discussed with eDiscovery and large document actions because these actions will tend to happen in the on-premise configuration of SharePoint rather than in Office 365. In this scenario, the day-to-day document creation and editing will happen in a very flat version of your IA configured in Office 365, and then you can migrate the final documents to your on-premise SharePoint ECM solution. This approach gives users the most up-to-date cloud and mobile experience but also requires a formal policy and training on where and when to create content and then moving or migrating it to when completed.

Whether your organization chooses Office 365, on-premise, or hybrid, there are very few technical limitations to accomplishing the goal. Just remember that the ECM principles outlined in this book and the IA planning need to remain the same.

Besides Office 365, the other area where SharePoint is very unique and deserves additional consideration is when working with third-party services and tools.

Third-party services and tools

What the SharePoint third-party market has in common with Office 365 is the rate at which it is changing. From the point when we first started this book, we have seen constant change in the variety of vendors, the tools, and the expansion of the market. Most SharePoint implementations incorporate a third-party tool, and most often come in the form of a custom web part.

In this section, we will look at the specific types of third-party service and tools. We will list the benefits of each type of solution and give you some advice on how to work with the vendors. We will also highlight some things to watch out for as they relate to ECM.

> **Note** We are not providing a list of vendor names and products, and we are not including this information to be used as any specific recommendation or endorsement of third-party SharePoint tools or software solutions. We encourage you to attend many of the SharePoint-specific events, like SharePoint Saturday and the Microsoft WPC conference, to get your own perspective on what is available.

Backup and recovery

This segment of tools for SharePoint is one of the oldest categories of third-party solutions. These types of solutions relate specifically to on-premise instances of SharePoint. In the world of ECM, they often get grouped with archive tools. While the technical approaches might be identical, the use case of backup and recovery is distinctly different. The use of tools for performing archive imply content that is designated as discoverable and should be kept intact with the original IA. Backup and recovery deals with the ability to restore content in the case of data loss or disaster from unplanned events. The content in a backup and recovery system might or might not be discoverable, and content can be modified. It's recommended that organizations first explore the built-in SharePoint functionality for backup and recovery before considering a third-party solution.

The primary considerations for ECM in backup and recovery are going to be the retention policies placed on backups, the discoverability of backups, and the frequency. Third-party solutions typically offer greater granularity of options for scheduling backups and the types of backups, even including special rules based on content types and metadata. Most organizations consider SharePoint backup and recovery as part of a broad backup and recovery strategy, which can include disaster recovery, which is the process of making sure that an organization can be up and running in an alternate location rapidly. If disaster recovery is part of your organization's planning, considerations for moving the environment farm or for farm replication will be required. There are both out-of-the-box SharePoint options and more robust third-party tools available for this.

Business intelligence

A growing category of third-party solutions is in the area of business intelligence (BI). These tools allow organizations to manipulate and visualize data and, in a larger context, also incorporate the concepts of BigData. Currently, this is largely dominated by transactional type data, but we are starting to see this blend into the world of unstructured content as well. SharePoint offers some out-of-the-box visualization technology in the Enterprise CAL with the Performance Point features. However, there are third-party tools that exist that take BI even further. These third-party solutions today are closely tied to SQL server and are often add-ins to SQL instead of SharePoint. Because BI and BigData have not yet found their place in the unstructured content or ECM world, they are not tremendously useful in visualizing and analyzing content. However, they do participate in ECM when you are considering the usage of the platform from an analytics standpoint. Creating and manipulating data around the types of content users are contributing to the system, the frequency of content, and even pattern identification across metadata are allowing organizations to get a window into SharePoint adoption that they would not otherwise have had. This is used to spot risky behavior or inconsistent usage. For example, analyzing patterns across content might help an organization identify that a particular document is misplaced in the wrong library, without browsing libraries manually or using search functions. Prior to acquiring these types of solutions, we recommend that you have a specific business goal or outcome that your organization is trying to achieve.

Business process management

A very popular category of third-party solutions related to ECM comprises the various Business Process Management (BPM) and workflow tools. As we stated in Chapter 2, "ECM stack–content in," the biggest difference between BPM and workflow is the administration layer of the workflows created. BPM tools allow you to create many workflows, version workflows, deal with change management, track in real-time document processing, and provide a larger range of workflow events and triggers. The typical workflow in ECM is related to content approvals. Organizations that are extending SharePoint into other applications such as human resources, bids, and proposals, and other line-of-business processes have a much greater need to integrate ECM content with the larger business process.

For these organizations, the functionality in out-of-the-box SharePoint workflows might not be enough, or because of the number of workflows, the administration of the workflows might be too time-consuming. In these instances, we tend to see a large adoption of third-party BPM tools. As always, we recommend that organizations start with the out-of-the-box workflows until they hit a limitation. However, there is the additional consideration of the number of workflows. SharePoint does not allow you to version or manage workflows collectively. If your organization is faced with 10 or more moderately complex workflows, it is worthwhile to consider a solution that allows you to version those workflows and manage them in a single location. Versioning of workflows allows you to have different versions of workflows running on content based on the evaluation of specific metadata properties, which might be critical to maintaining compliance under certain circumstances.

Content enrichment

While ECM ensures that content is timely, accurate, and secure, it does not always consider the quality of information. The quality of the content and the metadata of documents are the responsibility of the user most of the time. However, there is a class of third-party tools called *content enrichment tools*. These tools help improve the quality of content without the help of users. They can provide auto-classification of content, automatically apply content types and taxonomy terms, or generate summaries. In some cases, they can extract critical or known elements included in the content, such as people, places, and values. Content enrichment tools operate on content when it is modified, uploaded, or in bulk, initiated by a workflow or by the individual user. They use natural language processing (NLP) or predictive coding to read the body of documents to produce results.

It is important for the organization to understand how it will use such a technology. If the purpose of using such a technology is to feed a workflow, accuracy is paramount, so the vendor's tool should be put through a pilot project or proof of concept.

If the purpose of using such technology is to improve the quality of search, performance and inclusion of keywords are important. Various tests of real documents should be run with the tool and compared to search without the additional metadata. For organizations in regulated industries, you will have the additional consideration of making sure that metadata is not added to a library that should not be visible to some users who have access to the library. An example of this might be personally identifiable information, like extracting or exposing Social Security numbers. Content enrichment is a great benefit to ECM processes and should be considered during the planning stages with the ECM committee.

Remote BLOB storage

While SharePoint has built-in functionality for remote BLOB storage (RBS), many organizations find that they do not have the ability to configure it correctly. This is a consideration for on-premise SharePoint only. There are various third-party solutions that make the setup and maintenance of RBS a lot easier. All the same considerations given to RBS as an extension of what SharePoint already provides should be considered with any third-party solution. Organizations will choose a third-party solution when the staff, or other internal expertise, is not present to configure connectors for RBS manually. Additionally, some of these solutions provide a dashboard that gives a sense of the usage of content externalization and a way to monitor performance and other system-related storage issues. The primary consideration organizations need to make with such a solution is its reversibility. When you commit to content externalization, you are limited to the things you can do with SharePoint, and you might be limited in the future when planning an upgrade.

> ### From the field
>
> *I have seen customers get into trouble by not fully understanding the outcomes that result from third-party solutions. You should ask the vendor what happens if you want to remove their solution. Can content be moved back into SharePoint? What happens to metadata? What is the fail-safe mechanism if the link between SharePoint and external content is broken? The vendor should have detailed answers to all these questions, and you should consider the benefits or risks of each response fully in relation to your current and long term content strategy. - Chris*

Governance and security

User governance, content governance, monitoring, and security tools are the largest category of third-party SharePoint solutions that have a moderate influence on ECM. We group them together because they all fall under the scenario of observing adoption of the platform. Chapter 6, "User adoption," covered the importance of user adoption, and these tools can help with that effort. Because they tend to be platform-level solutions for on-premise SharePoint installations, they end up being a part of all applications deployed on the platform. In the area of ECM, these tools can be very useful in the early days of an ECM deployment to see how users are adopting the system. It can help to point out where active usage is taking place and to detect functions that are not leveraging the platform fully. It can also point out inconsistencies in usage and, more specifically, identify the behavior of individual users. We see such tools used very early on in ECM adoption and on an infrequent basis when the platform success is being evaluated or there is a specific need to audit content and usage. The biggest consideration for ECM planning is to know how these tools will direct or influence IA. Very often, such tools have specific requirements on sites and site collections. The ECM team, if the tool is already in place, needs to be aware of any of these restrictions before planning the use of the application. If the solution comes later, the team needs to test fully the solution in a test or development environment to make sure that it does not break any functionality that is already configured in the farm.

Integration with LOB

We understand that most organizations are faced with many content silos. Because of this, not all of their content is located in SharePoint. An organization might have another critical line-of-business (LOB) application, such as accounting packages, enterprise resource planning (ERP), or customer relationship management (CRM). In an ideal world, these applications are integrated with SharePoint. Integrations are a broad category, and there are many third-party solutions available. Integrations tend to be very specific from SharePoint to another vendor's product, so the choices of any one specific solution can be limited. For example, Microsoft and SAP have partnered to create Duet, which is integration with SharePoint and the SAP ERP solution.

There are also the integration scenarios where content needs to be synchronized between one platform and another. What we have found is that the general content sync scenarios are done on a case-by-case basis by many one-off integrations. Microsoft and a group of other organizations called OASIS have created a standard called Content Management Interoperability Services (CMIS). This standard is available in SharePoint and many content management platforms offered by third-party vendors for exchanging content and metadata. The standard includes functionality around things such as holds, records, and metadata. If your organization does not use a tool that implements this standard, you need to independently be aware that content migration from one platform to another might not include metadata, hold, record declaration, and other audit information that is critical for compliance and security. If integration is an important component to your SharePoint implementation, it needs to be considered at the very beginning, because retroactive integration almost always fails. Extensive testing needs to be done prior to any implementation.

Records management

While the functionality in SharePoint is very robust, it has some limitations compared to more mature records management platforms. These limitations exist mainly from a custody management, auto-scaling, and linkage of content types to retention schedules. There is a handful of third-party records management solutions that install externally or within SharePoint to provide this functionality. They will allow better reporting on custody of content. They address the problem of putting content into separate records management locations where large amounts of content will exceed the best practices of SharePoint sites and site collection sizes. And they help relate and automate the creation and update of content types based on published retention schedules. The best part of these solutions is that they use the terminology and practices that are recognized by records management communities. Governments or other highly regulated organizations typically need these solutions. First, the organization should identify the limitations of out-of-the-box SharePoint records functionality. If they are numerous, consider a third-party solution.

From the field

Like storage externalization, the considerations around a records management solution should be how do you reverse or undo any content that has been stored using the tool? Are you able to upgrade SharePoint after using such a tool? What is the fail-safe for content if the tool stops working and you need to obtain access to it? Currently these solutions are limited to on-premise implementations of SharePoint. - Shad

Document imaging

As we mentioned in Chapter 2, document imaging and image capture are a big consideration for organizations with paper documents that they want to store inside of SharePoint. Image capture is one area where the built-in SharePoint functionality needs to be augmented with third-party technology. When considering image capture solutions, it's important to note that most of the best capture solutions live outside of SharePoint. The second element that you need to consider is acquiring a tool to get document images and related metadata that has already been captured and converted from an external capture product into SharePoint libraries as a bulk loading process that includes metadata. This can often happen if a third-party organization is contracted to perform a backfile conversion of paper records. The content and its associated metadata will already be available to be uploaded in bulk to SharePoint. The processes used for capturing document images with high-speed scanners are less technically complex than extracting data or providing auto classification of documents using optical character recognition (OCR) or intelligent character recognition (ICR) software. You will find that picking the best-of-breed capture solution without regard for integration with SharePoint is important as a stand-alone consideration. Investing in integration efforts that meet your specific requirements and finding a bulk upload tool and process that will meet performance demands is more important than choosing a capture solution for its integration with SharePoint. In document capture solutions, you should look for scan quality, conversion or OCR/ICR quality, and file size as primary considerations. In our experience, the capture solution that produces the highest quality images, with the best OCR results and the smallest image size, are the slowest of capture solutions. If speed is a primary consideration, incorporate this consideration from a capture and process design standpoint early on. You might find that multiple tools to support the requirements will be necessary.

From the field

When SharePoint 2010 was released, many of the existing ECM capture vendors were slow to recognize the impact the platform would have on the market. After it became clear that SharePoint was going to be, or already was, everywhere, many of these vendors began to build connectors to SharePoint without understanding the underlying limitations or downstream implications of bulk loading large volumes of document images into SharePoint. I recommend that you take into consideration the total volume of SharePoint content that will be document imaging related and make sure that your IA, records management and RBS architecture are well thought out. - Shad

Social

Over the last three years, there has been a lot of hype about the benefits of social in the area of content creation and management. These tools can be beneficial to the nature of the content and to adoption. A well-implemented approach to social will take communication type content and move it to feeds. This ultimately reduces this amount of content in the ECM system and focuses the system in line with business documents, which makes it easier to manage, organize, and secure. So implementing social in your SharePoint environment will reduce the frequency and need for certain kinds of content while increasing the ability to manage the system. Because social is engaging, it is a way to bring users frequently back to the system; this can be both good and bad for adoption. In some cases, this encourages adoption only on social elements, but with most social implementations, the conversations are accompanied with document references, so this helps increase the adoption of the ECM system. Social is functionality that most organizations say they want, but they do not put a lot of thought into how they will use it. If your organization is considering social, first work with the out-of-the-box functionality in MySites and see whether this is meeting your goals with social. If it is not, consider the elements that are missing and then look at third-party tools. Like so many third-party add-ons, these can make upgrading to newer versions of SharePoint complex. Records management teams need to consider also where social conversations fit on their retention schedule and whether this content needs to be maintained and or monitored.

From the field

Many organizations have adopted social media as a tool for internal and external communication in various forms. In many cases, they don't realize the impact this can have during an eDiscovery event. Not only are the actual documents related to an eDiscovery event considered discoverable, but all discussions and communication surrounding the document are considered relevant. If you are using social communication platforms in concert with your general business operations, you need to account for these message streams in your records management and eDiscovery policies and practices. - Shad

General considerations

Third-party tools abound in the SharePoint space. The categories we have already outlined in this chapter include specific considerations, but we also need to highlight other critical elements that are true for any third-party tools. We highly recommend that your organization take the time to under-stand the following: Too many organizations have ignored these issues, and they have been forced to delay upgrades to newer versions of SharePoint and either remove or replace a third-party applica-tion. Following are some considerations you should be aware of:

- **Native versus non-native**   Is the third-party tool a native or non-native SharePoint solu-tion? Native SharePoint solutions are built using the best practices and object models of SharePoint. In SharePoint 2010, this meant building solutions, features, web parts, and timer jobs. In SharePoint 2013, it typically means building according to the new App model, with the exception of some farm-level tools. Non-native applications, while they can still be created and viewed in SharePoint, launch code that is separate from the SharePoint inter-faces. Sometimes non-native applications are easy to spot, and other times they are not. For example, it could be an application that launches from SharePoint separate ASPX pages that are not SharePoint pages, or perhaps it stores data in the server registry instead of leverag-ing application-isolated libraries and lists. We recommend considering only native SharePoint applications. The reason for this is that if the application follows the structure of the platform, it means that it is immediately easier to upgrade and to migrate to and from. This is because when Microsoft releases new versions or updates to SharePoint, they do regression testing on all the platform features. Because native applications leverage all platform features, including using lists and libraries for settings and configurations, upgrading to and from them is tested as part of the standard processes. However, with non-native applications that create exceptions, those exceptions are never tested, unless tested by the third-party vendor, which is usually severely delayed from Microsoft release dates. This is why many organizations find that the SharePoint farm that contains non-native third-party applications gets damaged during each service pack or release that is applied. In the worst-case scenario, they are prevented from ever upgrading to a newer version of SharePoint. The best examples of native SharePoint applications are actually the Central Administration and eDiscovery Center. Both are custom configurations of SharePoint that solve specific problems, one to manage the farm and the other to manage eDiscovery. All their settings are stored in SharePoint libraries and lists, and editing and changing configuration happens using built-in SharePoint features. These are fantastic examples of native SharePoint applications.

- **External applications** It is not always clear whether the third-party solution lives outside of SharePoint and integrates with it via the object model or REST calls or whether the application lives within the SharePoint runtimes, as in the case of native SharePoint applications. As we noted in the preceding list bullet, imaging, and in fact, any capture tool, is better as an external application from SharePoint that uploads documents to SharePoint. In the case of external applications, the integration with libraries is critical. You will want to investigate the configuration options for telling the tool where to store content. Make sure that metadata is stored. Make sure that it is not possible to bypass governance requirements such as records declaration. The nice thing about external tools is that if there is an issue, they stop working completely and don't affect SharePoint data. In some cases, depending on the nature of the external application, this could prevent new content from being contributed to SharePoint or prevent certain processes or users from using custom interfaces to retrieve or get content out of SharePoint. When an internal SharePoint application stops working, this can result in content or database corruption. The bad thing is that your team has to support any additional application over and above the SharePoint platform. While it sometimes is preferred to have external applications in the case of capture, most of the time it's better to have SharePoint applications that live within the SharePoint platform.

- **Impact on content** Many organizations do not consider what a third-party tool might do to the content itself and how this could impact content governance and migration. For governance, it's important that third-party tools do not skip or take precedent over any content governance features. An example of skipping is SharePoint workspaces that allow the uploading of documents to a records center without metadata and without declaring them as a record. Both of these are requirements of a records center. An example of taking precedence over governance features is a solution that will arbitrarily set records as undeclared without explicitly being told to. Because many third-party tools were not built with ECM in mind, we have found these situations are all too common. The ECM team needs to thoroughly test the scenarios before selecting a tool. They should pay particularly close attention to those tools that modify content or metadata.

- **Upgrades**   Just like the impact on content, all these tools impact upgrade. Most organizations consider that upgrading to a newer version of SharePoint will happen at some point in time. Today, the consideration also includes the move to Office 365. Every third-party tool will add additional variables to the upgrade process. And unless all these tools are native SharePoint applications, they will require special upgrade steps to move from even one same-version SharePoint farm to another, and especially to higher or lower versions. First, the organization needs to know the third-party vendor's plans for keeping current with the SharePoint road map. Next, the organization needs to understand the impact of upgrade. In the best case, there will be an upgrade path already in place for new versions of SharePoint. In the most common case, the tool will stop working for a period of 3–6 months while the third-party vendor gets an upgrade path established and tested. In the worst-case scenario, the business tool never works with a newer version of SharePoint and the third-party tool prevents you from moving your content with your IA intact. We are sad to say that we have seen the worst-case scenario a lot because the organization did not take the preceding considerations into account. In such a situation, we recommend staying with the current implementation of the farm, creating a brand-new farm with new configuration and start with new content only, or manually and slowly moving the existing farm.

The bottom line is that the ECM team needs to test all third-party tools against an ECM criteria checklist. If they do not fit for ECM, the team should have the option to omit their inclusion to the ECM application portion of the farm. So many organizations just assume that third-party tools will not impact SharePoint's ability to be migrated to and from or that the tools will not impact the ability for the platform to be upgraded. Remember that your greatest tool for ensuring platform migration, upgrade, and continuity of your content is the approach to IA that we covered extensively in Chapter 4, "Cases in point."

We always recommend the approach of sticking with out-of-the-box features until those features are not satisfying a strategic business need, making a third-party tool necessary.

Systems integrators

Finally, while system integrators are not a third-party solution, the community of system integrators in the SharePoint space is one of the strongest in the world of enterprise applications.

Most SharePoint projects, if only for validation, involve some third-party expertise. SharePoint system integrators are firms that bill per project or per hour to help implement SharePoint. All system integrators are different. You will find that some system integrators specialize in platform and security, which makes them most fit to stand up the farm and configure users and security. Others will focus on ECM and architecture. It is very important not to contract with a system integrator who has no ECM background for your ECM project.

When evaluating system integrators, we recommend viewing existing projects they have completed, if possible. System integrators will tend to tell organizations that if it is SharePoint, they can do it. They will always lead with their talent and make it clear that if they don't have the answer, their team of architects is so well connected that they can get the answer, even if from Microsoft directly.

It is often very hard to weed through who is really good and really not. The best and only way is to view current implementations they have done and compare them to this book and your own standards. Make sure that you know where the systems integrator is most successful. For example, some integrators come into projects where things are already broken, while others are very strategic and come in early on with the proper project management, planning, and best practices. A proactive and highly experienced integrator is best for any new ECM project or initiative. And a more reactive integrator is good for when something on the platform level breaks and you need specific support for a feature or issue.

From the field

I've had three clients now that have had five or more integrators involved over different periods of time on the same project. All three were projects that I at some point had been involved with. Because I was so concerned that I did a bad job, I investigated these situations. Did the client work with 5+ SIs because none of them knew what they were doing? Or was there something else going on? Fortunately, I had good relationships with these organizations and I was able to get honest answers. In some cases, I did find that there were some instances of bad services, but the bigger problem was the organization not understanding what they needed, vetting outside help carefully, and setting expectations accordingly. - Chris

The best advice we can give for working with integrators is that they are usually motivated by good references and profitable projects. This twofold motivation can work to make sure that everyone works toward and achieves the desired results. If you are working with a potential integrator, it's a good idea to cultivate a long-term view of how the project can be beneficial for the integrator from a client reference standpoint. At the end of the project, you want to make sure that the integrator delivers what was promised and that they make a reasonable profit margin doing so. This ensures that integrators who do a good job will be around next time you need them. This is a good time to remind you to incorporate good solid project management practices. If your systems integrator doesn't have a qualified project manager, this could be an indication that they aren't prepared to deliver at a reasonably professional level.

There are many ways to accomplish a technical objective, so make sure you are working with an integrator who seeks out the simple and straightforward approaches instead of the more costly and complex ones. An effective way to balance this is to bring in an independent high-level ECM architect to design and plan the implementation and then hire an integrator who is responsible for implementing the application based on the design, the fixed requirements, and the budget. Because this is not possible in all cases, the next best approach is for the ECM committee to fully design and plan their ECM implementation prior to receiving consultation on implementation. In any case, find a way to separate the strategic design from implementation. The problem you will face with this approach is contention between the planning and implementation teams, but this tends to be the lesser of two evils when the parties are interested in a successful implementation.

CHAPTER 11

Tools and final thoughts

Putting together the pieces of SharePoint to deploy an ECM solution can be overwhelming. There are three primary aspects we advise you to remember so that you can minimize the daunting nature of the project. First and most important is the ECM team that is formed; together you will be able to collectively take on the various complexities and pressures of the project. Second, we believe that you should start with a grand vision, making sure that everything and everyone is taken into consideration. Make sure that you set expectations so that everyone knows you are setting a vision for the project, that it is a part of the overall business plan, and that their efforts (adoption, usage, feedback) will help the company run more efficiently. You also want to make sure that they understand that the plan will be to implement a small and manageable design, essentially picking off key areas of ECM success one piece at a time.

Start off with the very basics, and remember that it's OK to start with an overly simplistic version of the design and plan in the earliest versions of your drafts for how the SharePoint farm implementation will occur. Sometimes this is easier to modify and build on than trying to put on paper all things you want the ECM platform to be. As you gain more insight and feedback, you and the team will become more familiar with how you will achieve success in your project. Iteration is a good thing, so make sure that you are open to change and addressing needs as they uncover themselves.

The final way to keep everything on a level playing field is to incorporate the use of a few tools that are available to you and the SharePoint community at large.

Tools

In Chapter 10, "Extending SharePoint 2013 solutions," we mentioned quite a few tools to help you with your ECM application and adoption. But what about the tools that are available to help you build, test, and evaluate your ECM system designs?

There are two very powerful tools that we recommend all SharePoint project teams leverage to help them throughout the life cycle of the project. These tools will be useful even after the SharePoint ECM solution is live, so becoming familiar with them early will give you a big advantage over others who have not used them. The tools are CloudShare and the SharePoint community, respectively.

CloudShare

CloudShare is a public cloud provider that has built a service specifically for organizations to configure, test, and deploy their SharePoint line-of-business applications. They are not a production cloud provider, so this is not where you will host your SharePoint application, but it is where you can do quick tests, have an iterative deployment built, and avoid all the acquisition and configuration of physical infrastructure that the project team will require.

To get you started, we have created a simple single-server farm configuration on CloudShare. You can obtain it by visiting *http://hoardinginformation.com/ecmbook/*.

When you select the CloudShare link, you will be given a copy of your own virtual machine with SharePoint 2013, SQL Server, and basic ECM configurations we outlined in this book. They are based on the Information Architecture (IA) and configurations for a large organization that we described in Chapter 4, "Cases in point." This SharePoint configuration will be distributed among site collections versus sites. All readers of the book receive a 14-day trial of the environment and can choose to subscribe to CloudShare if they want to have it longer.

We recommend using this environment to explore the IA and configurations mentioned in this book. It will also be useful to make some changes and configurations of your own to mimic a proposed design of your SharePoint environment. You will be able to do all of this without acquiring any hardware, software or spending the time it takes to perform the installation of a SharePoint farm.

When you are ready to start the ECM project and you have a high-level design, you can create your own environment. All environments that customers of CloudShare create are independent from everyone else, which means that you don't have to worry about breaking it.

The goal of the new environment should be to implement your ECM application in a sandbox iteratively. You can make changes and run tests to determine exactly how a specific design or feature will effect the overall SharePoint deployment. When you have 90 percent of the implementation done, use this as a tool to share with internal users, get them used to the system, test adoption, and get an idea of any changes that are needed based on feedback.

No matter how many sandbox environments you kick around to build and test your idea, there will be times when you and your team just get stuck. It's times like these that you should turn to the extremely powerful and diverse SharePoint community.

SharePoint community

The SharePoint community is like no other for line-of-business applications. They are an audience of very skilled professionals who are active with social media and local SharePoint groups. The best way to access this pool of skills is to use the hash tag #SPHelp and the various user groups.

#SPHelp is a Twitter hash tag used for communicating about various questions around the platform and configurations. If you tweet a question on SharePoint by using the hash tag #SPHelp, you can expect that within a day you will receive a collection of responses. Some will be direct answers, clarification for further information, or links to articles and blogs written by SharePoint professionals and enthusiasts. In addition, Microsoft SharePoint MVPs and professionals monitor the Twitter stream on a regular basis.

Because the community is so close knit and nearly all the leaders in the space are all acquainted with one another, you will also see a very strong local element to the SharePoint groups.

The local elements manifest themselves as either user group meetings called SharePoint User Groups (SPUGs) or SharePoint Saturday. You will find that most SharePoint Saturday events are planned and hosted by local SPUG leaders. The difference is in format. Where a typical SPUG meeting is single-topic focused and usually draws between 30–50 individuals focused on the topic, SharePoint Saturday events can have as many as 500 individuals and there are tracks covering various topics. SharePoint Saturday events draw out-of-state speakers and professionals for each of those topics and provide a great source of information. It is very common for you to be able to meet them face to face and discuss any particular issue you might be having.

Do a web search for your local SPUG group. The leadership of this group will be able to connect you with all the local events and talent in the SharePoint market.

Successful SPUG meetings and SharePoint Saturday events are usually followed by a casual get together at a local pub. These are called *SharePint events,* an obvious pun on having a beverage together and engaging in conversations about SharePoint.

Individuals like you who share their knowledge for the sake of all who implement SharePoint drive the power of the community. If you have a specific area of expertise or even just practical experience of pitfalls, it is always useful for the community to learn from your experiences. Consider volunteering for SPUG or SharePoint Saturday events as a speaker or organizer. You will find that giving back to the SharePoint community is the best way to build relationships with experts, and learn even more.

As we mentioned in Chapter 10, in the section "System integrators," always keep in mind that not all SharePoint experts are created equal. SharePoint experts will tend to be either more strategic or more technical. They will also be either more platform specific or more application specific. When considering an expert to help you implement your SharePoint ECM solution, you will be looking for someone who is both technical and platform specific. When you are looking for an expert to help you design your SharePoint implementation, you are looking for someone who is more strategic and ECM application specific.

It is very important to identify exactly what area of expertise a SharePoint professional is focused on and where they have had successful experiences, because all experts will want to tell you that they are good at everything. In some cases, it might take multiple subject matter experts who are familiar with various aspects of SharePoint facilitate to learn what is needed for your ECM solution. We believe that knowing a professional's area of expertise is critical because it's very easy to trust and believe an expert, and they will tend to always have a good response. Therefore, a poorly chosen expert can quickly lead you down a path that is either against your goals or contrary to your requirements. It will not be uncommon for organizations to have many SharePoint experts participating in different aspects of the farm deployment and design strategy.

In additional to the community and user groups, there is also a community around ECM and records management. For ECM, the trade organization AIIM (*www.AIIM.org*) is a great place to meet experts in ECM. Their community site has a whole section dedicated to SharePoint. For records management standards and practices, visit ARMA (*www.ARMA.org*). They hold the standards for all records management regulations and best practices.

Conclusion

Many elements of this book might have surprised you. If your background is more from a pure IT perspective, you probably were surprised that ECM applications cannot be solved by technology alone. If you have experience in the ECM and records management industry, you might have been surprised at how subjective the platform implementation can really be.

Always in the back of your ECM team's collective mind should be the notion that SharePoint is a platform, not an application, and ECM is a set of principles and a methodology, not a technology.

For the authors of this book, it took more than five years of experience in ECM and two solid years of implementing ECM principles using SharePoint technology before we each got to this level of understanding.

It is the rushed ECM project or the project with the wrong objectives, like moving all network file shares to SharePoint, that are doomed to fail. If you find yourself in this situation now, it's best to fail quickly so that you can establish a project restart sooner rather than later.

To provide a conclusion to *SharePoint 2013: Enterprise Content Management*, we have created the following short list of the high-level points we want all readers of this book to take away:

- It all starts with a solid team, and SharePoint projects are a team effort. A single individual should not drive your organization's ECM project.

- Find a naysayer, and bring them onto the team.

- Build a pre-mortem practice of reviewing how things might fail and then trying to mitigate their failure.

- Make sure that your team is diverse and includes IT and users as part of the ECM group.

When it comes to building an ECM application, IA is perhaps the single biggest element that demands most of your project team's time and attention. Keep the following points in mind:

- Structure of file shares is not the structure of ECM.

- Do not web-enable network file shares.

- Keep as flat of an IA as you possibly can.

- Standardize your IA across the farm.

- Leverage the power of content types and metadata instead of folders and more libraries.

SharePoint is a platform, not an application. Your team will be molding SharePoint features into the ideal ECM solution. Keep the following points in mind:

- Start with out-of-the-box features until they no longer meet the needed requirement.

- Think about what you need now and in the future.

- There is no 100 percent template that is a fit for your organization or industry, so do not waste your time trying to find it.

- You should be able to fully architect the features and concepts of your SharePoint ECM application without ever touching SharePoint.

- The best implementations are done where the ECM team fully plans the implementation. Therefore, when it comes time to work with the platform, it's just a matter of executing the design.

Start adoption of ECM now, before it's deployed in SharePoint, using the following guidelines:

- Internally crowd-source a cleanup of shared drives to match the proposed IA.

- Start educating users about how much time is wasted and how much risk network file shares pose to the organization.

- Start showing SharePoint and the possibilities in small, quick demos. Focus on the end result and what is possible—for example, faster navigation and filtering with a taxonomy, or search with better results.

Records Management and eDiscovery is for everyone. Don't ignore these features and principles just because you don't have a mandate. Not all organizations need to implement records management, but all organizations can be subject to it in the future. So, at the very least, you need to understand it, even if you don't implement it right away.

SharePoint ECM projects take time, and the bulk of the time is usually spent outside of SharePoint working out policy and handling the plethora of people, politics, and personality issues that arise in any project.

Successfully implemented ECM has been proven to make organizations more efficient and more stable when it comes to compliance and legal risk. What is often not realized is that great ECM implementations become a transparent tool. When this happens, not only are organizations eliminating the frustrations of creating and consuming critical line of business content, but they are spending more time on their core business objectives, which makes them more profitable and opens the doors to goals that previously seemed unattainable.

By this point in the book, you might not yet be an ECM expert. You probably thought twice about how you've organized your content, perhaps became more aware of how much time you spend with the management of your documents over creating and using them. At this point, our goal as authors is for you to understand what it takes to be successful in evaluating, planning for, designing, and implementing the ideal ECM solution in SharePoint 2013.

Index

Symbols

A

B

C

N

O

P

About the authors

CHRISTOPHER RILEY To say someone is predisposed to be in the field of Enterprise Content Management (ECM) is a little silly. There is no ECM gene, but there are certain characteristics that lead one to be interested in the space. You have a strong sense of order and organization. The statement "information is power" awes you, and you probably graze the boundaries of obsessive-compulsive disorder, or in my case full-on OCD.

I started my career life in content management, specifically in the area of *image capture*. As you will soon learn, capture sits in the early portion of the document life cycle, and at first glance seems so basic. But it is not. The sole job of image capture is to transform paper into value for a content management system, marrying physical documents with electronic. When you start to get into the details of how capture is done, its complexity becomes overwhelming fast. Do you capture all information? Some? What is the right format? What if you need to repurpose it? What do you do with the original? What happens when the types of content you capture are varied? Capture is just one piece of ECM, and as I've learned, all pieces follow the same pattern; they seem so rudimentary, but quickly you find that to execute on them well takes thought.

Think of all the unclaimed content or information out there. Think of the information that has haphazardly been pushed aside, a form of capture, and the implications that made on its findability in the future. We know how to generate information but not yet how to use it.

> *"When information is cheap, attention becomes expensive."*
> — *James Gleick, The Information: A History, a Theory, a Flood*

If you were not born with the ECM gene, don't worry; this book is still for you. The benefits of ECM, I can safely say, are the same for all. Although it might be a taste of medicine for some, the results of proper ECM are felt everywhere.

Whether you insist on hoarding information and organizing it like I do or whether you operate within the confines of normal organizations, with their hodgepodge of personified drive letters and multiple unplanned repositories, the benefits are the same. A well-designed and implemented ECM solution is a chugging engine that gets you on the path to better content utilization.

We all intend to transcend ECM and the simple aspects of managing content and move into a world where the content we spend so much time creating delivers real value. And by real value, I'm referring to all those technology terms that really excite us: BigData, Cloud, Unified Information Access, and Semantic Web. These more entertaining technologies make one major presumption: that we have succeeded in capturing and storing the content in a way these evolving technologies can consume. So far we haven't.

Today I believe that the technology world has finally mastered the capture of information, but we still are very poor at storing it, and we are only just now flirting with the grand potentials that come when we try to actualize it. Everyone needs the processes of ECM to be successful with their content actualization. This book takes the "why?" and "how?" of ECM and smashes them together into a comprehensive tool. A tool allowing you to form SharePoint into the best content storage and delivery machine it can be.

Writing this book in itself was an ECM exercise. And like all ECM projects, it was hit with detractors and challenges from every angle. While writing this book, I had a job change, fought the economy with the rest of the U.S., and finally said hello to the possibility of being a father. I dedicate this book to everyone who felt the blunt end of my stress to get it done, to Shad for making the efforts see the light of day, and to my beautiful wife and future child.

 SHADRACH WHITE   Enterprise Content Management is an industry-adopted term that is often referred or rather mislabeled by many. The reasons for this are due to the evolving landscape of information management. Whether it's early card catalogue techniques, microform, document imaging, or records management, the goal is always the same. Take vast and varied amounts of information and organize it so that anyone can find what they are looking for. The truth is, managing and organizing information in any form so that it is easy to find after you store it is one of the biggest challenges that all organizations grapple with, regardless of the technology used. My co-author Chris Riley is a rare example of someone who analyzes and then organizes every bit and byte of information. He refers to this as the ECM gene, and I am lucky enough to have a few of those chromosomes myself. This is one of the reasons he can accomplish so many complex tasks across a wide variety of subject matter and operational boundaries. In this book, our goal is to share our experience, best practices, and our obsessive desire to organize information so that it becomes easy to find and share.

My first role in the ECM field was working as a systems analyst and network engineer in my home state of Alaska. I worked in all facets of the business, from sales to implementation, training, and rollout. After successfully selling, implementing, and supporting dozens of document imaging and optical storage solutions across Alaska, I moved to Seattle. Working closely with upper management, I implemented some of the earliest and most successful document imaging solutions in the Northwest at companies like Eddie Bauer, Boeing, and Costco. It was during this time that I became frustrated with the lack of proper expectations being set with customers prior to selling them an ECM solution. I recognized the need to create best practices for architecting a document management solution and building a project delivery model. Prior to that, the approach was to sell the software and figure out the details later. Unfortunately, this is still a common practice today, and the results are either shelf-ware or poorly architected solutions. After reading this book, you will have tools and examples that can be used to prevent these outcomes and help you deliver an ECM solution that balances your business objectives, technical requirements, and budget.

The importance of developing a plan and following best practices can be challenging, and in the rush to just get the software deployed and the project completed, many important factors are too often overlooked. To write this book, I have relied on my experience in over 300 content management projects where I variously participated as a lead technical architect, project director, and later as an executive sponsor. Because not all projects are winners, my goal for you as a reader is to share the knowledge that came from both success and failure.

In nearly every project, you will encounter challenges from one of three primary areas:

- **Resources**   Time, infrastructure, money

- **Technology**   Functionality, integration, devices

- **People**   Users, management, project team

I have been asked many times about what the main difference is between a highly successful project and others. Without hesitation, it's about the people. Without a great team, solid executive sponsorship, and engaged users who together take ownership, you can have all the resources and technology in the world and fail spectacularly.

Now that you've read the book...

Tell us what you think!

Was it useful?
Did it teach you what you wanted to learn?
Was there room for improvement?

Let us know at http://aka.ms/tellpress

Your feedback goes directly to the staff at Microsoft Press,
and we read every one of your responses. Thanks in advance!

 Microsoft